Reborn of Crisis

This book examines the dominant popular culture convention of the superhero, situated within the most significant global event of the last 20 years. Exploring the explosion of the superhero genre post-9/11, it sheds fresh light on the manner in which American society has processed and continues to process the trauma from the terrorist attacks. Beginning with the development of *Batman* in comics, television, and film, the authors offer studies of popular films including *Iron Man*, *Captain America*, *The X-Men*, *Black Panther*, and *Wonder Woman*, revealing the ways in which these texts meditate upon the events and aftermath of 9/11 and challenge the dominant hyper-patriotic narrative that emerged in response to the attacks. A study of the superhero genre's capacity to unpack complex global interplays that question America's foreign policy actions and the white, militarized masculinity that has characterized major discourses following 9/11, this volume explores the engagement of superhero films with issues of authority, patriotism, war, morals, race, gender, surveillance, the military industrial complex, and American political and social identities. As such, it will appeal to scholars and students of cultural and media studies, film studies, sociology, politics, and American studies.

Annika Hagley is Associate Professor of Politics and International Relations at Roger Williams University, Rhode Island, USA. Her research interests revolve around the mediation of 9/11 through pop culture lenses, political rhetoric, and decision-making in Congress.

Michael Harrison is Associate Professor of Spanish at San Diego Mesa College, USA. His research has examined superhero iconography in Spanish literature and cultural, political, and social discourses of sexual and gender identity and queer sexual citizenship in comics from Spain.

The Cultural Politics of Media and Popular Culture

Series Editor: C. Richard King

Columbia College Chicago, USA

Dedicated to a renewed engagement with culture, this series fosters critical, contextual analyses and cross-disciplinary examinations of popular culture as a site of cultural politics. It welcomes theoretically grounded and critically engaged accounts of the politics of contemporary popular culture and the popular dimensions of cultural politics. Without being aligned to a specific theoretical or methodological approach, *The Cultural Politics of Media and Culture* publishes monographs and edited collections that promote dialogues on central subjects, such as representation, identity, power, consumption, citizenship, desire and difference.

Offering approachable and insightful analyses that complicate race, class, gender, sexuality, (dis)ability and nation across various sites of production and consumption, including film, television, music, advertising, sport, fashion, food, youth, subcultures and new media, *The Cultural Politics of Media and Popular Culture* welcomes work that explores the importance of text, context and subtext as these relate to the ways in which popular cultures work alongside hegemony.

Also available in the series:

Death in Contemporary Popular Culture
Adriana Teodorescu and Michael Hviid Jacobsen

Afro-Surrealism
The African Diaspora's Surrealist Fiction
Rochelle Spencer

Reborn of Crisis
9/11 and the Resurgent Superhero
Annika Hagley and Michael Harrison

For more information about this series, please visit: www.routledge.com/The-Cultural-Politics-of-Media-and-Popular-Culture/book-series/ASHSER-1395

Reborn of Crisis

9/11 and the Resurgent Superhero

Annika Hagley and Michael Harrison

Routledge
Taylor & Francis Group

LONDON AND NEW YORK

First published 2021
by Routledge
2 Park Square, Milton Park, Abingdon, Oxon OX14 4RN

and by Routledge
605 Third Avenue, New York, NY 10017

First issued in paperback 2022

Routledge is an imprint of the Taylor & Francis Group, an informa business

British Library Cataloguing-in-Publication Data
A catalogue record for this book is available from the British Library

Library of Congress Cataloging-in-Publication Data
Names: Hagley, Annika, 1983– author. | Harrison, Michael, 1975– author.
Title: Reborn of crisis : 9/11 and the resurgent superhero / Annika Hagley and Michael Harrison.
Description: Abingdon, Oxon ; New York : Routledge, 2020. | Series: The cultural politics of media and popular culture | Includes bibliographical references and index.
Identifiers: LCCN 2020013364 (print) | LCCN 2020013365 (ebook) | ISBN 9781138606500 (hardback) | ISBN 9780429467615 (ebook)
Subjects: LCSH: Superhero films—United States—History and criticism. | September 11 Terrorist Attacks, 2001, in motion pictures. | September 11 Terrorist Attacks, 2001, in mass media. | National characteristics, American, in motion pictures | Popular culture—Political aspects—United States—History—21st century.
Classification: LCC PN1995.9.S76 H34 2020 (print) | LCC PN1995.9.S76 (ebook) | DDC 791.43/652—dc23
LC record available at https://lccn.loc.gov/2020013364
LC ebook record available at https://lccn.loc.gov/2020013365

ISBN 13: 978-0-367-53934-4 (pbk)
ISBN 13: 978-1-138-60650-0 (hbk)
ISBN 13: 978-0-429-46761-5 (ebk)

DOI: 10.4324/9780429467615

Typeset in Garamond
by Apex CoVantage, LLC

Acknowledgments

This book developed from the unlikely collaboration between a political scientist and a Spanish comics scholar who discovered a mutual academic interest in the world of superheroes. The discussions contained here have also been informed by the many amazing students who have taken our courses focused on superheroes, philosophy, and politics at both Monmouth College (Harrison) and Roger Williams University (Hagley).

Annika – I would like to acknowledge the support I have received in the last three years from the Roger Williams University Provost Fund for Professional Development and from the CORE coordinator, Jason Jacobs, who wholeheartedly supported my proposing, developing, and delivering a course based on superheroes for the general education program at Roger Williams University. My departmental colleagues, David Moskowitz, June Speakman, Beppe Roberts, Mark Sawoski, and Wendy Godek have my thanks for daily doses of laughter and picking up some of my service responsibilities to enable me to finish this project. My colleagues from other disciplines have provided both moral support and feedback, especially Dr. Trudi Peterson and Dr. Erika Buhring, and I am eternally grateful to them. Finally, to all the children in my life, Chloe, Lauren, Evie, Jack, Floyd, Frances, Brady, Kaitlyn, Jackson, Kade, Chloe, and Colin, thank you for being sweet, goofy, loving, and cuddly and for playing superheroes with me over the years.

Michael – Although my interest in superheroes has been around since I first donned a towel doubling as a cape, I would like to acknowledge the support of my academic interest in them: to Dr. Matt Yockey for giving me the opportunity to work as a TA for his superhero course at the University of California, Irvine; to Dr. Jill Robbins who supported my inclusion of superhero iconographic analysis in my otherwise non-superhero focused doctoral dissertation and who has continued to be supportive in all of my research in the years since; to the faculty of Monmouth College who approved and subsequently supported the development and teaching of my course "Great Powers and Great Responsibilities: Superheroes, Philosophy, and Identity;" and to the faculty of the Department of Languages at San Diego Mesa College

Contents

and the Mesa College administration for their continued moral support during this process. I would also like to thank my parents and siblings for their continued love and understanding of my lifelong interest in these sometimes enigmatic superpowered heroes.

Finally, we would both like to extend a special thank you to our husbands, Tom and Clay for their unwavering support throughout this endeavor.

Introduction

The terrorist attacks of 9/11 sent shockwaves of incredulous grief, horror, and stupefaction throughout the world, becoming a catalyzing moment in the young 21st century. In all corners of the globe, people of all walks of life, most not directly affected by the horrific loss of life, were shaken to their core, and every person who experienced that shock has a story of how they interacted with those events as they took place. Ours are but two of millions, each distinct in their own contexts and specificities but all sharing the indescribable horror at the magnitude of the attack.

For Michael, who had a unique behind-the-scenes glimpse at the media machine that would package and repackage the images of the attack, the effect was surreal in nature. He says: in September, 2001, I was working at the Weather Channel in Atlanta, GA, and on the 11th, had the day off for a dental and a doctor's appointment. My initial interaction with the news, then, was predominantly audio in nature, as I listened to news reports in the waiting rooms and in my car driving to and from appointments. My dentist was nearby my childhood home, so I was able to pause and visit with my family as we attempted to process the horrific nature of the attacks. Many of those who experienced the non-stop news reports with the video footage on repeat often describe it as surreal. For me, the surreal feeling came the following day when I returned to my desk at work, which, at the time, was in an editing room in the basement of the headquarters of the Weather Channel.

In that editing room, the channel had a bank of televisions ringing the ceiling of the room, each with a live feed from all of the major news agencies, providing the channel with footage to edit and include in its broadcasts. On that September 12th, I was surrounded all day by images of newscasters on the street not only making their on-air reports but also in their off-air moments, discussing the camera angle and shot with the camera operator and adjusting their hair and clothes before going live with another affiliate. While obviously part and parcel to the preparation to go on air with a report, on that day it highlighted for me the constructedness of the media images as well as the narrative function of the media to package and present those visual images to the American public.

Although Annika experienced reports of the attacks and the aftermath from across the Atlantic, her interaction with the images of it was similarly impactful. She describes her reaction thusly: emerging from the dark, cavernous tube station at Oxford Circus on the morning of September 12th, 2001, I was met by a scene that has never left my memory. An undergraduate, finishing up a degree in the heart of London, I had spent the previous evening glued to the television, watching in horror as the Twin Towers fell into apocalyptic clouds of dust. As I traipsed up the stairs into the daylight with a sense that the world had changed but not knowing quite how, I saw a young man standing on the corner of Oxford and Regent Streets holding an enormous Star-Spangled banner. Tears were rolling down his face, but he remained still as the flag flapped in the wind. As I walked past, I attempted a sympathetic smile and figured that he must be an exchange student from America or travelling. How horrifying it must have been to be so far away from home when home had become the battlefront of a war that no one was expecting or had time to prepare for. How crushing it must have been for him that all he could do was stand at the corner of two foreign streets and hold the symbol of his country to acknowledge his pain and his nation's humiliation and sorrow.

As an untraveled student I barely knew what the Twin Towers were. There was a sense of muted despair in lectures and all over London that day, and I made my way back to my fellow students in our shared house to watch as the BBC tried to explain the significance of the attack on America and the rest of the world. We watched again and again, an endless loop of dust and screams and sirens filling the living room. I had no idea at that time that my further education would take me to America, that I would leave for a Master's degree, stay for a PhD, and never come home again. I had no idea that my research and my first co-authored book would center around the biblical scenes of destruction that I was currently watching. What I have never forgotten is my housemate Gwyn, taking a long drag on his cigarette, shaking his head in disbelief at the television screen and stating quietly: "it looks like a movie."

Although our two experiences varied in the specifics, it is undoubtedly true that across the globe, the extraordinary visual impact of the Twin Towers falling and the fact that most of the developed world was watching it replay on a continuous loop ensured that the event quickly became a collective "spectacular memory event"(Schlund-Vials, 2011, p. 13). Cathy Schlund-Vials (2011) coined the term in an essay following the attack and further stated that: "9/11 is a significant occurrence, a national event remembered via a formulaic tragic narrative" (p. 13). Given the immensity of the visual and all it represented in concert with the collective nature of how most of the world viewed it, it is unsurprising that it existed in people's consciousnesses as a fantastical, unbelievable "movie" like experience. It is further unsurprising that it was pop and media culture that were the first cultural spaces in which room was made to process the contesting emotions of Americans and the rest of the world. Writing about the super heroic response to 9/11, Jenkins (2006) states that: "popular culture is the space of dreams, fantasies and emotions." He also suggests that this space is not "unequivocal," that within the pop culture world there are opposing views and ideologies, sometimes in concert and sometimes in conflict with one another, which is, perhaps, what makes pop culture the most interesting place to turn an analytical lens toward after such a cataclysmic, fantastical shock (Jenkins, 2006, p. 98).

As the media machine rolled into response mode, the political and societal impact of 9/11 slowly made itself known with frightening speed. A sense of fear was drummed into the American people on a daily basis, a fear compounded by a collective insistence upon rallying around both the government and symbols of patriotism. Such "in group" conditions naturally led to the identification and vilification of "out groups." The hostility was in the first months directed at Arabs and in later years at all those who did not fall in line with a white, patriarchal militaristic world view that was deemed necessary for America to regain its standing in the world. With those in favor of swift vengeance far outnumbering the voices calling for a more strategic response, America found itself faced with: "A call to replace the institutions of equal protection before the law with those of crusading but secretive administrative practices sometimes (finding) acquiescence from a zealous public" (Jewett and Lawrence, 2003, p. 234). With a media machine that abdicated its responsibility not to get caught up in the zealous narrative, little attention or space was given to alternative visions of how America could or should proceed. As America was caught between: "a prophetically realistic commitment to world order and it's tendency to go its own, nationalistic, zealous way" (Jewett and Lawrence, 2003, p. 320), it was popular culture that stepped up to the plate, offering mediation, obsessive reliving, and, in some cases, critical commentary on the evolving tendencies toward fear and division that the government was befitting from and the media was in most part ignoring.

Why popular culture?

Hollywood was not initially prepared nor willing to take on the job of deconstructing the attack in its immediate aftermath. The first medium to respond was print, ranging from *Time Magazine* to *The Economist* to comic books whose writers were advantaged by the quick turnaround time in their production capabilities. The second was television, ranging from the almost condescending explanatory stand-alone episode of *The West Wing*: "Isaac and Ishmael," a 50 minute, literal classroom for Americans in which complex historical realities were explained in a manner that both simplified the solution and exonerated America's role in world affairs, to *24*: a hyper masculine revenge fantasy in which Jack Bauer tortured suspected terrorists with little to no oversight until they gave up their life-saving information. If pop culture is "one of the ways in which people come to understand their position both within a larger collective identity and within an even broader geopolitical narrative" (Dittmer, 2005, p. 626), it was clear that, immediately post attack, pop culture was the predominant vehicle for the American innocence myth and the us vs. them narrative to ride. The pop culture landscape post 9/11 was almost monolithic in its conformity to the Bush administration's narrative of the attacks and offered little criticism of the jingoistic calls for vengeance that were beginning to percolate in the American cultural psyche. When a more nuanced presentation of American identity in relation to the rest of the world came it arrived as a Trojan horse; Captain America himself and a band of super nationalistic American bred superheroes. It was exactly because of their reassuringly patriotic origins and seemingly unequivocal devotion to the American dream that superheroes slipped past the defenses of a public, a public being primed every day to accept over-simplistic narratives of good vs. evil and support the notion that the attack was as a simple result of evil doers in far flung lands being hateful of the freedoms that they all took for granted.

The superheroic resistance to the Bush administration's Manichean narrative began early in the immediate days following the event and within the pages of ongoing comics series. Positioned as an almost embarrassing presence next to the "real" heroes of the hour (firefighters, cops, and rescue workers), the likes of Spider-Man and Captain America lingered in the background of the rescue attempts in the pages of the comics, weeping, broken, and repeatedly excusing their uselessness on the day in terms of lacking the capacity to even imagine such evil. As the issues continued, we saw Captain America refuse to deploy to Kandahar, Superman situating himself as a healing balm for New Yorkers, and superheroes generally pushing for a response that focused on the carnage at hand instead of the thirst for vengeance that was quickly building (Jenkins, 2006).

The most obviously nationalistic superhero (Captain America) was written into an extremely circumspect and thoughtful post 9/11 set of narratives in which he constantly questioned the past and present behavior of America. Directly confronted with the memory of the fire-bombing of Dresden in WWII and America's complicity in the killing and maiming of thousands of non-combatants in the Middle East, he represented a radical set of ideas that strongly challenged the myth of American innocence. Other heroes, shown involved in the war on terror in both direct and tangential ways, also deviated from an expected reinforcement of narratives being established in the name of patriotism and vengeance. Wonder Woman arrives in a Middle Eastern nation to liberate Muslim women being used as human shields. Dressed in a burka, she reveals herself to the women and is met not as a liberator but as a "moral transgressor" (Jenkins, 2006).

The fact that superheroes were born in eras of crises of American identity and have traditionally been drawn and written by disenfranchised groups of young men and women ensures that, at their heart, they have always contained a somewhat radical, counter-culture appeal. This made them the perfect literary figures to carry the alternative post 9/11 narrative to a wider audience. As Jenkins notes:

> The marginal status of comics is paradoxical because they are fringe media, they have more space for experimentation than most mainstream products but because they are a feeder system for the rest of the

entertainment industry those experiments are closely monitored and have enormous influence.

(Jenkins, 2006)

The clash of competing ideologies within the comic world goes a long way in both explaining their post 9/11 appeal to those who wished for vengeance and those who were keen to consume a medium that was thought provoking and different. Watching a superhero movie reveals an almost schizoid sequence of events in which bursts of progressive liberalism are tempered with fascistic scenes of violence and reactionary conservatism built in.

The first signal that superhero movies were going to be a vital means of contesting American political narratives in the post 9/11 world arrived with Christopher Nolan's *Batman* trilogy. Nolan used a terrifying, dark cinematic style to reboot the Batman franchise. A particular stand out is *The Dark Knight*, in which Heath Ledger's psychotic Joker is pitched in a murderous battle with the paragons of law and order (Harvey Dent and Jim Gordon) and Batman himself. From the very beginning of Nolan's story, the notion of traditional villains, as an audience understands them, is completely undone. The Joker has henchmen, just has he always has had in the past, but, in an immediate departure from past uses of henchmen, they begin killing one another within the first five minutes. This radical breaking of the traditional notion of "honor amongst thieves" is a cue to the audience that there is no code expected between the agents of evil anymore, and old modes of "villains united versus everyone else united" no longer applies.

As the action continues, the audience is left in no doubt that a new style of villain has been established with a new set of motivations, which the audience does not and is not supposed to understand. The actions and character of The Joker create a series of incidents designed to explore deep issues about fear, terror, morals, and what chaos can do to otherwise "civilized" people living within the rules and institutions of a democracy. The Batman movies were truly shocking, both in terms of their departure from the campy versions of the past and in the sense that they unsettled the usual expected genre conventions of that past. Audiences were no longer confronted with slapstick, camp unbelievable villains who could not exist in real life but with a clear representation of the terror threat (chaos, uncertainty, and terrorism) that they were currently facing in real life.

The Dark Knight opened the flood gates for a genre that had existed at the margins, been mainstreamed in camp and comic ways in movies to radically alter its course within that medium, and return to the more counter culture tone of the comics. What followed was a series of reboots beginning with *Iron Man*, followed by *Captain America*, various Avengers tales, *Wonder Woman*, *Black Panther*, and several television programs bookended by *Avengers: Endgame* in which the post 9/11 line-up of actors/superheroes are in large part retired within a satisfactory story arc. Within those 16 years, Marvel movies particularly operated as a consciously evolving meditation upon the complex, painful, and contradictory post 9/11 American cultural narrative. The fact that this period of reflection occurred in the immediacy of the attacks up until the year that the first children born post 9/11 entered their freshman years at college gives us both a lengthy pop culture period of analysis to work with and an appropriate and important pop culture framework to work within.

In this book, we argue that in the post 9/11 world, superheroes were reborn, reconfigured, and used to process every aspect of the resulting trauma within a "safe" nationalistic and patriotic genre convention. We position post 9/11 superheroes as an analytical framework through which to view important questions of government authority, patriotism, war, morals, race, gender, surveillance, the military industrial complex, and American political and social identities formed over time in response to the terrorist attacks. We show that superheroes are naturally and uniquely situated to unpack complex global interplays that question America's historical and contemporary foreign policy actions for audiences who are seeking both entertainment and catharsis. We also discuss the notion that what the post 9/11 superhero films offer is that they come packaged in a reassuringly patriotic, American centric genre convention that allows them to push the audience much further in considering their support for American foreign policy decisions. Each chapter focuses on one superhero or superhero team and explores how that character or characters' stories provide lenses through which to understand the cultural and political moment of the post 9/11 era. Some of the chapters explore the comics' source material in a more in-depth fashion in an effort to position the post 9/11 film versions of the characters and their worlds within an historical context. Other chapters will be more focused on the films themselves and the varied ways that popular entertainment media can provide rich analytical ground to better understand myriad complex contemporary issues. Although our approach to each chapter varies somewhat in its specific structure and focus, each chapter is situated within a framework that first explores significant themes important to post 9/11 audiences and then fully unpacks these concepts in analyses of the film series within which the themes are most fully explored.

In chapter one we focus on the Batman franchise and trace the development of the Batman character from Bob Kane's early vision, through the creation of his "trauma" story and up to the present day. By initially comparing early Batman stories and the 60's television "camping" of the caped crusader and the 90s Tim Burton Batman movie franchise with the much darker post 9/11 Christopher Nolan trilogy, we argue that, post 9/11, Nolan had license to create a much darker film series that was more reflective of actual societal fears than past Batman movies had been. We suggest that *Batman Begins* is the starting gun for the avalanche of superhero movies produced between 2002 and 2014 in which writers and directors moved away from the colorful, "campy" presentation of both superhero and villain and began to consciously process the stark political, philosophical, and social questions that the 9/11 attacks raised and that the films of the Nolan trilogy open up analytical space to begin to understand a number of the elements that pervaded American culture in the years following the terrorist attacks.

Captain America is the focus of Chapter 2. We suggest that the film re-established one of the most iconic Marvel characters and one who, given his unambiguously patriotic traits, is perhaps the most interesting in terms of the exploration of American identities in the post 9/11 period. In this chapter, we trace the development of the character from his inception in the World War II era, through McCarthy's America, the Civil Rights Movement, and counterculture and his resurrection in the years following the 9/11 attacks. We analyze the films in terms of the somewhat simplistic Manichean us vs. them narrative with particular focus on how the reawakening of Cap at the end of the first film sets him up for the much more complicated roles he plays in *Winter Soldier* and the *Avengers* franchise. *Winter Soldier* builds upon some of the themes already discussed in the *Batman* analyses and sets the stage for our analyses of *Iron Man* and creates a terrifying allegory of government surveillance capabilities being used against democratic norms and, ultimately, as a tool for the summary execution of people that the New World Order (HYDRA) considers to be subversive. Attention will also be given to the fact that the two forces at work against one another (Hydra/SHIELD) are intertwined and indistinguishable because they are both engaged with the tools of oppression and the symbolic reaffirmation of democratic principles emphasized in the culmination of action, which allows Captain America to prevail. Explicit links will be explored between the fictional portrayal of hyper-surveillance and the extra-legal surveillance systems set up in America in the post 9/11 period.

In Chapter 3 we switch focus to *Iron Man* and the ascendance of his character from his creation during the Vietnam War era, through his post 9/11 resurrection. Iron Man quickly established a narrative that foregrounded the complexity of technology, war, and the military industrial complex at a time when anti-war sentiments were running high. He is, therefore, uniquely positioned in counterpoint to the sentiments of Captain America in his role as an Avenger. In our analysis of the *Iron Man* movie franchise we will focus on three major themes. The first will be the presentation of the American Military Industrial Complex, the "war machine" and the historical and contemporary prosecution of and consequences of US foreign policy. The second will be a specific analysis of the "villain" from *Iron Man 3*, "The Mandarin" whose plotline serves as a meditation on media complicity in the hyperbolic concept of evil. The third exploration, which underpins the first two and is woven into the foundation of each film is the individual, national, and lingering trauma that was inflicted upon the United States, its citizens, and the members of its armed forces in the aftermath of the 9/11 attacks and the subsequent wars.

The remaining chapters explore significant issues to American culture in the post 9/11 period adjacent to the more direct issues that ground the earlier films. In Chapters 4 and 5 we switch gears to focus on two movies that are unique by-products of 9/11 in the sense that they were released at a time when the stranglehold of white patriarchal militaristic dominant American culture was beginning to fracture. *Wonder Woman* was only possible because of the space created by the feminist movement in the mid and late 2000's, which allowed women to begin reasserting their place in American society. In Chapter 4, we discuss Wonder Woman's unusual origins as the creative brain-child of William Moulton Marston. Marston believed that humankind would be better off if men submitted to women and allowed them to take control of political, social, and cultural institutions. He lived in a polyamorous rela-tionship with three women, all of whom took responsibility for some aspect of family and professional life on behalf of the family. Being one of the first commercially successfully female superheroes in the midst of a male centric conflict (war), the character of Wonder Woman was loaded with potential meaning from her conception through the free love and second/third wave feminist movements, the socially conservative and religiously dominated cul-tural landscape of Reaganism, and, more recently, as a refutation of the war and destruction America has engaged in post 9/11. We dissect the changes Wonder Woman went through in the hands of both male and female writers in the 70s, 80s, and 90s and analyze the recent post 9/11 reboot. The post 9/11 analysis is anchored in contemporary feminist discourse and makes ref-erence to the current political climate for women's rights as well as how the feminist movement has been divided over the reboot movie (some co-opting Wonder Woman as a positive feminist symbol and others contending that she represents what they see as an oppressive white centric feminism that excludes transwomen and women of color).

In Chapter 5 we home in on one of the most obviously glaring aspects of the superhero genre – its overwhelming whiteness. Minority superheroes have been scarce, and, when they do appear in comics and onscreen, they are often relegated to the margins as sidekicks, sacrificial lambs or worse, stereo-typed in damaging and regressive ways. The first inklings of black super hero-ism in the major publishing powerhouses occurred during the civil rights era and presented, although clumsy and exploitative, the first diverse characters who, by their mere presence, held up a spotlight and a mirror to an evolv-ing and painful glitch within the American social psyche. In this chapter we analyze early representations of black superheroes including the Falcon and the Green Lantern co-starring the Green Arrow series in which John Stewart becomes the first black Green Lantern. This particular series has been widely recognized as a somewhat ham-fisted but first truly complicated super heroic mediation of what is meant to be black and wield power in America. The aftermath of this foray into progressive and radical cultural discourse was the creation of more complex, reflective, and self-aware black heroes tempered by the continuing fetish of "Blaxploitation" films.

We examine the shift from the bodily dominance of traditionally white superheroes to the less jacked, street smart characters of Milestone Com-ics then place the marginalized black superhero within the context of post

9/11 America. Anchored in an analysis of *Black Panther*, we examine how the black superhero is mediated after a prolonged period in which notions of Americanness were predominantly white and militarized. We continue with a discussion of race relations in the last two years, which we view as the culmination of a period of American history in which visible difference contributed to a hardening of long held prejudices and understandings of race that were mobilized by political elites in the last presidential election.

Our final chapter examines the prolific X-Men films, beginning with an examination of the X-Men comics, which, from the beginning, have served as an allegory for marginalized communities. This implicit, (and sometimes) explicit allegory for a marginalized (queer, gendered, racial, bodied) "other" will be used to explore how the idea of the X-Men as "other" was interpreted in the post 9/11 superhero world. We focus on specific identities (queer, racial, disabled) that emerge in the X-Men filmic universe, linking them through various theoretical frameworks to the central theme of the marginalized Other and explore how each of these X-identities is shaped by the global and political reality of the post 9/11 world.

It is our contention that, post 9/11, the dominant popular culture discourse was obsessively processing the impact of the attack and that marginalized groups all suffered from a lack of capacity to assert their voices and represent issues relevant to their discourses. We argue that the X-Men franchise was one of the very few successful presentations of issues affecting non-dominant cultural groups and foregrounded a discussion of the domestic politics of queer discourses, gender, race, and disability (both physical and mental) that arise primarily as a result of the rising visibility of casualties of the "war on terror".

Bibliography

Dittmer, Jason. "Captain America's Empire: Reflections on Identity, Popular Culture, and Post-9/11 Geopolitics." *Annals of the Association of American Geographers*, Vol. 95, No. 3, 2005. pp. 626–643.

Jenkins, Henry. "Captain America Sheds His Mighty Tears: Comics and September 11." In *Terror, Culture, Politics: Rethinking 9/11*. Eds. Daniel J. Sherman and Terry Nardin. Bloomington, IN: Indiana University Press, 2006. pp. 69–102.

Jewett, Robert and John Shelton Lawrence. *Captain America and the Crusade Against Evil: The Dilemma of Zealous Nationalism*. Grand Rapids, MI: Wm.B. Eerdmans Publishing Co., 2003.

Schlund-Vials, Cathy J. "Crisis of Memory: Memorializing 9/11 in the Comic Book Universe." *Modern Language Studies*, Vol. 41, No. 1, 2011. pp. 12–25.

1 The demons that haunt us

Christopher Nolan's Batman and the faces of evil

Introduce a little anarchy.
Upset the established order, and everything becomes chaos.

The Joker, The Dark Knight

Before Christopher Nolan got his hands on what is likely one of the most lucrative superhero film franchises ever, the wider world was familiar with a different type of "Caped Crusader". Outside of the character's comic book adventures, which had begun in 1939 in Detective Comics #27, the average American likely knew of the character from one of two very distinct live action incarnations, that of Adam West in the 1960's camp-fest *Batman* television show and/or the successful film franchise (1989–1997) hallmarked by the stylistic design of director and producer Tim Burton.

Adam West was, of course, the first Batman with widespread appeal, and his crime fighting was marked by a definite frame of reference, which relied heavily upon colorful comic book art. Scenes of violence were overdubbed with comic style "pows" and "whooshes," making the series appropriate for the millions of children and adults that tuned in for their weekly fix of campy violence and morally black and white tales.

This type of representation of Batman continued in the initial Hollywood versions starring Michael Keaton, Val Kilmer, and George Clooney, where Batman became more brooding than in the television series but still faced an onslaught of capers from "overly cartoonish, preposterous and exaggerated" (Booker, 2007, p. 25) supervillains whose motivations were sinister but whose actions were presented within the traditional comic villain framework and where the films often, in the words of critic Roger Ebert, favored "style over substance"(Booker, 2007, p. 20). The premiere of the darker Batman in the 1989 film and its immediate sequel was, even in its stylized "darkness," too dark for audiences of the time in the minds of producers and filmmakers, and by 1995, the franchise had become much more frivolous and light, because Batman's darkness "threatened to make him an unattractive figure, virtually indistinguishable from the criminals he so despised" (Booker, 2007, p. 21).

In the 1990s, Joel Schumacher was only able to steer the films in a lighter direction because the concept of the superhero was immutable at the time. After 50 years of presence in popular media, he saw that too much darkness for Batman would likely result in audiences shying away from the character, due to a sharp deviation from the superhero ethos that audiences at the time associated with superheroes. The director overcorrected, arguably, resulting in a colorful, campy farce, but his intentions appear to be based on the idea that, pre-9/11, superheroes in popular media were expected to inhabit a specific moral and ethical discursive space and could not be accused of straying too close to the "dark side."

Under Nolan's influence, however, Christian Bale's incarnation of Batman resurrected the franchise, making Batman melancholy, crippled by inertia and only possessing a vague sense of what his duties should be. These films pitted him against truly dark villains who sought much more intangible rewards and outcomes than the one-note villains in the previous movies.[1] The Nolan villains are, indeed, terrifying and deranged, but what is perhaps more frightening for an audience that has traditionally been absolutely sure who is good and who is evil is that Nolan's villains exist in a liminal space between good and evil. They are driven by a need to destroy, but this drive is linked to philosophies and behaviors that raise interesting and significant questions about human nature and psychology, most especially when tied to the psychological trauma suffered after the attacks of 9/11.

The immediate long-term psychological trauma that the events of 9/11 inflicted upon audiences all over the world can be understood as one of the explanations for the swing toward a darker, more hyper realistic portrayal of good and evil in post 9/11 superhero movies in general, and in some ways, the realism may help process the trauma through cathartic reenactments. In others, it could be explained by a pervasive sense of helplessness against terrorist acts making their way to the screen in these big budget films. As Shaun Treat (2009) has said in his study of this phenomenon,

> It seems hardly coincidental that superheroes flourish during traumatizing wars abroad and an economic crisis inherited from Gilded Age corporate corruption at home, but a post-9/11 superhero *zeitgeist*? Since 2001, more comics-based superhero movies have been released than in all the prior years combined, doubling their domestic box-office average ($3 billion conservatively) with "darker" superhero franchises ahead.
>
> (p. 105)

What is indisputable is that the popularity of the superhero post 9/11 in general and of Batman in particular reached new, dizzying heights and launched a series of films that have become deeply pervasive allegories of post 9/11 political and social realities. As the world takes an even more frightening turn toward utter totalitarianism in the Middle East and as Western democracies are faced with an enemy they, seemingly, do not know how to engage, the potential for superhero movies to continue to dig even deeper into the complexity of evil and terror is even more pronounced.

The Nolan Batman films trace the inception and development of Batman as a distinct hero from the others studied in this volume. The character has no superpowers, but is built out of darkness, revenge, and fear, which provides the filmmakers with a number of rich opportunities to explore these abstract concepts in a concrete superhero format. It is not only the character of Batman and his quest for justice that make these films an engaging part of the post 9/11 superhero landscape, however, but also the interactions Batman has with the various villains he faces that provide the richest commentary about the nature of evil and the threat of terrorism in the 21st century. The trauma of 9/11 on the broader cultural consciousness can be seen reflected in Nolan's Batman trilogy in its highlighting of fear, trauma, and the threat of uncontrolled terrorism. As Andrew Pulver has pointed out,

> Superheroes fill a gap in the pop culture psyche, similar to the role of Greek mythology. There isn't really anything else that does the job in modern times. For me, Batman is the one that can most clearly be taken seriously. He's not from another planet or filled with radioactive gunk. I mean, Superman is essentially a god, but Batman is more like Hercules: he's a human being, very flawed, and bridges the divide.
>
> (Pulver, 2005)

The representation of the origins of the Dark Knight Detective and his interaction with his gallery of villains provides a fascinating reflection upon the evolving societal notion of evil and the innumerable and complicated fears that have arisen and consequently have been explored by Hollywood at a time when the nation of "evil" became multifaceted, problematic, and difficult to understand. Nolan's trilogy refashions the big screen Batman, opening the character up for representation of exploration of the psychology of fear, societal interaction with terrorism, and contemporary inequities of the modern economic class struggle through the exploration of the superhero character himself as an avatar for the American psyche reacting to the tragedy of the 9/11 terror attacks, as well as through the villains themselves as representative of the different facets of the new "evil" faced in the post 9/11 world.

Inner demons – fear and the making and practice of Batman

In a sometimes very crowded field of superpowered aliens, gods, and magical beings, the character of Batman has always been somewhat of an outlier, both in his lack of extraordinary powers and in his mythic, shadow status in his world. Because he has no powers, "Batman has always been a much more human figure than Superman," for example, and it is that humanity that has made the character so attractive to audiences for the last 80 years (Booker,

2007, p. 18). While the Man of Steel can inspire power fantasies among audiences and musings about what they might do with near limitless power, the humanity of Batman has always made him more accessible to identification. The birth of fan culture and the rise of the comic book "nerd" in popular culture, then, opens up even more of a space for identification with superhero characters, which serves to further deepen the draw of a character like Batman. For example, Glen Weldon points to late 90s/early 2000s participatory culture (such as the creation of fan fiction and cosplay) to show

> a sincere desire for participatory engagement, a wish to enter the story and forge a persona, intimate, and emotional connection to the character. Far more personal, more intimate, and more emotional, these cosplayers believe, than is achieved by passively consuming the story.
>
> (Weldon, 2016, p. 233)

This type of engagement brings the development of the Batman character into the more personal sphere of the audience. In these films, audiences aren't just hoping for Batman to defeat the villain and save the day. They identify with him. In essence, the participatory nature of fan culture at the time of the release of these films results in identification. They *are* Batman.[2] This personalization may be the distinction that makes the Nolan Batman films most symbolically significant post 9/11. If viewers are more participatory in nature, then the stories take on power to represent real preoccupations and fears. Fear itself, then – and the struggle to conquer and reclaim it – become central themes of the Nolan trilogy.

Fear is prolific in the post 9/11 landscape, and in Batman, audiences can watch one man, a victim of evil/crime, use his fear to become mythic and heroic, allowing them to imagine the same in themselves. In these films, Batman is not only a force to fight villains and save the day but is carefully constructed to highlight his own journey through fear and his escape and reclaiming of it. In the development of the character on screen in *Batman Begins*, screen time early on is dedicated to Bruce Wayne's life before Batman, and by seeing Bruce's struggle to deal with his own trauma and victimhood, the audience in turn cares more about the character.[3] By privileging his origin story, audiences are presented with a much deeper look into the psyche of one man's struggle to build an identity and a purpose built from the shattered pieces of his life, and this focus on his origin story at the beginning of the trilogy "explicitly link(s) the hero to his trauma in order to understand the trauma as part of the hero"(Horton, 2016, p. 76).

Although the originating trauma that sets Bruce Wayne's life on a course that will eventually lead to the creation of the Batman is fairly consistent throughout all iterations of the character, Nolan chooses to explicitly link fear to the hero's origin in a way that had theretofore not been done. Early on in *Batman Begins*, Bruce flashes back to an early childhood memory where he falls down a well full of bats, needing to be saved by his father and cementing a fear of bats in the impressionable young Wayne. Upon being saved, his father says "don't be afraid," setting up an initial symbolic connection between the bats, fear, and Bruce's father Thomas Wayne. Later, Nolan reframes a familiar scene in the Batman mythos, when instead of the adult Waynes being murdered after seeing a movie, the family instead is implored to leave an opera featuring grotesque bat costumes in the middle of the performance because young Bruce is too scared to keep watching. When this fear results in the mugging and death of his parents, Bruce's fear is solidified, and, now interwoven with guilt, this trauma and a lack of purpose and direction will eventually lead him on the vision quest to seek guidance, which will be the creation of the Batman.

Once Bruce is able to train with the League of Shadows, he learns that fear is a weakness to be mastered, but Bruce does not just master the fear that has consumed him and that he views as part of the cause of his parents' death. Instead, he goes one step further and decides instead to practice "conquering fear by becoming fear" (Wainer, 2014, p. 143). He fashions a shadow persona that utilizes the tools that he learned under the League's tutelage. In one of the earliest Batman comics stories, Bruce Wayne similarly plots to terrorize villains, saying "Criminals are a superstitious cowardly lot, so my disguise must be able to strike terror into their hearts."[4] What distinguishes the comic book origin story from Nolan's filmic one, however, is that Bruce channels the fear that he himself holds deep in his psyche and that he latches on to when partly blaming himself for his parents' death into the heroic persona of the Batman. Instead of being just a tool to terrorize criminals, in *Batman Begins* the persona of the bat is almost a form of psychotherapy. Bruce Wayne wields his own fear as a weapon, immunizing himself against it while he seeks vengeance against evil. This one symbolic difference that distinguishes Nolan's from the numerous other representations of the Batman origin story in various media is significant, due to its ties to the cultural trauma pervading US culture in the aftermath of 9/11. Owen Horton, for example, examines Nolan's choice to inject Bruce's fear as part of his origin and part of his heroic mission as explicitly tied to the post 9/11 landscape. He says, "This initiation and reconfiguration of values mirrors the experience of Americans after 9/11 and during the buildup to the Iraq War, as the Bush administration attempted to redirect feelings of vulnerability into aggressive responses" (Horton, 2016, p. 80).

Another aspect of the Batman origin story as presented in *Batman Begins* that distinguishes it from the others that came before it is the presence of the figure of Thomas Wayne. In previous iterations, the deaths of Thomas and Martha Wayne most definitely figure into the birth of the superhero, but the focus is most often on their death itself, traumatic, by a thief, in the middle of the seedy streets of Gotham City, that is the most ever-present image, and that act does similarly play a featured role in Nolan's origin story. However,

Nolan goes one step further and includes a number of scenes that establish Thomas Wayne and his interactions with his son and with his city that tie this film to the preoccupations of the US post 9/11.

In flashback scenes and in scenes in which people discuss Thomas Wayne's legacy, he is presented as a model citizen who sought to use his wealth to improve life for all Gothamites. Wayne is a doctor, and the film ties medical imagery of Dr. Wayne with his young son, with stories of how he spent his family wealth and his own time and efforts to "heal" a sick city.[5] Thomas is Bruce's model of beneficence, and although he does so with very different techniques, he shares his father's love for his city and his desire to "cure" it of its ills. This reflection of a previous, more optimistic and less jaded, generation and its failure to achieve its goals in part due to that optimism can be understood within the rhetorical framework established earlier as representative of the generational dichotomy before and after the 9/11 attacks. The world in which a member of the Wayne family attempted to make choices that would put Gotham back on track, when viewed through the hindsight of his traumatized son, is similar to the cultural viewpoint of US culture after being attacked. The methods and perspectives of the past would no longer be sufficient, and, as a culture, Americans began to question the ways and policies of previous generations.

The flaws of the policies and perspectives of a previous generation being viewed as potentially to blame for the darkness that came afterward is further emphasized when Ducard tells Bruce during training that his father was in part to blame for his death and that of his wife, because he was afraid to act. Instead of allowing an idyllic, perfect idea of who his father was to remain in Bruce's psyche, Ducard attempts to plant seeds of doubt as to the character and fortitude of Thomas Wayne. As one of the archetypal victims in the Batman mythos, by injecting this new perspective as to Thomas's partial culpability in his own death, questions are raised about where one might place blame as the victim of a traumatic act. By framing Thomas Wayne not only as a victim but also as culpable for not acting, this problematizes the idea of pure victimhood. As a culture after the 9/11 attacks, Americans were faced with victimhood for the first time on a large scope, and much of the discourse ignored any culpability that US foreign policy might have played in inspiring the attacks. Here, invoking Thomas Wayne as partly to blame simultaneously positions him as one who should have done more (should the US have been more aggressive?) and also as a mirror for what might have inspired the attack in the first place.

Once Bruce decides to harness his grief and trauma, he begins his journey to get heroic vengeance for his parents' death by training his body, mind, and techniques with the League of Shadows. Through this training, he turns his own body into a weapon to fight in the war against evil in Gotham City. This need to train and acquire the tools to wage war can be understood as his quest for symbolic military technology, as he learns the tools to fight and wields them against evil. However, they are not free from symbolic baggage. He is tied to a moral system, but the "weapons" in the hands of those without it are instead a destructive force.[6]

Although Bruce must train his body and mind to become a weapon against evil, in his mission, he must also employ technology to achieve his goals. He does so through the help of his company, Wayne Enterprises, more specifically through their technological research division. That division specializes in the development of military technology for the US government, and Bruce uses that connection lucratively in developing his suit, gadgets, and, most visibly, his new "Batmobile," which, in these films, is a military transport vehicle called the Tumbler. To fight the rising evil, including the shadow terrorists of the League of Shadows (even though Batman doesn't realize it's them until the end), military technology must be utilized. This move not only grounds the film in reality (how else would Batman in the real world protect himself from gunfire, knives, etc.?) but also mirrors the military buildup in the Iraq and Afghanistan Wars that were in direct response to the 9/11 attacks. The role that military technology plays in Batman's war on crime and its ties to real world US military action is not without its criticism, however. When first being presented with what will become the Bat-suit, Lucius Fox responds to Bruce's inquiry as to why the armor had not been adopted by the military with, "Bean counters didn't think a soldier's life was worth 300 grand." This line speaks to criticism of real world issues surrounding troops being underfunded in necessary supplies and gear (troops having to purchase their own body armor, for example) during the Iraq and Afghanistan Wars and in its cynicism about the value of a soldier's life to whether or not the US should be involved in the two wars in the first place.

In addition to Batman's use of tech tied to real-world military purposes, Wayne technology is also used by the League in the attack on Gotham, in the form of a microwave emitter that was developed for desert warfare. This speaks not only to historical precedent of the previous American involvement in conflicts in the East through its arming of Afghan rebels fighting against the Russians in the 1980s who would, over time, become many of the forces against whom the US was fighting in the post 9/11 era but also to the military industrial complex in general. No matter how much care is taken to secure technology, this aspect of the film seems to say, if the technology exists, it has the potential to fall into the wrong hands and be used against its creators.[7]

Traditional iterations of Batman have similarly highlighted his originating trauma, training, and technology as essential elements that make the hero who he is, but one particularly significant distinction between those representations of the Dark Knight and that of Christopher Nolan is his moral code. Nolan distinguishes his Batman from previous iterations and from other film and comic book superheroes in the character's eschewing of association with a symbolic vaulted moral or ethical code. In *The Dark Knight*, he says "I'm not a hero. I'm whatever Gotham needs me to be," which questions the traditional idea of heroics as emblematic of a type of person, belief system, or behaviors. Batman is a liminal character who acts with a goal in mind and does not question whether or not his actions fit a prescribed moral/ethical system. Instead, he tries to do good the way he is able, even when perceived to be bad or when viewed by society as a negative. This Batman is willing to bend the traditional sense of superheroics if that deviation from the norm results in more security for his city. For example, when Batman chastises Harvey Dent for torturing a Joker henchman in *The Dark Knight*, it isn't because torture is wrong per se but rather because the subject is mentally ill. Would he condone torturing a sane henchman? At other moments, the hero does seem willing to compromise what otherwise would be considered a moral code to get results. This consideration mirrors many of the cultural conversations that took place in the aftermath of 9/11, as many Americans considered what formerly taboo behavior might be acceptable in the light of their newfound victimhood and that led to vigorous debates in the public and private spheres on whether torture, surveillance, and rendition were called for, in spite of their direct contradiction with the traditional American moral code. These practices and the real-world issues associated with them resurface throughout the trilogy, continuously reminding audiences that they are issues that still need to be grappled with and better understood.

The demon's head – Ra's al Ghul

The central villain in *Batman Begins* is Ra's al Ghul, the head of a shadow terrorist organization whose name means "The demon's head." As the leader of an evil organization, al Ghul has overseen the assassination and destruction of world leaders and sites with the goal of "cleansing" the world of those who would lead it to its downfall. Setting his sights on Gotham City, the interaction between terrorist and target provides a number of symbolic connections to the US in the post 9/11 period, beginning with the city itself as a representation of the decadence of class inequities and corporate greed.

Throughout *Batman Begins* Gotham City is portrayed as a city in decline, riddled with crime and corruption. The police and the government are, for the most part, complicit, and organized crime reigns supreme. In this landscape, the film reveals both extreme poverty and extreme wealth existing simultaneously, a commentary on wealth inequality and the real-world class disparity that exists in much of the US today. Before the arrival of the Batman, powerful men use their power and wealth to stay on top, each one seemingly more corrupt than the next.[8] Keith Booker (2007) draws a parallel between Gotham City and the US at large, arguing that the country faced a moral crisis by the early 21st century after surviving depression and that Gotham's moral crisis is, similarly, a crisis in leadership (p. 30).

Among the powerful forces keeping Gotham City from rising out of its decline are politicians, leaders in law enforcement, and most visibly, corporate leaders and organized crime bosses. Representing both "legitimate" financial power and "illegitimate" power in *Batman Begins* are Earle, the heartless capitalist who attempts to seize control of Wayne Enterprises and Carmine Falcone, the kingpin of the Gotham mob. Much more screen time is devoted to Falcone's power and influence – making him the primary figure representing the corruption of money and power – and how it can contribute to the decadence of a city and society.[9] Falcone's power is presented as near absolute, with control of government and law enforcement alike, and that power and influence provides the means for the League to attempt to enact their city-wide terrorist attack.

While Carmine Falcone is emblematic of corruption, crime, and the decay and decline of Gotham City, his greed and thirst for power is self-serving, which allows him to be used by Ra's al Ghul and the League to their more nefarious ends. Ra's al Ghul views Gotham City as irredeemable and wants "to cleanse the world of its moral contamination" and has resolved "to do whatever is necessary to impose his system on the world" (Booker, 2007, pp. 27–28). In his role as the architect of a massive attack on a major US city, al Ghul's symbolic ties to real world terror networks is clear, but similarly to the portrayal of the shadowy, global terror network in *Iron Man 3*, the surface parallels are, in fact much more complex, in turn mirroring the intricate complexities of global terror in the 21st century.[10] Much as the techniques Bruce is trained to use by the League, deception and theatricality obscure a clearer understanding of the terrorist group. The man first introduced to Bruce as Ra's al Ghul is in fact an imposter, with the man who took on Bruce as his pupil, Henri Ducard, revealing himself as the real Demon's Head. At another moment, al Ghul indicates that he is, like Batman, a symbol, casting even more doubt as to the identity of the leader of the League of Shadows. Rather than focus on a clear representation of evil that must be defeated, as is the central plot of most other iterations of Batman, the choice of a more nebulous, shadowy figure speaks to the changing nature of the world and the adversaries of the US in a changing global climate. If the representative of evil in the figure of Ra's al Ghul cannot truly be defeated, since he is only one of many who fight for a particular point of view, then American audiences are forced to confront their understanding of evil and how to orchestrate its defeat, distinct from the symbolic systems of the previous century that were built around a clear adversary.

If the League of Shadows stands in as an analog for global terror, with Ra's al Ghul and his transitory and symbolic identity serving to problematize understanding of who is the enemy in 21st century conflicts, the attack on Gotham itself evokes the attack on New York on 9/11, on both the surface (terror group attacks a city they see as emblematic of corruption and excess) and in the reactions to the attack. When Wayne manor is destroyed in the attack by Ra's and the League, Alfred tells Bruce afterwards that "the Wayne legacy is more than bricks or mortar," which is representative of the resilience of the US after the 9/11 attacks in the face of the new threat of terrorism. Furthering this metaphorical connection, Alfred refers to rebuilding the Manor and improving its foundations. He is, of course, talking about improving the Batcave, but rhetorically this can be understood as an optimistic look at the opportunity to move forward as a culture after the 9/11 attacks based on our morals and ethical framework (our foundation). The next film will problematize that overly optimistic idealism, however, in the figure of Harvey Dent showing that our "foundations," although strengthened after the attack, are still able to be compromised. This arc, beginning in *Batman Begins* and continuing in *The Dark Knight*, will further an argument for less absolutism (we are good and they are evil) and instead invite a deeper examination of all of the elements that have contributed and continue to contribute to this type of conflict in the 21st century.

Dancing with the devil – chaos and the Joker

Released in 2008, *The Dark Knight* is the second in the trilogy of Batman reboots directed by Christopher Nolan. Nolan cloaks his creation in the dark moodiness that characterized Frank Miller's 1980s adaptions of the Batman saga as part of this reimagining and darkening of the Batman story, and in doing so is able to comment on the nature of good and evil, terrorism, and the seeming flexibility of a society's moral and ethical code when threatened with attack. Martin Fradley points out that

> While a film like *The Dark Knight* is certainly imprinted with the anxieties of a post 9/11 world, the key attractions for the audience were more banal. *The Dark Knight*, Prince argues, "is about what happens when civil and government authorities break the rules in their efforts to cope with terrorism."
>
> (Fradley, 2013, p. 17)

The central focus of the film, however, is the rise of the villain known as the Joker and how the reactions of both Batman and Gotham City at large will reveal the deeper motivations of a society threatened. Nolan's Joker is a stark deviation from previous iterations of the Clown Prince of Crime, and his twist on the character, as interpreted by Heath Ledger, takes audiences on a much darker journey into the post 9/11 American psyche.

In Tim Burton's 1989 film *Batman*, the audience was introduced to the first big budget incarnation of the Joker. Burton, whose name has become synonymous with gothic, campy style films, set the scene for an epic battle between two disturbed figures. Even in the most cartoonish elements of the Burton film, "particularly in Nicholson's spectacular over-the-top performance as the Joker" the film is "hilarious, but in a deranged way" (Booker, 2007, p. 25). In this version of the Joker story, audiences see the Joker before he is deformed, as a human being who is given a reason to seek revenge when his face is severely burned in a vat of acid. Almost 20 years later, when, in Nolan's version of the Joker story, the audience is presented with the horror of Heath Ledger's interpretation of the character with no context for who he is, how he was disfigured, or what compels his intentions, the once comical villain has become something different.[11] The Joker being less of a caricature, as in previous versions, creates a space for audiences to be truly terrified. As a cartoon, the Joker doesn't truly threaten to the core, but here, he does easily. In the monologue the Joker says to Harvey in the hospital, he says he doesn't plan, but Ledger shows that it is a lie. "We at last catch a momentary glimpse down to the depths of the character's soul, and find nothing there" (Weldon, 2016, p. 251).

Viewers are terrified by this lack of a "soul" and never learn anything truly revealing about Ledger's Joker because he gives several different versions of the story of his disfigurement and repeatedly tells Batman and commissioner Gordon that all he is interested in is "chaos." The effect of not featuring an origin story for the Joker is to leave audiences with a lack of understanding as to why he does what he does. This could be seen as reflective of the confusion that abounded post 9/11 about what could motivate terrorists to do the unspeakable. It would be too easy to ascribe to the Joker a clear rationale (society caused him, he faced trauma, etc.), but instead, the confusion is what lingers, drawing focus to his acts at the expense of his motivations. Nolan's presentation of the Joker, shrouded in mystery as to his origin, in contrast to Burton's, sets up a very important distinction that undergirds the shift in the representation of evil. While Nicholson's Joker is shown as an (albeit disturbed) human and elicits a basic human empathy from the audience, Ledger's does not. The audience does not see Ledger's Joker in anything resembling a human form and thus does not identify with him even on the most basic human level.[12]

From the very beginning of Nolan's story, the notion of traditional villains, as an audience understands them, is completely undone. The Joker has henchmen, just has he always has had in the past, but, in an immediate departure from past uses of henchmen, they begin killing one another within the first five minutes. This radical breaking of the traditional notion of "honor amongst thieves" is a cue to the audience that there is no code expected between the agents of evil anymore, and old modes of "villains united versus everyone else united" no longer applies. As the action continues, the audience is left in no doubt that a new style of villain has been established with a new set of motivations, which the audience does not and is not supposed to understand. The actions and character of the Joker create a series of incidents designed to explore deep issues about fear, terror, morals, and what chaos can do to otherwise "civilized" people living within the rules and institutions of a democracy.

Further underscoring this questioning of traditional expectation of "good guys" vs. "bad guys" is in the form of how first responders are portrayed in the film. First responders took on an almost mythic status in the aftermath of 9/11, due in large part to the number of first responders who lost their lives trying to evacuate the towers during the attack and those who made sacrifices afterwards. Here, by presenting police forces who are bad guys in disguise, firetrucks used as obstructions, trash trucks used as weapons, Joker disguised as a nurse, and police officers who are corrupted and used as pawns for the Joker, the chaos that the Joker espouses is made even more clear.[13] The Joker redeploys these codified, heroic symbols that had been reified in the media discourse post 9/11 and in doing so further questions the established order and understanding of "good" and "evil."

The first real indication of the Joker's psychosis, however, is when, having walked into the heart of a mob lair with several crime bosses seated around him, he murders one of them using a pencil he has stabbed into the table. Again, this is an early signifier that *this* Joker is an entirely new breed and that the film has moved to a level of violence and darkness that cannot be foiled by the traditional super-heroic ethical code. The Joker's indiscriminate violence will quickly escalate into something more organized and more broadly impactful, building to a fiery crescendo to events that mirror post 9/11 tactics of terror. When the Joker kidnaps the "fake" Batman and videos the captive, bound and terrified, viewers know that there is no chance that the man will live. Reminiscent of videos of hostages captured in the Middle East, the audience understands that the likelihood of a rescue or trade is non-existent.[14] The impact of a public, televised, and gory execution is employed by the Joker to sensationalize his own deeply vicious form of evil. Laughing as he warns the audience; "This may be graphic," he effectively terrorizes an entire city with one terrible act of violence: the ultimate goal of terrorism in general.

The Joker also uses a mental patient to escape from the city jail by implanting a bomb in his stomach, echoing suicide bombings, which have always been a bedrock tactic of terrorist organizations. The man is obviously and deeply mentally disturbed and allowed the Joker to implant the device telling the surrounding police officers, right before it blows, that the Joker said he would make the voices disappear "replacing them with bright lights, like Christmas." The difference in this scenario between the mental patient and the would-be suicide bomber is that the Joker is offering the man a "cure" and leads him to believe he will get his life back. The similarities, of course, are that in both cases, death is the end result, and both have been used by people in positions of power who prey on the weaknesses of their "foot soldier" victims, wielding them as sacrificial weapons in their campaigns of terror with the promise of a better life or afterlife. As a consequence of the Joker's reign of terror, the people of Gotham quickly divide and are thrown into a constant state of fear, waiting for the next attack. The Joker obliges by threatening to blow up Gotham General Hospital but, interestingly, allows time for the patients to be evacuated as his goal is not necessarily to kill in high numbers but rather to create situations of chaos and terror to reveal what he perceives as people's "true" natures (selfish, immoral, evil just like him).

In reaction to the terror created by the Joker, once captured, Batman beats the Joker while in captivity, and in this image of Batman beating the Joker, there is no doubt in the audience's mind that the Joker is pure evil, and it is likely that most audiences would not question the methods of the Batman in this situation. However, when it is later revealed that the Joker had intended to get captured and the interrogation was all part of his plan, the expectations of what is right and wrong, acceptable or unacceptable are questioned and parallel the discussion, frequent in the post 9/11 era as to whether torture is legal, acceptable, or effective.

The Joker's last act of terror is to rig two ferries (one evacuating prisoners and one evacuating civilians) with explosives, give each group on each boat a detonator to the other boat and 30 minutes to decide which one of them will blow the other up first. His "game" is layered with a further threat of mutual destruction (double detonation by him) if the 30-minute time period expires. In this scene, the Joker sets up a situation that inspires regular people to step up to commit what would normally be considered bad/evil actions in the name of saving numerous other (in the case of the civilian boat) "innocent" lives. Again, the Joker seeks to alter/destroy the existing set of morals by which society usually functions to bring Gotham down to its basest level. He says,

> their morals, their code . . . dropped at the first sign of trouble. They're only as good as the world allows them to be. When the chips are down these "civilized" people . . . they'll eat each other. See, I'm not a monster. I'm just ahead of the curve.

Halfway through the boat situation the people on the civilian boat offer the conundrum up to a vote. In this, the mechanism of democracy (voting) serves to symbolically "decode" the American populace with civilians facing the "evil other" (prisoners). The central question is "whose life has value and whose doesn't?" The confounding conclusion to the hostage situation is that the prisoners are elevated to a moral position higher than the one of the terrorist/inhuman evil that provoked them because they have a moral code in the end. Both groups of people get to live because they refused to subvert the societal moral code.

The Joker's ferry dilemma is, on the surface, an interrogation of contemporary morals and ethics, established by the Joker to be a test to prove that Gothamites (representing broader American culture) are morally and ethically corrupt and will likely sacrifice another group for their own safety. However, when a convicted criminal eliminates the decision-making mechanism, he seemingly reveals a triumph of what can be understood as Western moral/ethical systems that eschew violent murder of innocents as a preemptive action against a violent threat to the self. However, Shaun Treat views this act not as an active redemption of Western values in the face of terror from the outside but of passivity in the face of the threat. He says, "Batman celebrates non-explosion as vindication of Gotham's redeeming decency and virtue, yet such comforting sentiment instead affirms this public's passivity as victims of terror." In other words, if the people had been courageous enough to live their moral/ethical values, they'd have no need for a "savior" in Batman. "Instead, the victim-of-terror-turned-Super-Antihero makes hard choices, so we need neither contemplate self-sacrifices for our convictions nor examine our complicity in affective citizenships"(Treat, 2009, p. 107).

As this scenario is unfolding, we are witness to Bruce Wayne's unveiling of his massive sonar network, which has the capacity to track every citizen of Gotham. Lucius Fox tells him that this is "unethical, wrong" to which Batman replies: "I have to find this man." In a clear nod to the provisions of the post 9/11 USA Patriot Act, we understand, at this point, that the Joker has succeeded. The moral structure of Gotham City has fallen, and the figures guarding the prosecution of justice have thrown out the rulebook in pursuit of their terrorist. This points to the notion that 9/11 was viewed as so monstrous and out of the realms of expected behavior that America was willing to set aside its founding charters in the pursuit of those responsible for the attack. The change in the prosecution of American foreign policy after 9/11 was justified by many as temporary and necessary, just as Bruce Wayne tries to justify it to Fox in the movie scene. When the Joker has been found and killed, Fox is able to blow up the tracking system presumably so that it can never be used again. In reality, we know that the provisions in the Patriot Act set in place a surveillance system and a series of exceptions to the Bill of Rights that were not temporary and, unlike the fictionalized Hollywood version, cannot be returned to a pre 9/11 configuration.

Although Gotham and its criminal underbelly are characterized as uniformly evil in the first film, here, as a means of exploring the nature of good and evil, some ambiguity is injected into the presentation of the criminal element. Lying on the ground after being shot by a disguised Joker in the opening scene of the film, the bank manager of a mob controlled bank says, "Criminals used to believe in things: honor, respect." This establishes the idea that there are codes by which groups live their lives. "Good" people behave in one way, and "Bad" people, even in their counterpoint to the "good," have their own code by which they live their criminal lives. However, this dichotomous existence, with foundations in codes of behaviors and identities, is quickly dispensed with. The Joker's henchmen kill each other, as the Joker robs from a mob bank. The Joker confronts the mob and doesn't care about money – everything that he is flies in the face of the criminal code these people have heretofore lived by and understood their world by. The mob in *Batman Begins* was supported in the shadows by the League working through them to attempt to fulfill their plan (although unsuccessfully). Here the mob similarly allies with the Joker, but the previous model is quickly turned on its head when the Joker refuses to play by anyone's rules, resulting in a precarious power vacuum that will result in even more wholesale destruction in *The Dark Knight Rises*.

Similarly tied to the characterization of organized crime in the film is the influence of international forces in the conflicts in Gotham. In *Batman Begins*, the international element appears in the form of the League who used terrorist practices to try to effect change in Gotham based on their perception of its corruption, while in *The Dark Knight*, the international element takes the form of financing of the film's criminal enterprises. This could be seen as a commentary on how the global banking system can facilitate supporting the funding of terrorist groups (money laundering, hiding funds, shell corporations) but also how intervention (sanctions, ceasing business) can be an effective tool to stopping global terrorist networks. In the metaphoric microcosm that is Gotham City and the Batman film universe, mob funding moved offshore cannot escape the intervention of Batman. In the real world, these interventions are more in line with diplomacy, negotiations and legislation, but the filmic metaphor serves to highlight the role that money has in both supporting and stopping global terrorism.

Perhaps more interesting than the presentation of the villainous forces in *The Dark Knight*, however, is the counter-presentation of the heroes. Commissioner Gordon is the only character who comes through the events with his moral compass unchanged. He remains wedded to the notion of law and justice and, ironically, it is his "death" that starts of the cycle of Batman throwing his own moral code to one side to pursue the Joker. Batman has always wanted to fight evil within a certain set of ethical guidelines. To this end, he states that he does not want to become the kind of man that he would have to become in order to beat the terrorist. When Gordon fakes his death, both Batman and Harvey Dent beat the mob informer to try to get information about the whereabouts of the Joker from him. The idealistic good guys that represented law, order, justice, and morality for the first three quarters of the film turn to torture as soon as they think Gordon (the moral heart of Gotham) is dead, showing the audience that it doesn't take much for the moral code to fall apart in the absence of people who guard it.

Harvey Dent begins the film as an unequivocal good guy; he is representative of the party line, the government, justice, and the institutions of power. His trajectory toward villainy reveals something else about the breakdown of the traditional notion of good vs. evil and us vs. them. Dent is an idealist, but his idealism is corrupted through the presence of evil and directly because of his fight against evil. Dent is motivated by emotion, revenge, and humanity, and in his turn toward evil, he is presented as a villain and undertakes villainous and murderous acts. However, half of him is still human, and his evil is not shown in concert with the evil of the Joker but as a parallel story line in which Dent displaces his moral code to chance. After Dent's two-headed coin is burned in the wreckage of the fire that scars him and kills Rachel, he views the world as a place in which sometimes there is good and sometimes there is evil. By using his coin (following through in heads and not on the burnt side) he is not murdering indiscriminately but instead is leaving the outcomes to chance. Dent invests his moral structure in the coin, a game of chance that reflects the balance of the universe, whereas the Joker acts indiscriminately and is only interested in destroying that balance.

The exploration of the aspects of good and evil in these films, through the development of the chaotic Joker, the "White Knight" Harvey Dent, and the various surrounding characters and events, each contribute something to the problematization of the moral and ethical codes established in the first film. As Martin Fradley has indicated,

> Both *Batman Begins* and *The Dark Knight* were criticized in some quarters for their apparent endorsement of "necessary evils" such as rendition, torture, and the erosion of civil liberties. Rather than simply validating Bush-era military vigilantism, however, in Kellner's view the melodramatic fallout from Batman's violent war on crime in *The Dark Knight* – the death of Wayne's beloved Rachel (Maggie Gyllenhaal); the pathologization of "liberal" politician Harvey Dent (Aaron Eckhart) – signals instead that the film's murky political allegory "suggests that going over to the Dark Side twists and corrupts individuals and society."
>
> (Fradley, 2013, p. 17)

Batman Begins shows us a Gotham City at the depths of darkness, and *The Dark Knight* presents a city on the rise but faced with a more nuanced evil: one that does not follow rules and instead corrupts the "good" characters to the point that audiences ultimately question the categorization completely. It will be in the culminating film, *The Dark Knight Rises*, that this exploration ultimately culminates in the near complete destruction of both Gotham City and its hero.

From the pits of "hell" – Bane

In the first two films of the Nolan Batman franchise, the physical spaces of the films serve a functional and a symbolic purpose, primarily as the originator of the Batman (crime in the city is responsible for the death of his parents and inspires him to protect it) as well as the target of the terrorist forces of both the League of Shadows and the Joker. In *The Dark Knight Rises*, the physical spaces of the film take on additional symbolic meaning – discursively tied to the distinguishing final word of the title – and will provide commentary on 21st-century American society.

Gotham City of *The Dark Knight Rises* is a dichotomous one. While above, the city seems to have more fully emerged into the light from its beginnings in *Batman Begins* in both the outward prosperity and the visual tone of its presentation on film, below the city, children toil working in secret for Bane's mercenaries. This can be understood as a commentary on contemporary class disparities, poverty, and homelessness, and these class issues are woven throughout the film not only in its spatial imagery but also in the action that takes place in those spaces. In contrast to the extremely wealthy in the figure of Bruce Wayne, who has the luxury to begin the film holed up in Wayne

Manor, the impoverished young masses of Gotham are literally underground as they are framed as "less than." It is equally not an accident that the children working in the tunnels are orphans, like Bruce Wayne. However, just as his wealth keeps him "above," so does the poverty of the children keep them "below."

The orphan laborers working underground in the film are helping to build an underground infrastructure to facilitate Bane's attack on the city, and the central hub "lair" of the mercenary serves as a contrast to the "lair" of the Batman. For Bane, his "lair," which is evocative of the Batcave though their shared central waterfall, is below the grimy, gritty city of Gotham and is created from man-made sewer tunnels. It is literally born of filth, while the Batcave is a natural formation, born of water naturally eating away at rock and is found below the opulent wealth of Wayne Manor. In fact, visual and textual imagery in this film tied to the idea of "under" or "below the ground" abounds (Batcave/prison/sewer tunnels/Bane's headquarters/buried police officers/"rising") as a reminder of this disparity between those who are symbolically "under" others and who must fight to rise out of their circumstances.

Although the prison that is the birthplace of Bane is tied to this symbolic figuring of "under" or "below," connecting it to contemporary class issues, the near inescapable pit is also deliberately linked to geopolitical spaces relevant in the post 9/11 era. In the Batman comics, Bane's birthplace, the Peña Duro prison, is located in Santa Prisca, a fictional Spanish Caribbean nation. By changing the location in the film to "a more ancient part of the world," which is clearly intended to be somewhere in the Middle East, the film explicitly ties the world into which Bane is born (and Talia as well for that matter) to the region. Linking the global terrorists Ra's al Ghul and Bane to this region evokes the desire for a clearer understanding of the origins of real world terrorism. The complex nature of thousands of years of religious tension, economic hardship, and geopolitical maneuvering is often a dense subject for the average person to unpack and understand. Here, in a fictional narrative, elements of that narrative history are presented in an abstract way, allowing audiences to reflect on their real-world counterparts. Although the prison is predominantly populated by criminals, the fact that an innocent woman, a baby born there (Talia), and the prisoner who protects her (Bane) are linked to this otherwise dark hellscape establishes that, even in a discursive space established as the place horrible men go to serve a sentence until death, the light of innocence and good can be found. The appearance of these glimmers of good found even in the literal pits of darkness serves to problematize some of the homogeneous characterizations that appeared as a reaction to the terrorist attack in the US ("all Muslims are bad," "all people from the Middle East are terrorists"). This symbolic portrayal, however, simultaneously communicates the inverse idea. Here, darkness, when thrust upon those good people, ultimately corrupts them and pushes them into a life of vengeance against a society that has wronged them, representative of the real world examples of terrorists who, when faced with what they see as a societal/cultural/religious "attack" on their beliefs/worldview, turn to terrorism as a remedy. This metaphor, which points to two seemingly opposite sides of a coin: innocence and good found in a dark place vs. innocence and good corrupted into vengeance through violence, demonstrates that "evil" may not be as monolithic as often portrayed in the media and that only by understanding the origins of terror are we able to effectively fight and eliminate it in the future.

If the underside of the spaces in *The Dark Knight Rises* paints a portrait of the lower classes, the poor, and the downtrodden, the above-ground spaces of Gotham serve as the site of interaction between the have and the have-nots and are reflective of class disparity, communicating the hardships that poverty in the modern era can engender. Interacting in these city spaces are "regular" Gothamites, whose appearance further underscores the film's commentary on class. When Bane's forces attack the stock exchange, for example, his men are each disguised as "ordinary" citizens: a delivery man, janitor, and shoe-shiner, and they attack the heart of extreme wealth, the stock exchange. This "regular citizen" symbolic position is expanded beyond just the mercenaries whose appearance might otherwise symbolically link the working class with the film's villain exclusively when one of the wealthy victims bemoans the loss of "our" money, and the "ordinary" police officer says, "Mine is in my mattress."

The Dark Knight Rises establishes Gotham City as an allegorical space representing class disparity (underbelly/above ground), but beyond just a symbolic space for these more abstract ideas, the film presents Gotham City at its most literal, as the target for Bane's terrorist attacks. Although Nolan had used Chicago in the previous two films, for this film, he chose Pittsburgh specifically for the symbolic power of Gotham being able to stand in for a number of US cities.

"He wanted Gotham to look like a number of familiar places but stylized to be uniquely something else. In that sense, he wanted to capture the spirit of Gotham as it exists in comic lore; relatable, but fictional" (Saporito, 2015). In the desire to communicate the class disparity and wealth disparity discussed earlier, a change of location was needed, and Pittsburgh provided the ability to see in the establishing shots of the city both the poorer areas juxtaposed with the wealth of the "gleaming skyscrapers." And one could also argue that the less visually iconic nature of Pittsburgh helped audiences see Gotham as its own city, without tying it too closely to a real world one. The universality and more fictional nature of Gotham City allows for a more allegorical understanding of the issues and ideas presented in the film, especially when related to social issues/class disparities. However, as a victim of a terrorist attack from a group of mercenaries tied to a global terror organization with vague Middle Eastern ties, one moment in particular anchors this attack in the specific echoes of the al-Qaida attack on New York City.

At the moment when Bane blows up the bridges, stranding Gothamites on their island city, there is a wide shot of the city demonstrating the bridges going down. Although Pittsburgh had stood in for Gotham in virtually every other establishing shot, here, due to the need for the city to be viewed as an island with collapsing bridges, an aerial shot of lower Manhattan is used instead. In this image, which is meant to stand in for Gotham as Bane blows up the bridges into the city, the One World Trade Center tower under construction is clearly visible. A symbol of rebuilding after the terrorist attacks of 9/11, here it serves not only as a visual reminder of those attacks – discursively tying them to the attack on Gotham by Bane's mercenaries – but also of the resiliency after attacks such as this one.[15] This shot comes only a short time after Bane has explained to Bruce Wayne that hope is what causes true despair, and the tower rebuilt after the two towers were destroyed is the architectural embodiment of hope from tragedy. In reality, the single tower can be understood as standing as a reminder of American resiliency in the face of evil. Its presence here, however, as viewers watch the attacks on Gotham in real time, is one of hope. Reminding viewers that, as a culture, we did rebound and move forward communicates a sense of hope for the fate of Gotham. However, with Bane's words freshly echoing in the viewers' ears, that hope functions to deepen the darkness and despair associated with the assault on Gotham City.

As a symbolic space representing the breeding ground for wealth inequality and class disparity, Gotham City is an apt metaphor with its seedy underground alongside the shining temples to wealth and prosperity, and it is also the physical victim itself of terror from outside who see the city as emblematic of that disparity and seek to destroy it. But, Gotham City in the Nolan Batman films is more than just a stage for the action to take place, and through the course of the films, it takes on more and more symbolic significance, not just of the issues that divide but of those that unite as well.

In *Batman Begins*, audiences are invited to identify with Batman as he overcomes his trauma and fear and redeploys it in a mission of justice and revenge against the forces of evil seeking to destroy Gotham City. In that film, Gotham is the backdrop and home for the corruption that gives birth to The Dark Knight and is the stage on which he proves his superheroic mettle. But, by the third film, the resiliency of Gotham City in the face of Bane's attack and takeover appears to take on the role as identification object for the audiences. In *Batman Begins* "We are Batman," but by the end of *The Dark Knight Rises*, it appears that "We are Gotham." And, much like the orphaned Bruce Wayne who must overcome obstacles to save his city, at the conclusion of *The Dark Knight Rises*, Gotham City is, itself, like an orphan, abandoned by its "father and protector" awaiting the protection of a new, adoptive father. This idea is intertextually ironic, because the new adoptive "protector" of the city is *Robin* John Blake, and in the Batman comics mythos, Batman's sidekick Robin is similarly orphaned, taken in by Bruce Wayne and adopted and trained to be his crimefighting partner. Here, Gotham City itself believes it has been orphaned by Batman in a final redemptive act, when in fact, if the imagery at the end of the film is to be taken to its next logical step, *Robin* will soon be "adopting" the city as its new protector (and, presumably, as the new Batman).

Due to the iterative nature of superhero comics where any threat to the hero is temporary (even death is ultimately often thwarted as dead heroes return anew), superhero films have traditionally been constructed on a similar structure. Despite great turmoil, the hero triumphs in the end, ready to fight the next villain who may present themselves in the next film of a franchise. That hero is symbolic, powerful, and ultimately undefeatable. As we have discussed at length, however, the Nolan Batman films eschew a structure that vaults the superhero to the status of an unbreakable god, in favor of a grittier realism, one that rests on the very human back of its central figure. The choice of this aspect of the film (focusing on a more human Batman) not only underscores the realism Nolan seeks, but it is also another aspect that weaves the films into the post 9/11 cultural tapestry. Previously, not many would have wondered about the human physical toll being Batman would take on the body, but a number of scenes in *The Dark Knight Rises* do just this. When Bruce visits the doctor, who proceeds to lists his numerous, chronic, physical health issues resulting from his superheroics, the scene highlights that, in this world, Batman is human. He is a highly skilled and trained human but human, nonetheless. This scene reflects a trend in the post 9/11 era of more public focus on the physical toll of "hero" work (the lawsuits from 9/11 rescue workers and their families, persistent health problems deriving from rescue efforts, PTSD and the physical afflictions in servicemembers returning from Iraq/Afghanistan, etc.). This sets up Bane's "breaking" of Batman as realistic and inevitable. It is only a "matter of time" that a serious injury would likely occur, but through that injury, Batman's resiliency is highlighted. Even from what is, in medical science, viewed to be a catastrophic injury (breaking ones back) Batman is ultimately able to recover and save his city, and, once again, this trajectory draws parallels to the resiliency of the US post 9/11.

Conclusion

Batman has had a significant presence in popular culture since the creation of the Dark Knight Detective in 1939, with fans young and old following the adventures of the hero as he Banged! Powed! and Socked! his way through numerous heroic battles with colorful and wacky supervillains, and through various iterations both bright and colorful and dark and brooding. However, it is with Christopher Nolan's interpretation of this world that audiences are presented with stories that are grounded in real experience and that attempt to interpret the sometimes over-the-top escapades of more than 75 years of comics, television, and film stories through a lens that makes them relatable and understandable in the contemporary 21st-century context. As a result of Nolan's vision, the Batman franchise not only saw a boost in popularity and box office sales but also a renewed interest in a superhero who, distinct from most of the numerous heroes that flourish on film in the post 9/11 period, does not have superpowers and instead must rely on his intellect, training, and his technology to combat the various evils that plague his city. Inspired by the complex social, psychological, and political issues affecting audiences in the aftermath of a domestic terrorist attack, these films attempt to unpack and process them, continuously weaving them back into audiences' contemporary experiences. Their focus on exploring more abstract concepts such as the nature of fear, the psychic power of vengeance, and the effects of trauma provide audiences with a means to better understand their own experiences of these as a culture after the attacks. Through the abstract, fictional representation of other practices and forces that emerge in this period such as torture, the mythologization of first responders, military campaigns and technology, warrantless wiretapping, rendition, and the media, audiences similarly are provided the opportunity to interrogate these and better understand them, free from direct links to the originating traumatic event itself. And finally, at the center of the constellation of abstract psychological concepts and analogous practices are representations and the exploration of the complexities of evil and terrorism in the modern era. Through this symbolic work, Christopher Nolan's Batman films are emblematic of the rise in the popularity of superhero media not only purely for entertainment value as they had been in the past but as a means to understand ourselves and our own trauma. If, indeed, audiences identify with the Dark Knight, then as a culture we share his trauma and travel with him through his harrowing fight against villains and his own psychic wounds and ultimately triumph with a deeper understanding of who we are in the present moment.

Notes

1 Batman's interactions with cartoony, over the top villains in the 1990s sets up a clear contrast with Nolan's villains and could be understood as a commentary on the Other. In other words, the 90s villains are so removed from reality that they become abstract concepts and not human characters. They are so different and irredeemable that their representation seems to feed into a compartmentalized cultural conceptualization that will set a tone for the 21st century. Nolan's villains, by contrast, break out of this abstract "evil model" and become much more significant as avatars of contemporary societal ills and evils.

2 The participatory nature of audiences associated with the Nolan Batman films went beyond just establishing identifications with the characters. Before the release of *The Dark Knight*, audiences were encouraged to participate in various marketing "scavenger hunts" on the internet and real life to unlock trailers, images, and information about the film. For a discussion of this successful campaign that drew in Batman audiences even further, see Weldon (2016, p. 249).

3 Previous screen iterations of the character either ignored the hero's originating trauma (*Batman* (TV), 1966) or presented it as a quick flashback to explain the relationship between Batman and the Joker (*Batman*, 1989).

4 Detective Comics #33

5 After the well, Thomas asks Bruce "Why do we fall? So we can learn to pick ourselves up again," which speaks to the myth of the American "self-made" man. But the privilege of the Wayne family is worth noting in this utterance. Thomas Wayne is only able to "pick himself up" because of his inherited wealth. Bruce is only able to "deploy" Batman because of his wealth, but the true "construction" of that identity is named after stripping himself

(albeit temporarily) of that privilege. This raises questions about the nature of privilege and whether or not it plays a role in resilience after trauma.

6 The fact that Bruce trains to be the Batman with the terrorist organization against which he will fight in both the first and third movies of the trilogy is not insignificant. The fact that Bruce uses his skills for good but with the same "weapons" the League uses to sow discord and evil in Bruce's estimation, while believing they are fighting for a good cause, can point to the idea that the branding and understanding of terrorist groups is linked to their mission and the cultural perspective of those attacked. The difference between a "terrorist" and a "freedom fighter" might be merely one of the cultural group referring to them. Ra's al Ghul and the League believe they are doing good, so the presentation of both perspectives invites reflection about the nature of terrorism and the potential inspirations for it.

7 This is similar to a central plot point of *Iron Man*. See Chapter 3 for more on the relationship between American military technology when repurposed in the hands of terrorists.

8 The exception being the Wayne family, who, in narration and flashback is seen as attempting to use their wealth and influence to save Gotham City. Their removal by the very dark forces they were working to clean up speaks to the inadequacy of previous policies in the US such as the War on Drugs and Crime, which, although well intentioned, often resulted in more poverty and crisis among the poor.

9 In a conversation between Bruce Wayne and Falcone, the crime boss says, "I could blow your head off and no one would bat an eye." This quote unintentionally foreshadows Donald Trump, who said that he could shoot someone in the middle of Fifth Avenue and supporters would still support him. One could chalk this up to coincidence, but what they both have in common is that both of these similar phrases are uttered by powerful men who do not espouse a moral and ethical system, instead doing whatever is in the best interest of their own wealth and power but, because of that power and influence, those who might ordinarily condemn such misdeeds instead ignore them, further empowering the powerful men to continue to work in that mode.

10 See our discussion on the Ten Rings and The Mandarin in Chapter 3 on Iron Man.

11 Interestingly, filmmakers appear to be poised to make a 180 degree turn away from this dehumanizing approach, as they explore the Joker's back story and explain his transformation from human to psychotic supervillain in the film *Joker* due in late 2019.

12 The second of Burton's films presents an even more sympathetic villain in the form of the Penguin. The Penguin's origin story is presented in the style of Dickensian horror. The audience is drawn into an almost fairytale atmosphere where the underlying premise is dark but dark in a fairytale way. In other words, the audience watches the action unfold; safe in the understanding that nothing that happens for the next hour could possibly ever come true. Through his evil plan the Penguin elicits laughter and, more importantly, pity. He wants to be recognized as the human being that, despite his disfiguration, he is. The fact that he leads an army of penguins into battle with rocket launchers attached to their backs and uses clowns to kidnap the first born sons of Gotham adds to the tone of comedy evil, which is completely disconnected from the very possible, terrible evil that Nolan later brings to the franchise.

13 The heroism of first responders during the terrorist attacks has been commemorated in a number of comics volumes, the sales of which, in most cases, raised funds for funds supporting families of those who died attempting to save people and other survivor groups. These comics (*9–11: Artists Respond*, *9–11: Emergency Relief*, *Call of Duty* and *Heroes*, to name a few) published by DC, Marvel, and the other major comics publishers, collected the work of a wider variety of artists, which, in comics form, told both real life stories of the rescue attempts and more fantastical stories of the reactions of superheroes such as Superman, Spider-Man, and Captain America to the attacks.

14 In the first Gulf War, British pilots and a handful of Americans were captured, and, although they appeared on Iraqi television with bruises and were used for propaganda on

behalf of Saddam Hussein's regime, there was worldwide expectation that they would be released unharmed. Post 9/11, the expectation that hostages might survive was still intact, until, half way through a series of beheadings that were televised, Western democracies realized that they could not negotiate their citizens out of harm's way and reconciled themselves to post-execution statements of condemnation and horror.

15 Further tying the city spaces to the threat of real-world terrorism is a shot of men hanging from the Gotham bridges after defying Bane's forces. The contemporary imagery of men hanging is currently associated with images from newscasts of the Middle East, where people are often hanged publicly for violating religious law or refusing to conform to the imposed norms of the local leaders. Here, these images of men hanging from the bridge further deepen the symbolic connections between real world terrorism and the terrorist takeover of Gotham City.

Bibliography

Batman. 20th Century Fox Television, 1966–1968.

Batman. Dir. Tim Burton. Warner Brothers, 1989.

Batman *Begins.* Dir. Christopher Nolan. Warner Brothers, 2005.

Booker, M. Keith. *May Contain Graphic Material: Comic Books, Graphic Novels, and Film.* Westport, CT: Praeger, 2007.

The Dark Knight. Dir. Christopher Nolan. Warner Brothers, 2008.

The *Dark Knight Rises.* Dir. Christopher Nolan. Warner Brothers, 2012.

Fradley, Martin. "What Do You Believe In? Film Scholarship and the Cultural Politics of the *Dark Knight* Franchise." *Film Quarterly,* Vol. 66, No. 3, Spring 2013. pp. 15–27.

Horton, Owen R. "Origin Stories: Rebooting Masculinity in Superhero Films After 9/11." *Human: Journal of Literature & Culture,* No. 6, June 2016. pp. 72–85.

Pulver, Andrew. "He's Not a God, He's Human." *The Guardian* (UK), June 14, 2005.

Saporito, Jeff. "Q:Why was Pittsburgh used as Gotham city for the majority of 'The Dark Knight Rises'?" *The Take.* December 5, 2015. http://screenprism.com/insights/article/why-was-pittsburgh-used-as-gotham-city-for-the-majority-of-the-dark-knight

Treat, Shaun. "How America Learned to Stop Worrying and Cynically ENJOY! The Post-9/11 Superhero Zeitgeist." *Communication and Critical/Cultural Studies,* Vol. 6, No. 1, March 2009. pp. 103–109.

Wainer, Alex M. *Soul of the Dark Knight. Batman as Mythic Figure in Comics and Film.* Jefferson, NC: McFarland, 2014.

Weldon, Glen. *The Caped Crusade: Batman and the Rise of Nerd Culture.* New York: Simon & Schuster, 2016.

2   The high price of freedom

Captain America

But the price of freedom is high.
It always has been.
And it's a price I'm willing to pay.

Steve Rogers, Captain America: The Winter Soldier

The question of why Captain America was resurrected to lead the characters of the Marvel Universe through almost two decades of obsessive contemplation about how 9/11 changed America rests simply with who he is. He *is* America, in all its faults and all of its glories. Placing him at the center of the action and as the "moral center" of the Marvel Universe was both a wise commercial and artistic choice that lead to both the stunning popularity of the resurrected superhero genre and a capacity for a more complicated and introspective narrative about what it meant to be American in the years following the terrorist attacks.

His ability to fully occupy that space in the pop culture landscape rested firmly on the ideals he was imbued with before he ever donned the star-spangled uniform: his capacity to evolve as America did over the decades and his unique position as the only super heroic character that acted as a canvas on which to contest American ideals. Steve Rogers was ordinary; the amplification of his existing gentle and just traits were vital to the development of the Captain America character in concert with dramatic changes in the American political and social landscape. No other superhero has evolved and reflected to the extent that Cap has over the decades. Beginning as the unquestioning super patriot soldier of the Second World War, moving through the 50s with the debunked Commie Smasher iteration, throwing down his shield to become "man without a country," and finally picking it back up again in his realization that the people and not the government are the keepers of the American dream. In more nuanced terms, Captain American has wrestled with the themes of domestic dissent, the tension between the greatest generation and the more radical values of the baby boomers, civil rights issue as they exploded in the 1960s, and a growing disconnect between the American people and their government. His most important evolution, the one that grounded him perfectly for the post 9/11 American mission, was the realization that American values were and are still aspirational. His acceptance that the American dream was not equally accessible to all and deliberately withheld from many moved him completely away from his one note acceptance of American superiority and fully into the notion that America was a complex beast, both bringer of opportunity and oppression, provider of life and reaper of death.

The post 9/11 Captain America movies were a faithful reconstruction of the arc of his character development, heavily layered with post 9/11 societal concerns. *The First Avenger* reintroduces American audiences to their super patriot; magnifies those characteristics that made him gentle, progressive, and just; and perfectly structures a character who is able to evolve and operate in a post 9/11 world, albeit with traditional American values. In *The Avengers* (2012), he is already shown to be questioning the prosecution of American foreign policy, arguing about American values with Iron Man and desperately trying to hold on to a sense of who he is while the traditional powers structures that protected the public before are exposed as corrupted, fraudulent, and dangerous. *Winter Soldier* ratchets up the complexity considerably and has Cap leading a resistance against the infiltration of HYDRA into the American intelligence apparatus. The creeping under narrative of the reappearance of Bucky Barnes (The Winter Soldier) serves to highlight the fact that the reconstruction of American foreign policy, post World War Two, created incredible tension with the rest of the world and some culpability in the creation of the threat that the world is currently facing. By *Civil War* Cap has moved completely away from the American Government and sits firmly of the side of freedom as he views it. As in the comic "NOMAD" storyline, he gives up his shield and goes on the run. What we know from Cap's return in *Avengers: Infinity War* and *Avengers Endgame*, is that he is able to quickly and easily retake his position as the moral center of the Marvel Universe in the end of days narratives only because he has evolved more than any other character in the post 9/11 Marvel universe while remaining reassuringly immovable in the face of terror, fear, and loss.

What post 9/11 Captain America on the big screen allows for is the mediation of America itself. No other character is so tied with American ideals, and no other character would have been accepted and embraced through a journey of discovery that told the story of a corrupt and complicit American government, people, and foreign policy. In the immediate aftermath of 9/11, the interrogation of the hyper patriotic, pro America narrative that emerged from the attacks was forbidden within American pop culture. It is, perhaps, the greatest irony that it is the super patriotic, ham-fistedly rendered Captain America himself that serves as the ultimate Trojan horse in forcing American audiences to consider what freedom actually looks like and what is required to preserve the actual tenets of democracy.

The bittersweet dénouement of *Avengers: Endgame* hints at an alternative historical timeline where Steve Rogers goes back to the past and stays there.

In this timeline Rogers gets to live his life, presumably with Peggy and with his values intact. When Wilson comments that he is sad to exist in a world where Captain America never existed, Cap smiles and, with the passing of his shield to The Falcon, signals the beginning of the reconstruction of post 9/11 America, a place where the remasculinization and militarization of American attitudes badly served the American people and the rest of the world. To understand the full significance of the passing of the shield, it is vital to understand the full arc of a character who was "a continuing, reflecting, adjusting: 'performance of American identity'" (Dubose, 2007).

From the minute Captain America burst onto the cover of his own comic, draped in the American flag and punching Adolf Hitler square in the jaw, it was clear that both his origin and his continued existence would be forever tied with the perception and mediation of America itself. He was not the first patriotically themed superhero, having followed and drawn aesthetic and thematic influence from the Blue Bolt, Uncle Sam, and The Shield, but he would become the most enduring. Over six decades, even in times where his popularity waned, he has been an iconic presence, rebooted, post 9/11, as the: "moral center of the Marvel hero community"(McDermott, 2012). Cap's appearance in Captain America #1 shows the unambiguous preference of those who created him for America's proactive involvement in World War II. He was imagined both as a powerful rebuke to the almost theatrical evil of the Third Reich and brought to life by Jewish immigrants as a symbol of resistance (Moser, 2012). Cap entered the war long before American leaders signaled their commitment and, intended or not, acted as a propaganda tool to increase the American public's appetite for a war that was remote, misunderstood, and that tested the isolationist tendencies of some Americans and German sympathizers within the country.

Cap's interesting departure from the more fantastical origin stories of the genre privileged the ordinary over the super heroic and elevated the potential of the soldier over the potential of caped crusaders. He was the first superhero whose origins were not particularly magical. Injected with super-soldier serum, a scientific endeavor well within the realms of the possible, his physically weak body was enhanced to the limits of human capability. More importantly, his personality traits, which were gentle, just, and modest, were also magnified. In *Captain America: The First Avenger* (2011), Dr. Erskine and General Phillips are shown to be in disagreement as to which candidate should be chosen for the experimental injection of the serum. Phillips argues that a meat-head soldier by the name of Hodge is the best candidate: "He's big, he's fast, he obeys orders; He's a soldier." Erskine replies: "He's a bully." Erskine's preference for a man who knows what it is like to be at the mercy of those with more power than himself indicates that it is the existing character within the man that is the most important qualification. Erskine's vision of who his super solider should be mirrors the aspiration he has in how America should set an example on the world stage. As its influence and power grew alongside its increasing entanglements in foreign policy, the idea that America could lead the world into an era of peace was keenly felt by many, who also believed that its capacity to do so relied upon adherence to American ideals of freedom, mercy, and the judicious use of military force. As the Captain America character developed over the next five decades, this aspect of his origin (the fact he has few "fantastical" powers) became deeply important because: "his character is amplified as part of his power"(Dubose, 2007).

Also present in the Golden Age Cap comics and growing more apparent over the decades following, was the notion of Steve Rogers' inherent virtues, tying him to the aspirational use of American strength while grounding him with an unusually thoughtful and reflective personality. Discussing the virtues of Captain America, Mark D. White (2014) identifies qualities that began with Steve Rogers the man, became intrinsic to the Captain America persona, and allowed Cap to respond to the growing complexity of America's position in the world order. There is some irony to the notion of a star-spangled soldier, frozen in an ice floe after a glorious campaign against fascism, awakening decades later in the middle of a tumultuous American political age and being able to effectively articulate American values within a new, cynical era. His ability to disentangle himself from the black and white, unquestioning government patriot of the Golden Age rested heavily in the early establishment of his independent, aspirational, American ideals.

At the creation of the character, no one could have imagined that he would have staying power beyond the immediate conflict from which he drew his mission. Perhaps Jack Kirby and Joe Simon did not realize that in naming him Captain America and draping him in the Star-Spangled Banner, they were creating a canvas on which the very tenets of American identity would be drawn, erased, redrawn, and vehemently contested over the next six decades. It is astonishing to think that 73 years after the Axis powers surrendered, children all over the world have and will continue to excitedly don their American flag outfits and pose with their shields as they wait for the next installment of Captain America's adventures on the big screen. Such devotion begs the question of how it occurred and can be addressed by looking into the changes Captain America went through from his creation to 2019 while his writers were: "tracking developments in a culture he was designed to embody" (Stevens, 2015).

Captain America, the Cold War, and the American protest era

Cap's immediate future post WWII was always uncertain. The question of how a character so intrinsically linked to a specific period and event in history could operate outside of the conflict of his creation was one that writers struggled with enormously. A number of shifts in the prosecution of American foreign policy took place after WWII. This both alarmed and confused Americans as the government moved from the theater of hot conflict in Europe to an uncertain strategy of containment in the Cold War. As Jewett and Lawrence (2003) explain in their book *Captain America and the Crusade against Evil*, America's zeal for war was dampened in the 1950s and 1960s by a series of "police actions" and strategic retreats, including Truman's ordering of American troops across the 38th Parallel in Korea only to have them quickly withdraw to prevent an all-out military engagement with Chinese troops who had been mobilized in response. For a country used to winning wars and having parades, Truman's decision was viewed by many as an act of cowardice that signified a dramatic shift in American foreign policy. In short, in the reconstruction of post WWII Europe and Asia, America was forced to play a more ambiguous role in world affairs. An audience used to the dramatics and heroism of an unambiguously good America destroying unambiguously evil fascists found proxy wars and containment a tough and perplexing pill to swallow.

It was against the backdrop of this new American reality that "Commie Smasher" was brought to life, and Marvel quickly found themselves at odds with their audience. Communism was an entirely different beast than fascism and, carrying a blunt message without any context that communists were as bad as Nazis, was not a complicated enough story to engage a generation who: "understood the complexities of the Cold War and understood that it would not be easily won" (Stevens, 2015). With the growing realization that the tactics of the Golden Age Cap could not be so easily transferred to the next enemy of the American government alongside the reality that comic book fans were less drawn toward the jingoism that had been such a compelling part of the Golden Age stories, Commie Smasher was quickly withdrawn.

By the 1960s, Marvel's creative team had moved at pace away from one-note, black and white heroes and began to create superheroes with deeply human flaws and psyches. The lesson learned from the Commie Smasher series was that there had been a deep mismatch between the audience and their hero, and that realization led Marvel to resurrect Captain America.

In his reawakening and retconning, the 1960s Cap undertook a period of intense evolution. In the first few years, he was riven with guilt about the death of Bucky Barnes, showed signs of post-traumatic stress disorder, and spent nights alone at the Avengers mansion thinking about his service during the war. Reintroduced four months after President Kennedy was assassinated in Dallas, he came to represent the tension between the greatest generation and the baby boomers in a period of American history where domestic disagreements about race, feminism, and foreign interventions were rife (Hayton and Albright, 2012, p. 17). The early 1960s Cap underwent a transitionary period in which he confronted the ghosts of his past, committed himself so wholeheartedly to his mission that he became reclusive, and continually questioned what had changed so dramatically during his absence that Americans now seemed to be more focused on fighting with one another than uniting against a common, foreign enemy. As his disillusionment grew, Cap's attention slowly but surely moved away from his desire to protect the American home front, and, by the end of the decade, Marvel had positioned Cap deftly for the 1970s. Realizing that the mistake of the Commie Smasher lay in Cap's refusal to change, they changed him dramatically. In his "return from the dead" era, Cap evolved significantly; he developed, reacted, reflected, and firmly established himself as the ultimate symbol for the ongoing contestation of American politics, culture, identity, and behavior. As he moved from the 1940s patriotic super soldier on a clear and zealous mission against an evil threat into a thoughtful and idealistic character, he became: "centered on the home front as a site of contestation over the meaning of America" (Dittmer, 2009, p. 112).

In the years after the Civil Rights Act was signed and JFK, Martin Luther King Jr., and Bobby Kennedy had been murdered, tensions over racial discrimination in the United States threatened to boil over. The commercial power of the baby boomers and their tendency to question the existing American systems of power opened up a generational schism into which a hyper-patriotic relic of WWII was unlikely to easily fit. Racial tensions were exacerbated by America's involvement in Vietnam; a conflict that many Americans viewed as a campaign of terror against a civilian population disguised as a battle against communism (Jewett and Lawrence, 2003, p. 183). Marvel's approach to the Vietnam War was to sideline their super soldier, beginning a new era within Cap comics where his intervention in foreign incursions was no longer guaranteed simply by his patriotic soldier status. The reluctance to send Captain America into action was, perhaps, both a hangover from the Commie Smasher era and born of a growing realization that, in order to be commercially successful, Cap would have to continue to evolve away from his deep connection to the United States government. Cap's one major storyline occurring within Vietnam was a tale of heroic rescue, made all the more interesting by the fact that the pilot he had come to recover was presented as a capable, brave, and patriotic African American man. The interjection of a definitively more nuanced black character than one usually saw in Marvel comics of the time was an attempt to refocus Cap's attention to issues of race that were being played out domestically and away from wars in which the national myth of American passivity and innocence was being severely undermined (Jewett and Lawrence, 2003, p. 178).

During this time, Cap struggled intensely with the growing realization that there was a distinct difference between the American ideals he was created to defend and how those ideals had been ignored and corrupted by the American political machine. Entering, somewhat ham-fistedly at times, the civil rights debate by way of his new partner "The Falcon," Cap confronted social issues and came around to the idea that the status quo never guaranteed freedom and equality for all. The manner in which the Captain America series dealt with issues of race during the 1970s can be described as well-intentioned Blaxploitation. As: "an obviously Aryan ideal" (McWilliams, 2012, p. 66), the Captain America narrative was always awkwardly positioned to deal with issues of race. However, because of the fact that Cap came to exist as a space for the mediation of America itself, when racial issues *were* addressed, the potential and meaning was always that much more powerful.

The Blaxploitation era involving The Falcon, which awkwardly saw Steve Rogers attempt on more than one occasion to urge Sam Wilson to accept a nonexistent post-racial narrative of America, was the beginning of a racial discourse within the Cap universe that reached its zenith with the publication of *Truth: Captain America, Red, White and Black*. In *Truth*, written and inked by Robert Morales and Kyle Baker, the Cap backstory is retconned, aligned with the notion that America would never have tested a super soldier serum on a white man first, and weaves an allegory of slavery, racist foreign policy and the appalling abuse of people of color within the United States. At the end of the book, current (white) Cap visits Isaiah Washington (black cap) and takes a photograph with him, both wearing their Captain America uniforms. The distinction between the glorious sight of Steve Rogers juxtaposed with the frail Isaiah Washington in a state of mental decline only underscores the reality of the lengths America is willing to go to in order to protect a dream that only ever belonged to white men. It further serves as a reminder that, although Steve Rogers' Captain America has attempted to understand and stand against racial injustice, as a walking symbol of the white power structure, he exists in a liminal space as far as his capacity to mediate race relations in America (Morales and Baker, 2009).

As Cap moved from the certainty of the Golden Era, through his reanimation in the 1960s, he began to ask questions of the country he had been created to unquestioningly defend. If the 1960s pushed him away from a focus on American foreign policy and toward American domestic issues, the 1970s tested him to his limit. The realization that the American government was not intrinsically aligned and constant with American ideals caused him to question what it meant to be American. His interactions with The Falcon tested his perception of America's racial innocence, and living through the Watergate era (the reality played out in cap comics as an amusing allegory in which Richard Nixon turns out to be an alien) caused him to sever ties with the US government once and for all. Post-Watergate, Cap returned his uniform and shield and became "man without a country." Wandering from place to place in America in true counter-culture style, he questioned his origin, his behavior, the orders he followed, the dark underbelly of the American dream, and the government's complicity in racism, sexism, and the exploitation of other countries. His decision to return to his previous incarnation was made only with the realization that it was he himself who had let America down by "not realizing that *Americans* could corrupt America" (Stevens, 2015, p. 112). Cap vowed never to make that mistake again and severed all complicity with the governing structures of the nation. He was finally certain that the keepers of the American dream were not the people who govern the country or the military but the people themselves.

Reagan, progressive Cap, and the lull of the nineties

The turn toward moral, social, and religious conservatism during the Reagan era was a refutation of the cautious foreign policy decisions of Jimmy Carter and created an interesting dynamic for superheroes to operate within.

As Reagan turned his focus toward painting a narrative of a dark and violent America, desperate for the reestablishment of tough justice, most super heroic comics followed suit.

1980s Cap was able to retain some of the passion and idealism he had developed in the 60s and continued to question the substance of the American dream versus the American reality (Dubose, 2007, p. 928). The divisive political rhetoric of the 1980s gave Cap much cause for deep contemplation of American values, but, unlike previous eras, he did not seem to be able to plant himself solidly on either side of the debate. In his quest to be as representative of American values as he could, he developed something of an obsession with the protection of free speech in all its forms, oscillating from deep seated panic and discomfort over the flag burning debate to acceptance of the reality that the American flag is not imbued with the same meaning and honor for all Americans (Stevens, 2015, p. 165). Against a backdrop of hyper-partisanship and hyper-patriotism, 1980s Cap reflected on what America had meant to him at the same time as acknowledging the validity of the narratives of those who had been oppressed by the US government. In his conflict with "Super Patriot," Cap is disgusted with the virulent racism within the anti-migrant message Super Patriot is spreading. An obvious metaphor for the propensity for nationalism to quickly turn to fascism, Super Patriot tripped over the fabric of an American flag he had been using as a shield, fell to his death, and was viewed by Cap as embodying the new and somewhat dangerous American jingoism: "without the experience and wisdom of the past" (Stevens, 2015, p. 165).

Perhaps the most important development of this era was Cap's evolution in terms of the symbols of America being hollow in the absence of the American ideal of equality that he truly believed in. In terms of adapting to the 1980s and its "doubtful status of morality" (Dubose, 2007, p. 928), Cap finally recognized that his life experience did not elevate his opinions over the opinions of others. Alongside the acceptance of the truth of various narratives about the American dream, this seemingly small step in character development was the foundation of the all-out radical dissent Captain America offered in the painful and contested post 9/11 American political landscape.

If the Captain America franchise was in any danger of losing its relevance since the Golden Age, it was during the more domestically and internationally stable decade of the 1990s. The end of the Cold War signaled an era of great promise in terms of international relations, and although America did have an international engagement in Iraq, they were widely supported by their allies and executed a meticulously strategic military campaign to do nothing more than turn back the advancing Iraq army from its invasion of Kuwait and restore the existing and legally recognized sovereignty of the kingdom. As the external threat of the Soviet Union was deconstructed and the tumultuous domestic issues threatening to tear America apart were muted by the economic boom of the "dot com" explosion, Cap had nothing much to rail against.

The Cap of the 1990s was a placeholder for the incredible development that, unbeknownst to everyone, would occur in the post 9/11 Marvel universe. Cap did not change much, was consistent in the reiteration of the values that he had always claimed to represent, but showed little in terms of character development. 1990s Cap served primarily as an image conscious product, used to sell comics to children and merchandise to their parents. It is fair to say that, although there was an attempt to engage Captain America during the 1990s, it is entirely possible that his influential place in the Marvel universe may have dwindled to irrelevance were it not for the sudden, violent, and fantastical events in America on September 11th, 2011.

Post 9/11

Captain America's success had always relied upon the extent to which he was able to evolve in response to real world events. Both his political ideology and his tendencies toward jingoism, nationalism, violence, justice, and equality were sometimes paced exactly with the majority of American sentiments and sometimes progressively ahead of them. From the Golden Age to the 1990s, Cap made "continual adjustment to appeal to contemporary tastes of patriotism and violence" (Stevens, 2015, p. 42). His character traits were imprinted early, and some (jingoism and tendency toward nationalism) were moderated over the years. Others (fairness, morality, and merciful use of force) remained important foundational non-negotiables that, while tested by the dominant cultural forces of the times, tended to appropriately bend instead of breaking. The one-note Golden Age Cap had to develop into a much more complex character to operate within the divisive domestic conflicts of the 1960s and 1970s. He *was* America, emerging from the narrative of innocence created around WWII to immerse himself in a country that regularly displayed to the rest of the world that it had serious proclivities toward racism, sexism, and homophobia but viewed itself through the lens of exceptionalism and innocence (Stevens, 2015, p. 55). As a character who is largely defined by the "other" (whether that "other" be Nazis, Fascism, Racism, or corruption), Cap has been provided with a steady stream of cultural material to work with from the 1940s to the 1990s. The lack of interesting issues to deal with in the 1990s could have led to his retirement for good, but, as a character America yearns for in times of crisis, September 11th, 2001 thrust him back into the heart of the philosophical American debate.

The uncertainty of the day itself was followed by immediate domestic divisions between those who wanted vengeance, those who wanted to end the cycle of violence, those who continued to passionately believe in the narrative of American innocence, and those who were ready to contemplate America's complicity in the destabilization of foreign regimes. Further layers of complexity were added year after year as America pushed itself into two unwinnable Middle Eastern wars and the voices of domestic dissent grew louder and louder. In a scramble to make meaning of the disaster, a dominant political rhetoric emerged in which a Manichean us/them/Good/Evil, religiously imbued paradigm established itself within certain sections of the American body politic. Any deviation from that message was viewed as heresy. Into the void created by the mainstream press' reluctance to question America's post 9/11 zeal for conflict stepped Captain America. His success was assured by his unquestionable morality and reassuringly patriotic name and guise, and his service to America was never more important. At a time where legitimate institutions (the press) and democratic norms (questioning of authority and tolerance of opposition) were stretched to the breaking point, Cap created the "space" for those he disagreed with (Curtis, 2016, p. 45). That a progressive, patriot, super-soldier became part of and eventually the leader of a radical pop culture response to 9/11 that then permeated through Hollywood is an incredibly interesting phenomenon to consider. Audiences lapped up the reboot because it glorified the fight against fascism and the traditional American way. In the following films (*Winter Soldier* and his appearances with *The Avengers*), Cap's message became one of the few that was able to challenge the prevailing sense of nationalism and blind trust of authority that had settled into the era. To some, given their simple (and mistaken) understanding of his character, this was a heresy.[1] To those who understood the evolution of his character through the decades, it was a needed and expected deviation from blind support of the American establishment narrative.

Captain America's immediate response to the events of 9/11 was heartbreak, disbelief, and devastation. In a famous picture drawn by Mike Deodato, Cap looms large over the lower Manhattan skyline, his legs in place of where the Twin Towers once stood, and, with one hand gripping his shield and the other covering his face, weeps. Cap's transformation from the superficial 1990s era, post 9/11, is immense. It begins with the immediate decision by the creative team at Marvel to position him in opposition to the clambering voices of revenge and situate him firmly within the role of a healer. His priorities are firmly established as domestic, with the American people (not the government) and tempered by his own understanding of the history of American foreign policy entanglements. When Nick Fury orders him to Afghanistan he refuses to comply, stating: "I'm here to protect the people and the dream; not your secrets" (Rieber and Cassady, 2002). Cap's post 9/11 journey is centered in NYC. In his immediate post 9/11 activities, he protects a Muslim youth threatened by angry New Yorkers after working at ground zero all day (Stevens, 2015, p. 215) and is one of the first voices to offer resistance to the religiously situated, moralistic language that the Neo-Conservatives surrounding President Bush were urging him to frame the upcoming military operations within. As President Bush declared: "You are either with us or against us." Cap, however, refused to be drawn into the zealous, nationalistic language (Stevens, 2015, p. 215). In perhaps one of the most controversial post 9/11 storylines, Cap finds himself in the Midwest, facing down a terrorist by the name of Al-Tariq who is holding hostages to highlight the fact that the defense production plant located within the town is directly responsible for creating the weapons that maim and kill his people. With other pop culture mediums focused upon stereotypically evil villains of Middle Eastern origin, operating on orders from terrorists higher up the command chain and waging a war of ideology that could only result in the complete annihilation of one side, in this storyline, Marvel offered an incredibly nuanced character whose legitimate complaints were impossible to deny. Backed by a group of amputees who had been maimed by American munitions, Al-Tariq directly challenged the myth of American innocence. Invoking the US's involvement in proxy wars in the Middle East and Africa during the Cold War, he proclaims himself to be an orphan of such conflicts and calls America an "empire of blood" (Rieber and Cassady, 2002). Al-Tariq challenges Captain America to identify his nationality. The fact that he could be from any number of countries around the world is underscored by Al Tariq's last invective to Cap: "tell your monster where he's from" (Rieber and Cassady, 2002). Doubly explicit in the reference to Mary Shelley's Frankenstein is the notion that American conflicts all over the world have sown the seeds of the discord to the extent that the terrorist "monster" is both the direct result of American atrocities against civilians and, most troubling for an American audience, in the minds of those organizing and executing their version of Jihad, completely justifiable.

Blockbuster Cap

The final presentation of post 9/11 Cap, the one that dominates the pop culture landscape is, of course, the one created by Hollywood. The decision to reboot Cap for the big screen was taken after 9/11 and was part of an acceleration of superhero movies being pushed into production because the social and political atmosphere within America was perfectly situated for mediating on attitudes, enemies, and discourses of terror and evil within a reassuringly safe American genre convention. A film that explicitly recreated 9/11 would not have gone over well with audiences were it not for the presence of a super heroic team being, in this case, able to crush the enemy in the streets of NYC after a buildup in which they had unpacked several complicated facets of post 9/11 American political identities. The fact that *The Avengers* was one of the biggest grossing films of the decade was a clear sign that, in terms of creating a space for the dissemination of extremely divisive American issues post 9/11, Marvel hit the bullseye and created a monolithic film franchise for the 2000s. Without 9/11, the super heroic landscape would have looked extremely different and may never have been resurrected.

In order to have Cap operate in a post 9/11 cinematic world, it was important for Marvel studios to reboot him in a manner that would be faithful to his origin story and still be appealing to an audience, the significant majority of whom were born after the conclusion of WWII. Marvel's 2011 movie, *Captain America: The First Avenger*, was kept fairly close to the original genesis of Captain America over time (ignoring the Commie Smasher of course) and was also careful to dwell upon the aspects of his character before he became Cap that would be most useful in making him a believable leader of superheroes and mission in the early 2000s.

In one of the early scenes in the movie, Bucky drags Steve Rogers, who had been rejected again from military service, to the Great Exposition where they watch in amazement as Howard Stark demonstrates his "flying car." After Rogers makes clear his intention to try to enlist again, Bucky leaves him at the recruiting station for a night of dancing before he is deployed to the infantry unit that Rogers longs to serve in. The first half of the movie, in which Steve Rogers is identified by Erskine as a potential for the super soldier project and goes through training and the final injection of serum to become Captain America, dwells almost obsessively on what makes Rogers suitable for the mission above anyone else. Steve impresses Erskine by saying that he does not "want to kill Nazis, I don't want to kill anyone. I don't like bullies; I don't care where they come from." It is vital from Erskine's point of view that he not enhance a propensity to jingoism and racism already existing within a person, and Rogers' refusal to be drawn into the patriotic zeal to destroy his enemy is the first signal he gives of his appropriateness for the mission. Further difference from the other potential chosen breed of super soldiers is signaled in several scenes of basic training. The recruits play fight and shadowbox in the background as Rogers unpacks a series of books about history. His attempt to understand the world around him and possibly what led to the war shows a considered, academic approach to the potential to solve it set against a backdrop of displays of physical prowess where the only option to end the war is by the honing and unleashing of more violence. The presentation of Rogers is a deliberate contrast to all the men around him (except Erskine). General Phillips describes his new platoon as: "First in a new breed of super soldiers (who will) personally escort Adolf Hitler through the gates of hell." His invocation of an afterlife and demands to Erskine that he choose a big, strong recruit who displays a thoughtless adherence to the orders of others is gently eroded when Rogers continues to persevere despite being physically incapable of much of the training and then shows mental alacrity when, instead of trying to get at a flag by physically climbing the flagpole, he simply undoes the pin at the bottom. Finally, the moment when Rogers jumps on a dummy grenade that Phillips has thrown into the circle of recruits as a test of "guts" convinces Phillips of Erskine's choice. That Steve is willing to sacrifice his life for the others around him finally convinces Phillips of his suitability for the coveted first injection of the super soldier serum.

In a scene the night before the experiment is due to take place, Erskine is talking with Rogers and underscores both to Steve and the audience that the characteristics of the man are the most important aspect in choosing who should have the serum. Erskine discusses his personal tragedy of being called to the service of Hitler and watching as his own country (Germany) was invaded as the weakened populace was lured by the promise of greatness, marching, and flags. He is careful to delineate the difference between Hitler (a man who "uses his fantasies to inspire his followers") and the Red Skull who actually harnesses the power of science and is much more of a threat if he is able to mobilize technology against the world. Making a distinction between Rogers and the Red Skull, Erskine states that the serum amplifies already existing traits. In the Red Skull, it amplified his madness and his thirst for destruction: "Good becomes great, bad becomes worse." Erskine clearly views Steve as a good man and someone whose gentle traits will be amplified by the serum. He also regards Steve's hitherto weakness as a vital aspect of the decision to burden him with the coming power of Captain America: "A weak man knows the value of strength and knows compassion." Creating a narrative of the "rightness" of Steve Rogers for the experiment and juxtaposing him with the evil of the Red Skull is immediately comforting for the audience. Erskine is a man who has defied his government and adheres to his own morals; he chooses to empower a man who shows similar propensities and views the technology he is about to pass through Rogers as the first step on the path to peace. What cannot be ascertained at this point and is something that unfolds in later Captain America and Avengers movies, is: what happens when the technology/idea you create is used by people who do not share your world view?

After Erskine's assassination and the revelation that HYDRA had infiltrated the State Department, the super soldier program is shut down, and Steve Rogers is ordered to fulfill a propaganda role, appearing in revues across America to sell war bonds. When he is sent to Europe to entertain the troops, his patriotic act does not go down well with the men who have been fighting the Germans in the trenches. In a clash of propaganda versus reality, Cap is pelted with tomatoes by troops and forced to retreat from the stage. Echoing the general sentiment of what makes Cap who he is, Steve Rogers only becomes Captain America when he first defies the orders of the hierarchy and drops behind enemy lines to rescue Bucky and lead the 107th back to the safety of the Allied camp. It is the sight of him walking back into the camp and surrendering himself to disciplinary actions that signifies that he is finally a soldier in the eyes of General Phillips and, in the eyes of Peggy Carter, has lived up to the intention of his creation.

The rest of the film follows Captain America and his select group of soldiers as they go behind enemy lines again to defeat the Red Skull. Important foundations continue to be laid in the second act of *The First Avenger*, ones that signify to the audience that the lesson of Captain America is not his super strength but his super morality and his steadfast belief in justice. Gabe Jones, an African American character, states that he spent "three semesters at Howard." The addition of Jim Morita, a Japanese American soldier who declares in response to the racist goading of another soldier about his heritage and loyalty: "I'm from Fresno, Ace" highlights the juxtaposition with the Teutonic German enemy. In this iteration of the origin story, Captain America is fully invested with a character that does not seek out violence to conquer and is backed by an inclusive team including a woman with real agency and power and a group of men who signify that the diversity of America is its greatest strength. Set in opposition to the Nazis, particularly the Red Skull's troops who are all interchangeable and presented as a procession of storm troopers, they are led by a man who is presented as physically and ethically outside the bounds of humanity. This presentation of American identity is a much more progressive one that the Golden Age comic books allowed for.

In the final act of the film, Rogers' qualities are dwelt on almost obsessively. Bucky declares that he is not following Captain America into the jaws of death but following: "a guy from Brooklyn who was too dumb to say no to a fight." Constant reiterations of the fact that Steve Rogers is the most integral part of Captain America set the scene for the climax of the action when Cap boards the plane that the Red Skull is flying toward America carrying weapons of mass destruction marked clearly for each city on which he intends to drop them. As the camera pans in on the bomb that says "New York," anyone familiar with the comic history of Captain America knows at this point he will sacrifice himself to save his city. The fact that Cap does not explicitly kill the Red Skull (his death coming about as an accident more than anything else) hyper focuses the story not on violence as redemptive but of sacrifice as the most noble form of action in the fact of threat. Captain America's strength in this aspect is not that he can overcome the enemy and win the war; it is that his character will allow him to sacrifice his own life and his future to save the lives of fellow Americans and hasten the end of violence.

The First Avenger serves a dual purpose in the post 9/11 Marvel cinematic lineup. First, from a purely commercial standpoint, it rebooted one of the most commercially successful characters Marvel has ever created and released him to operate with the other post 9/11 Marvel characters in the 2000s. The second purpose was to take the creation, development, changes, and complexity of the Captain America story throughout the last six decades and foreground what it is about the character that will be most important in the coming years. The Captain America that is reborn in *The First Avenger* is not a carbon copy of the patriotic, jingoistic, and sometimes racist 1940s Golden Age Cap. The film reiterates the Golden Age values of Captain America but significantly alters some of the problematic aspects of his character by placing him within a battle in which he is backed up by a multiracial commando team, a woman, and a civilian inventor. He does not dwell obsessively upon beating the Germans. His mission is to defeat tyranny and evil wherever he finds it, and the futility of evil is underscored by the fact that the Red Skull is destroyed by the source of power he was seeking to control. The final scenes of the movie culminate with Captain America's sacrifice being recognized and revered (a child runs through the streets of New York City with a trash can lid painted in the colors of his shield) followed by the resurrection of Cap himself. As he runs into the middle of a post 9/11 Times Square and is overwhelmed by his own senses, the movie sets the scene for the clash of everything 1940s Captain America stands for and the coming mediation of the military industrial complex, technologization of war, and the global consequences of American foreign policy that play out in *The Avengers* (2012).

Captain America: The Winter Soldier (2014), the second in the Captain America titles, shows Cap come full circle in his realization that corrupt forces within America are as responsible for its demise as outside threats. Designed as a sophisticated meditation on the inevitable endgame of government surveillance systems, Cap is forced to reflect upon his entire existence since WWII and re-establish his individuality and moral code in the face of a hostile takeover of American democracy. The main theme explored in the film is the notion that times and realities have changed and that Captain America is uncomfortably placed at the nexus of traditional American values and the subversion of those values in the name of security. Sitting next to Peggy Carter's bed in the nursing home, Rogers questions his place in S.H.I.E.L.D. and the world in general. Peggy consoles him in a brief moment of lucidity by stating simply that: "The world has changed and none of us can go back." Nick Fury further responds to Rogers' questioning about the abuse of freedom in the new Project Insight by saying: "S.H.I.E.L.D. takes the world as it is, not as we would like it to be." Both scenes anchor the post 9/11 concerns and debate around the erosion of civil liberties in America's quest to be secure. Rogers is, after all, a relic of a previous era, free from the need to sacrifice one for the other. This theme continues to develop, and through the creation and destruction of a government surveillance system that falls into the hands of those who seek to use it for the purposes of murder, the film creates a not-so-subtle scenario in which the proliferation of a surveillance state is almost played out to its natural conclusion: genocide. As uncomfortable as this is for a post 9/11 American audience, the question of the fine line between democratic fascism and anti-democracy fascism is drawn early and obviously before it builds to the dramatic conclusion in which both HYDRA and S.H.I.E.L.D. are necessarily and rightfully destroyed.

The action begins when S.H.I.E.L.D. agency Director, Nick Fury, tells Captain America that, after the events in New York, he managed to convince the US government to fund and allow "Project Insight." Captain America reacts uneasily as Fury explains that the project gives the government the capacity to read terrorist DNA and eliminate threats before they occur. Rogers fears that keeping records of people's past behavior and using a predictive algorithm to quell their dissidence will lead to the erosion of the bedrocks of democracy, in place to prevent summary judgments, do not take long to be realized. It becomes clear that the infiltration of S.H.I.E.L.D. has occurred on every level from foot soldier to Secretary of Defense, and the means by which S.H.I.E.L.D. intended to round up terrorists is turned against them and deployed in the name of HYDRA's twisted version of societal order. Secretary Pierce explains, in a parallel but chilling version of the same justification given by Nick Fury, that he only intends to kill a few million for the sake of harmony for billions of people on the planet. The audience is cued into the fact that the HYDRA targets are not evil and deserving of death by their sheer numbers on the map and the fact that Rogers', Black Widow's, and Tony Stark's names flash up in the database of people to be eradicated by Project Insight's lasers. HYDRA's list is not about evil or danger, it is about the eradication of inventors, creators, and anti-establishment voices who move society forward and provide necessary checks and challenges to the potential for fascism in all its forms to rise.

The fact that the forces of good (supposedly S.H.I.E.L.D.) and the forces of evil (HYDRA) are indistinguishable and intertwined early on in the action ensures that there has to be a series of signals to the audience that good and evil *can* be deciphered from somewhere within the chaos. The finale of the film is underscored with several symbolic gestures designed to accomplish the recasting of American values and ideals. Returning the locus of heroism to the symbolic representation of American goodness, it is Captain America, thus far an increasingly disillusioned member of S.H.I.E.L.D., who takes the initiative to bring both HYDRA and S.H.I.E.L.D. to their destruction. He announces to Black Widow that: "We're taking down S.H.I.E.L.D. . . . S.H.I.E.L.D., HYDRA, it all goes." In this act, the mission is taken back by somebody who has always and continues to faithfully uphold the American ideals that both HYDRA and S.H.I.E.L.D. are attempting to subvert. In a symbolic physical reaffirmation of the past, Cap breaks into the museum exhibit about his own life and borrows his 1940s suit for the mission. This scene separates Cap from the enemy (both S.H.I.E.L.D. and HYDRA) and all of their interlinked machinations and reverts the motives of the heroes back to the unambiguous morality of the WWII era. A similar moment occurs in the launch room at the S.H.I.E.L.D. triskelion headquarters when a S.H.I.E.L.D. officer refuses, on threat of execution, to enter the launch codes that will kill millions of people. This is a clear nod to the fact that traditional democratic values have always relied upon those people willing to sacrifice their lives to uphold them in the face of terror and fear. It also serves as a reminder that such a sacrifice in the name of deeply held values that are subject to perversion when a populace is afraid is the single most powerful weapon against terrorism that any country has.

The final act of the movie sees the destruction of both HYDRA and S.H.I.E.L.D. by Captain America and his allies and the attempted restoration of democratic values. The ending is riddled with ambiguity about the character of the people who played a part and how events will unfold in the world from this point onward. In this ending, the Winter Soldier does not kill Captain America because he appeals to his human memory: "You're my friend." This is another affirmation of the humanity and love in the face of terror and death that is woven through most of the post 9/11 Marvel storylines. The Winter Soldier walks away, but we do not know whether he is leaving to commit more evil or to rehabilitate himself. The balance of power is restored to the established institutions of American democracy, the CIA and the FBI. Fury burns his entire identity, and the Falcon refuses the call to arms of army intelligence by saying: "I'm more of a soldier than a spy." The duality of Black Widow's service record as it is laid bare in the hearings after the events in DC leaves us to ponder the nature of superheroes in the face of the new post 9/11 threats. They are neither unambiguously good nor unambiguously evil; they are simply needed.

Cap's capacity to separate himself entirely from S.H.I.E.L.D., the government, and the state at the end of *Civil War* relies upon the consistency of his beliefs as developed in the comic books over the decades and in the first two movies in the series, *The First Avenger* and *Winter Soldier*. If the ideals and philosophical trajectory of Cap's actions were not so firmly established and did not so closely align with a growing sense of unease at the behavior of American leaders, post 9/11, it would be unthinkable for a man draped in the star-spangled banner to drop his shield and walk away from the country he was created to represent.

The graphic novel on which *Captain America: Civil War* (2016) was loosely based was published in 2006, a year where the tension between President Bush's international agenda and the American people was growing wider by the day. In an excellent analysis, John McGuire (2015) perfectly assesses the timeline of what he refers to as the security ideology, how it played out in politics and how *Civil War* captured the two sides of an ongoing tension between security vs. freedom, both ideological components of the American dream. Arguing that the events of 9/11 sparked a sequence of events that directly led to significant tension between the competing notions of security and freedom, McGuire situates Hurricane Katrina as the death knell for President Bush's right wing security rhetoric. With a background tension already brewing, the reality that the mighty American government was both unprepared and seemingly unconcerned with the deaths of thousands of its own citizens diminished the capacity for the government to maintain its insistence that Americans give up their freedoms in exchange for a safety that didn't seem to exist. Katrina irrevocably changed the political narrative in America to such an extent that, finally, alternative discourses to the one in which the country viewed itself through a lens of innocence and infallibility were taken seriously and given space in the national discourse (McGuire, 2015).

The ability for Marvel to capitalize on that narrative change came precisely because two of their most loved and commercially successful characters each served as an unmistakable allegory for the various post 9/11 themes that were, at last, being explored. *Civil War*, the graphic novel, sets out a slightly different version than the blockbuster movie that followed it, but both rest solidly upon the tension between two characters who had long worked alongside one another but had every reason to disassemble.

The fight between Cap and Iron Man is, of course, one in which the ethos and ideology of the "greatest" generation comes squarely into conflict with a representative of the more complex Vietnam era uncertainty and government corruption. Cap exists as a moral absolutist whose values are contained within a physical representation of: "the dream of enlightenment philosophers, the free and independent citizen who voluntarily chooses to identify with the nation state" (Martin, 2015, p. 100). Iron Man has no allegiance to nation state, views the world in a global sense, and is willing to engage in dubious acts of immorality to achieve his goal of passing the Superhero Registration Act. Specific to 9/11, the initial elite driven framing device for the attack was a constant comparison to Pearl Harbor. This quickly shifted with the realization that a World War II narrative would not successfully sustain a campaign in which the very morals for which the World War II generation were convinced they had fought were publicly upended and covertly sneered at. Within the choice every American was forced with post 9/11, Mark Editz argues that a foundation was laid in which each side was demonized for their beliefs and the initial split became the cornerstone on which consequent polarization of the body politic and the institutions of government began to reconstruct.

The film *Captain America: Civil War* (2016) begins with an acknowledgment of the awesome powers and responsibility that super heroic beings have and should be aware of. The levelling of Sokovia in *The Age of Ultron* is visually continued as the Avengers destroy buildings in Lagos, Nigeria. The opening scene hinges around a surviving member of HYDRA from *Winter Soldier* attempting to steal biological weapons. We are shown a series of images in which the plot seems secondary to the destruction and catastrophe that the Avengers themselves are visiting upon more innocent civilians. The catalyst for the Superhero Registration Act is when Wanda Maximoff, who fails to control her power, destroys a building and cannot help in the rescue efforts.[2]

In the following clash of ideologies, the histories of both ideologies are laid bare within several leitmotifs throughout the movie. The locations of action are something of a rehashing of much of WWII and the Cold War (Africa, Vienna, London, Berlin). This signifies that America's past occupations with conflict both in the European theatre during the 1940s and in the proxy wars of the 1950s onwards have set in motion a series of events that can only culminate in the clashing of the hot and cold war ideologies.

Aside from the conflicting ideologies in play, the mechanism by which the Superhero Registration Act comes about is a grieving mother who accuses Tony Stark of being responsible for the murder of her son. Confronted with the death of the innocent, Stark crumbles easily into a pro-government, pro-registration stance. The plot is further propelled by the actions of Helmut Zemo, a high ranking Sokovian soldier who lost his family when Ultron attacked. While the grieving mother exists to induce guilt in Tony Stark and reinforce that it is the innocent who suffer when the Avengers are engaged without oversight, Zemo occupies a much more complex position in the narrative. Using an American solider (Bucky) who was weaponized by the Soviet Union as the Winter Soldier, Zemo seeks to destroy the Avengers from within to avenge his own family. In a clear signal to the mechanism of terrorism employed by Bin Laden, Zemo taunts Cap: "An Empire toppled by its enemies can rise again but one that crumbles from within, that's dead forever."

Beginning with the united/victorious World War II era (Bucky) that is corrupted and moved to a place of moral ambiguity and anti-democratic practices in the Cold War (the Winter Soldier), Zemo takes two American eras, foregrounds them in terms of what they meant, and unleashes both forces in the present as a wrecking ball with which to bring down American superheroes. There is little subtlety in the notion that, having lost the "righteousness" of the motivations of World War II[3] and moved past the expected notions of Jus Ad Bellum, the United States was responsible for the suffering and death of millions of people in their proxy wars, arms dealing, and interventions in the democratic processes of other countries. Zemo exists to underscore and intensify the already bubbling tension between Cap and Iron Man, as exemplified by their different views of what is justified for the good of the nation and the rest of the world.

Throughout the movie, Cap shows dogged allegiance to his moral worldview and protects Bucky from Stark's vengeance, even in the event that he realizes that it was the Winter Soldier who was responsible for the murder of Stark's parents. Roger's sense of responsibility and self-doubt is exemplified as he watches the replay of the destruction and defends Wanda Maximoff but refuses to be drawn into an action (signing the accords), which he views as ill-conceived and potentially dangerous to individual freedoms. Having lived through more in terms of history than the other members of the Avengers, Cap reminds the team of the important point that, while the United Nations may seem like an appropriate body to have control over super heroes, it is like *all* other organizations and governments: under the direction of people who hold temporary powers but seek to leave permanent agendas. In *Winter Soldier*, Cap discovered that he was used by a corrupt organization to kickstart their heinous plans. In *Civil War*, despite the experience of betrayal and despite the massive potential for things to go wrong, he asserts that superheroes and, by extension, individuals, are still the best guardians of the will of the people and the best hope for peace in the world.

In the scene where Tony Stark offers Cap one of the pens used by FDR when he signed the Land Lease Act of 1941, the deliberate gesture of hearkening to Rogers' creation and attempt by Stark to situate him within the framework of the Second World War is met with resistance from Cap who reminds him: "Some would say (the act) bought us closer to war." Stark further blows his chance of having Rogers sign when he offers amendments and safeguards: "after we put out the PR fire" and reveals that Wanda is being confined (interned) at the Avengers mansion. Perhaps not fully realizing the extent of Cap's transformation from blunt nation state propaganda machine to concerned, questioning global citizen, Stark triggers in Cap a remembrance of the worst aspects of American behavior during World War II instead of the intended reminiscent myth of American innocence. Sealing his fate, Cap leaves the room knowing that he will become a criminal, a fugitive, and an exile in a country that owes him its existence and from a team whom he has come to regard as the only family he has.

In scenes that somewhat truncate the more complex plot of the graphic novel, Bucky is weaponized by Zemo to tear the Avengers apart; the Avengers fight one another at an airport to a heartbreaking crescendo that results in Rhodey being paralyzed and Cap sacrificing his allegiance to the Avengers in order to pursue the only living link to his past and the only friend he has ever had. As two young men from Brooklyn who served their country in combat, Rogers and Barnes represent two very different outcomes of warfare in terms of what it does to the humans who are sent to fight. While Rogers suffers from some signs of depression and mild PTSD, he is mostly revered and able to be proud of his service. Bucky is tortured, abused, and used as a tool in malign agendas to the extent that he is unrecognizable as his former self. When Cap chooses Bucky over his super-heroic team he both reveals the depth of loyalty that he possessed before he became a hero and a belief that, no matter how badly Bucky has been abused by others, something of him remains enough for Rogers to want to save.

The end of the movie reveals several frightening developments in the progression of the Superhero Registration Act including the fact that Captain America, having dropped the iconic shield that Stark insists he does not deserve, has become "Nomad," the man without a country. The audience also sees the superheroes who refused to sign the accord being held in the negative zone, a prison in which due process and rights do not exist. Stark is shocked by the discovery that his friends have been imprisoned, and, again, shows his ignorance to the aspects of history that Cap witnessed and made his decision to oppose the registration act based upon. In the final scenes, Black Panther spares Zemo's life so as not to be consumed by vengeance himself, and Cap leaves a letter for Stark outlining the reasons for his continued resistance. Leaving a phone for Stark to contact him in the future is the final act of a man who, having stuck to his moral convictions, bears no grudge against those who also stuck to theirs.

As the principle character who leads the resistance against the Superhero Registration Act, Cap moves full circle from *The First Avenger*, the wide-eyed and innocent Steve Rogers of the 1940s; through *Winter Soldier*, in which his faith in the entire system was blown to pieces; to *Civil War*, the last stand (in which he positions himself fully in opposition to and willing to go to battle against government control of individuals). The symbolism and power of his dissent is summed up beautifully by Karl Martin (2015):

> The decision to make Captain America the primary spokesperson for the opposition to the Superhero Registration Act provides wonderful dramatic tension for it places the very embodiment of the nation state at odds with the current leadership of the nation state.
>
> (p. 101)

The fact that he walks away from *Civil War* without his Captain America identity closes the loop on the cinematic evolution of the character, which is loosely but faithfully based upon the evolution of the character from the 1940s comics to the graphic novel Marvel event of 2006.

Notes

1 In response to the Centerville storyline arc of the Captain America series, Michael Medved wrote an article in 2003 for the *National Review* in which he accused Captain America of being a traitor to America. The storyline was a complex one in which the complicity of America in arms dealing and killing civilians was highlighted and was met with fury by those who considered the super soldier a one note government agent.

2 As soon as the extent of the damage is revealed, Captain America calls for "fire crews on the South side of the building" – In a nod to the "real" heroes of 9/11, the moral center of the Marvel Universe steps aside and calls for firefighters and paramedics, non-super powered, to clean up the mess that the Avengers have inadvertently created.

3 World War II should not and has not been viewed as a morally unambiguous campaign by scholars. Many argue that American intervention was propelled by primarily capitalist concerns, and others have convincingly stated that the romanticizing of the war instead of a thorough post mortem of what propelled it led to further conflict down the line. In the super heroic world, this is not the case. Captain America has been drawn within the dominant framework of being victorious in a righteous war, and it is this framework that is signified in *Civil War*.

Bibliography

Captain America: Civil War. Dir. Anthony Russo and Joe Russo. Marvel Studios, 2016.

Captain America: The First Avenger. Dir. Joe Johnston. Marvel Studios, 2011.

Captain America: The Winter Soldier. Dir. Anthony Russo and Joe Russo. Marvel Studios, 2014.

Curtis, Neal. "Defending Freedom." In *Sovereignty and Superheroes*. Manchester: Manchester University Press, 2016. pp. 34–57.

Dittmer, Jason. "Fighting for Home: Masculinity and the Constitution of the Domestic in Tales of Suspense and Captain America." In *Heroes of Film, Comics and American Culture*. Ed. Lisa M. Detora. Jefferson, NC: McFarland, 2009. pp. 96–116.

Dubose, Mike. "Holding Out for a Hero: Reaganism, Comic Book Vigilantes, and Captain America." *The Journal of Popular Culture*, Vol. 40, No. 6, 2007. pp. 915–935.

Hayton, Christopher J. and David L. Albright. "O Captain! My Captain!." In *Captain America and the Struggle of the Superhero: Critical Essays*. Ed. Robert G. Weiner. Jefferson, NC: McFarland, 2012. pp. 15–23.

Jewett, Robert and John Shelton Lawrence. *Captain America and the Crusade Against Evil: The Dilemma of Zealous Nationalism*. Grand Rapids, MI: Wm.B. Eerdmans Publishing Co., 2003.

Martin, Karl. "Competing Authorities in the Nation State of Marvel." In *Marvel Comics' Civil War and the Age of Terror: Critical Essays on the Comic Saga*. Ed. K. M. Scott. Jefferson, NC: McFarland, 2015. pp. 98–107.

McDermott, Mark R. "The Invaders and the All Star Squadron." In *Captain America and the Struggle of the Superhero: Critical Essays*. Ed. Robert G. Weiner. Jefferson, NC: McFarland, 2012. pp. 36–52.

McGuire, John. "Captain America in the 21st Century: The Battle for the Ideology of the American Dream." In *Marvel Comics' Civil War and the Age of Terror: Critical Essays on the Comic Saga*. Ed. K. M. Scott. Jefferson, NC: McFarland, 2015. pp. 150–163.

McWilliams, Ora. "Not Just Another Racist Honky: A History of Racial Representation in Captain America and Related Publications." In *Captain America and the Struggle of the Superhero: Critical Essays*. Ed. Robert G. Weiner. Jefferson, NC: McFarland, 2012. pp. 66–78.

Medved, Michael. "Captain America, Traitor?" *The National Review*. April 4, 2003. www.nationalreview.com/2003/04/captain-america-traitor-michael-medved/.

Morales, Robert and Kyle Baker. *Truth: Captain America, Red, White and Black*. New York: Marvel Comics, 2009.

Moser, John E. "Madmen, Morons, and Monocles: The Portrayal of the Nazis in Captain America." In *Captain America and the Struggle of the Superhero: Critical Essays*. Ed. Robert G. Weiner. Jefferson, NC: McFarland, 2012. pp 24–35.

Rieber, John Ney and John Cassaday. *Captain America*, Vol. 4, No. 1. New York: Marvel Comics, June 2002.

Stevens, J. Richard. *Captain America, Masculinity And Violence: The Evolution of a National Icon*. Syracuse: Syracuse University Press, 2015.

White, Mark D. *The Virtues of Captain America: Modern-Day Lessons on Character from a World War II Superhero*. Chichester: John Wiley & Sons, 2014.

3 We create our own demons

Iron Man

We create our own demons. Who said that?
What does that even mean? Doesn't matter, I said it cause he said it.

Tony Stark, Iron Man 3

Stan Lee's Cold War inspired creation of Tony Stark/Iron Man introduced a politically and culturally complex set of issues to the Marvel Universe that ensured Iron Man would remain relevant all the way from his inception and up to a post 9/11 American audience. Lee described the process of designing the character as a challenge to the prevailing Marvel readership's disapproval of the national trend toward capitalism, business, and war, particularly at the height of the Vietnam conflict (Lee, 2008). In his quest to complicate notions of heroism, Lee managed to create one of the most political Marvel characters of all time. While we can look to many superheroes for commentary on a number of issues such as nationalism, patriotism, environmentalism, and morality, it has always been true that the more complicated, morally ambiguous characters allow for much deeper probing of the crucible of their creation, America. In Iron Man, readers and audiences are presented with an imperfect hero with a deeply flawed psyche who presents an ongoing interrogation of technology, war, and the role of the United States in world affairs.

Aside from the obvious visual markers of Iron Man as representative of the technologization of war and the increasing sophistication of arms weaponry, the cinematic trilogy (Iron Man 1, 2, and 3) deliberately mirrors the real life, historical trajectory of the development of America's military industrial complex. In the comic series of the 1970s, Tony Stark is kidnapped by Vietnamese communist Wong Chu after stepping on a land mine, which propels shrapnel into his chest. Stark escapes, with the help of scientist Ho Yinsen, by building the first iteration of his famous iron suit, which he lovingly refers to as "shell head." In *Iron Man* (2008), the first film of the franchise, this origin is easily updated and transferred to the Afghanistan conflict, signaling the thematic appropriateness of the Iron Man character for a contemporary audience in the midst of an actual war. *Iron Man 3* (2013) returns to the Middle East and dwells explicitly upon the complicity of the media in the creation and sustenance of fear and the "celebrity" of evil. It is not surprising that the first and third films are framed within the contemporary conflicts in which the United States is involved. The audience is primed to accept Iron Man as a significant actor within the parameters of this slightly altered version of reality. Perhaps the most surprising and interesting aspect of the trilogy is the choice to address the pre Middle East history of the military industrial complex in *Iron Man 2* (2010). The second "Russian" film has been widely derided as the worst of the three films, yet the critical and audience response reveals that this may be because the decision to have Iron Man confront the origins of the military industrial complex sandwiched between two contemporary stories that resonate with a contemporary audience may have been lost on a majority of viewers who expected their hero to squarely confront the now and not ask questions of the past.

To a post 9/11 audience, Tony Stark is relatable, damaged, and human. When he dons his Iron Man suit he becomes a vehicle through which the audience is forced to consider a number of complicated global interplays between governments, foreign policy, arms dealers, and the innocents who will be caught among such forces. That Iron Man was born of conflict and enmeshed with questions regarding the ethics and consequences of the American military industrial complex means that he is the ultimate re-imaginable "hero" in the schema of Joseph Campbell's (1949) monomyth.[1] As long as there is war there will be Iron Man, and as long as there are questions about the technologization of conflict, he can be inserted into popular culture, rewritten, and updated to reflect the contemporary concerns of an audience embroiled in such traumas. Such prescience makes him one of the most interesting characters to analyze within the scope of current affairs; it also makes him one of the most complicated.

While the Iron Man character has enjoyed a certain level of popularity since his introduction in 1963 in the printed comics market, it was the release of the first *Iron Man* film in 2008 that thrust Tony Stark into the role of premier superhero. Historically, Iron Man had never enjoyed the appeal of the bigger name characters like Superman, Captain America, and Batman and had only existed as the favorite character of a small but devoted niche market of comic book fans. This changed with the release of the first major successful film in the Marvel Cinematic Universe, which made Iron Man a household name. Critics have pointed toward a multitude of conceptual lenses through which audiences can appreciate and read the Iron Man film franchise that may help to explain its unlikely commercial and critical success. The most obvious, one that we will meditate on significantly in this chapter, is the fact that Tony Stark, in both his civilian and Iron Man incarnations, is a signifier of the growth of the military industrial complex, the technologization of war, and the depersonalization of the death and carnage that war creates. For an audience primed to deliberate on machines of death and the consequences of decades of US foreign policy decisions, Iron Man represents an opportunity to process and ultimately question US authority within the safety of a reassuringly patriotic genre convention.

Iron Man and the military industrial complex

On January 17th, 1961 President Dwight D. Eisenhower delivered his final address to the nation as Commander in Chief (Eisenhower Library Archive). His military credentials and expertise were beyond question, and, having been a five star general and Supreme Commander of Allied forces in the European theater during World War II, it was somewhat ironic that he was the first president to warn the public of the danger of the creeping "military industrial complex." Eisenhower was referring to the interest of various, sometimes shifting coalitions of actors in American politics and culture who have a vested interest in the creation and maintenance of a heavily armed military, always ready for – and expecting – war. There is some dispute amongst military historians as to when exactly the military industrial complex took hold in the United States. Some argue that it began during the Second World War and intensified through Vietnam and the Cold War era. Others trace the beginning of the interdependence between private defense contractors and the government to the late 19th century, when the changing nature of technology forced governments to subcontract their weaponry needs to private industry (Epstein, 2014). What is beyond doubt is that, post World War II, the ramping up of the military industrial complex and the privatization of defense contracting reached new levels of intensity in America. This set the stage for a disastrous engagement in Vietnam followed by 20 years of Cold War conflict in which the American government convinced citizens that the only way to prevail against the USSR was the procurement and stockpiling of ever-increasing amounts of complex weapons systems.

In his book, *America's War Machine*, James McCartney (2015) argues that the military industrial complex is rarely interrogated in public forums or in a manner that the public can easily understand. He further argues that the consequence of a lack of understanding and deliberation about what the military industrial complex is creates a lack of capacity for the ordinary American citizen to follow the budget busting flows of money within it, and the effect it has on the security of the nation.

McCartney traces the development of the military industrial complex from its late 19th century beginnings to the Second World War where, according to traditional conventions, the war machine should have been demobilized and ramped down significantly (back to pre-war levels). Instead, defense spending intensified in the period after the war, decreased slightly under the Clinton administration, then exploded and morphed into an uncontainable behemoth after the 9/11 attacks (Council on Foreign Relations, 2014). McCartney outlines a number of issues that an uncontained military industrial complex creates, including the creation of an industry that is spread out over hundreds of congressional districts, which makes members of congress complicit in the problem of offering no resistance when the arms industry floods the armed forces with weapons it repeatedly states are outdated and not required for the war in terror. The most important issues he discusses in terms of being resonant with the cinematic presentation of the military industrial complex and the arms industry are twofold: conflict over diplomacy and the lack of media attention to what is going on.

When the Pentagon and the Department of Homeland Security receive far more government funding and permission to spend discretionarily than the State Department, a clear message is sent that the Pentagon, with its focus on non-diplomatic conflict resolution, has primacy in the American foreign policy psyche. Recent negotiations with Iran to prevent their acquisition of nuclear capability revealed an interesting schism in terms of how Americans are, generally speaking, less enthusiastic about viewing a proactive, non-violent diplomatic defense strategy. Months of painstaking diplomacy were viewed by some pundits as a signal of American weakness, and the expectation that America should be able to bomb Iran out of their nuclear aspirations was one that was widely disseminated in the public and media debate over the issue (Smith, 2016). One of the ever-present themes in the Iron Man franchise is deliberation on the expectation of violence to solve American conflicts, showing both American military strength as the principal means to prevail that appear parallel to unfolding storylines that highlight the danger of constantly deploying a legacy of force. The technologically enhanced Tony Stark is uniquely placed as a non-enhanced (genetically, magically, or otherwise) human, subject to very human reactions and fears so as to lead the audience into some of the complex political, moral, and ethical questions that America's reliance on its superior weaponry has created. For this particular line of questioning, the story arc is that of a man who has always relied upon and been entirely convinced of the need for arms, conflict, and force, reduced to gasping on the roadside in the third installment as he struggles with a panic attack induced by the horrors of the reality of his engagement with his armor. To even suggest that there is an alternative to military force and that the defense budget could be redirected to other areas is an American political heresy that both Democrats and Republicans are usually happy to steer clear of for fear of being labeled weak and, worse, "unpatriotic." The power of Tony Stark/Iron Man and War Machine in the trilogy is an assumption by the audience of already superior patriotism and moral "goodness" (assumed as a function of being a superhero). When a lead character's morality and patriotism are already so strongly assured by their ties to a somewhat traditionally nationalistic genre convention, it is much easier for the film to interrogate the very questions that the more dominant forms of entertainment and media in America have been reticent to address since 9/11.

The abdication of the media

McCartney also argues that the media has abdicated its role in terms of investigating government claims about the needs for arms, where they come from, and the damage that the procurement of them does to American citizens. Scholars have noted a steady decline in the quality of reporting, investigative journalism, and media in recent decades (Houston, 2010). While the media in America maintained its neutrality and respectability for as long as it could hold out, eventually the corporate buy out of the major networks around the early 1990s led to a profit-based news model that necessarily focuses on what viewers want rather than what is complex, informative, and necessary for them as guardians of democracy (Gentzkow and Shapiro, 2010). With the advent of the Internet, the line between sensationalist reporting and accurate journalism became further blurred, and we now live in an age where the media races to report breaking news with little background, content analysis, or reflection. Such a news media is apt for manipulation both by governments and enemies of state, something that the third Iron Man film dwells on heavily. Just as the media never seriously questioned or investigated the claims of the Bush administration post 9/11 with regard to the invasion of Iraq, the media in *Iron Man 3* is seen immediately accepting the symbol of fear (The Mandarin) even in his excessively stylized presentation. Indeed, it is accepted without question that The Mandarin is who he says he is, and an immediate government response is to mobilize the military and War Machine/Iron Patriot in response. *Iron Man 3* suggests that the media has become complicit in the constant vibrating fear that allows the American government to continue to ramp up both its military and the expectation that military action will always be the first and most appropriate response to even the perception of an attack upon America.

From the jungles of Vietnam to the caves of Afghanistan

As previously mentioned, the origin story of Iron Man in the Marvel Comics universe was centered on the (then) present threat of communism. As the world moved on from the Cold War, so did Hollywood's preoccupation with pro-Western reflections of its rivalries in films such as *Rocky* (1976), *Miracle on Ice* (1981), *WarGames* (1983), and *Red Dawn* (1984). After the 9/11 attacks, the narrative focus of action films moved squarely into recreating the initial trauma of the attack and then the processing of the global implications and questions arising in the aftermath.

The first two Iron Man films have several shared themes relevant to a discussion of post 9/11 superheroes. Both the introductory film and the sequel are interesting in that they directly comment upon the contemporary and historical context of the military industrial complex and build an obvious platform for the third film to deliver its damning indictment of both the weapons industry and America's complicity in violence and instability in the contemporary world.

American excess vs. the "other"

A number of visual markers appear in the opening scene of *Iron Man* that hint at some of the main themes of the unfolding story. Tony Stark, clad in a pinstripe business suit and tie, sipping what one can imagine is very expensive whiskey, is riding in a convoy of Humvees. AC/DC's "Back in Black" blasts from the CD player and obnoxiously juxtaposes the sparse beauty of the Afghan desert with signals that American excess and all that comes with it has arrived. An immediate "other" is referenced as the dusty, poor, terrorist ridden Afghanistan, complete with a goat herder watching the convoy from the side of the road. The military function of the Hummers represent a generic "over there," and, as the camera moves to an interior shot of the vehicle that is carrying Stark, we see him relaxed, perhaps even a little tipsy: confident in the fact that he is protected both within the Humvee and by the US soldiers protecting him.

What follows the shocking opening scene is a flashback to the 36 hours prior to Stark's arrival in Afghanistan in which he is shown being honored as an innovator who changed the weapons industry with his superior engineering and technological brilliance. The flippant manner in which the announcer interposes the notion that Stark has "changed the face of the weapons industry, ensuring freedom and protecting America and her interests around the globe" is the first hint that the shallow façade created around the weapons industry is about to crumble. The vague language about freedom, without any explanation or reference to the fact that the weapons industry is a much more complex and interlinked beast that ensures freedom (as long as the weapons are in the "right" hands), comes crashing to the ground in the last scene of the terrorist hijack where we see a mortar shell with "Stark Industries" emblazoned on the body land at Tony's side, a first indication that Stark's weapons are not in the "right" hands and that no one can control the flow of weapons and the innovation and technology behind them once they are unleashed on the world.

In more pre-capture flashbacks we are, again, subjected to a sequence of markers of wealth and excess. A banquet to honor Stark with a prestigious award is held in Las Vegas, but not at one of the booming, larger, more modern casino hotels. Instead the ceremony takes place at Caesar's Palace, a symbol of the Golden Age of wheeler-dealer American wealth. This sense of bygone Vegas wealth and fame is strengthened by Tony's classic limo, further emphasizing Tony's membership in the "old boys' club." Surrounded by excess, Stark himself cannot even be bothered to turn up and collect his award. Instead, he indulges in all the corruptions that Vegas has to offer before jumping into his sports car and speeding to his private plane for his appointment with reality in the caves of Afghanistan. En route to the airport, his confrontation with a journalist who offers an alternative view of how Stark Industries has impacted the world is interesting in that it offers an insight into the somewhat conservative and hawkish justifications that Stark has deployed, both publicly and privately, to defend the creation of weapons that he knows cause death and destruction, not indiscriminately but not without collateral damage. Stark deflects the criticism by referencing his father's legacy, claiming that it was due to Howard Stark's help that the Nazis were defeated. His defense is, of course, complicated by the fact that, as Captain America comes to find out all too painfully, we no longer operate in a world in which clearly fascistic (evil) regimes threaten the existence of clearly democratic (good) regimes. The complexity of the arms trade and the historical reality that the US has been culpable in the arming of terrorists in a number of situations makes Tony's attempt to liken himself to his father seem a stretch to an audience that has already watched Stark's weapons fall into the hands of the "other" and kill Americans.

The theme of gaudy American excess continues in the opening scenes of *Iron Man 2*, albeit transferred from the deserts of Afghanistan to the freezing Siberian province. This film's opening scenes introduce audiences to Russian physicist Ivan Vanko: a tattooed bad boy of science, in many ways a kindred spirit to the pre-Iron Man Tony Stark. Instead of being a mirror symbol of American/Russian innovation, Vanko is purposefully established as a product of the imperial, technological, economic, and material decline of post Cold War Russia. Although the choice of a Russian foe for Iron Man's second feature film might, at first glance, seem to be an odd choice, the placement of Vanko (and later on Hammer) as Tony's nemesis continues the established narrative of American military intervention in foreign conflicts and the proliferation of military technology at great human cost.

In Vanko's introductory scenes, the scientist is shown caring for his ailing father in a run-down Russian apartment, surrounded by news clippings of Tony Stark's successes as Iron Man. Ivan's father, Anton, is revealed to have worked closely with Tony's father, Howard Stark, and the remnants of that partnership are soon shown in the plans for the Arc Reactor both scientists worked on. This connection establishes a common bond in science and innovation, as well as a similar familial connection: both men are sons of important innovators and creators. However, a drastic contrast is drawn between the billionaire Stark and the destitute Vanko, once again pointing backward to the profiteering of past American war making. Vanko's lived experience is of the "losing side" of war with the US, and this fuels a hatred for Tony Stark that inspires Vanko to use the technology of US dominance against his enemy. Although Vanko's hatred for Stark is implicitly tied to post 9/11 terrorism through the use of American technology to attack a symbol of American profit and success (here, Tony Stark instead of the World Trade Center), Vanko is briefly more explicitly tied to international terrorist networks when he is given papers to enter Monaco illegally from a member of the 10 Rings, the terrorist group that held Tony captive and that once again will take center stage in *Iron Man 3*.[2]

As Vanko builds his own weaponized arc reactor, Tony is revealed in the Iron Man suit in a demonstration worthy of any Superbowl halftime show. Following the dreary, snow-ridden landscape of Russia, Tony's appearance at the Stark Expo is the epitome of American excess. Iron Man appears before the masses in a spectacle of sex, rock music, and explosions. Although still arrogant and boasting about American superiority, Tony speaks to the public seemingly couched in terms of peace, not war. He has, after all, stabilized East–West relations. He takes credit for these successes and in doing so represents an arrogance often ascribed to the United States and pointed to as one factor in the incitement of terrorists against US interests. Tony has achieved "peace" and televises this idea to the world. As a product of American excess, Stark must take credit for and brag about his successes in establishing that peace in a spectacularly over-the-top extravaganza in the grand tradition of American showmen.

The excesses of both the spectacle of Iron Man and Tony's own personal arrogance are soon shaken, however, in an unexpected and seemingly unprovoked attack at the Grand Prix in Monaco. Much like Tony's appearance in the "classic" Vegas, Monaco is a clear symbol of wealth and the decadence of the monied classes. Indulgent and extreme, Monaco is the perfect place for Tony's hyped-up ego, and he decides to drive his own car in the prestigious race. When least expecting it, while the privileged classes are lost in entertainment and sport, Vanko, now revealed as Whiplash, attacks. Tony must try to decipher the reasons behind the attack, and only through analysis and reflection on the role he and his family had in creating the hatred that inspired Whiplash's attack can he ultimately defeat the villain. Here, Stark remains the symbol of the American psyche: armored against the known enemy but blind to the enemy created by American arrogance. In a pivotal scene when the two enemies first meet, Vanko explains, "You come from a family of thieves and butchers, and like all guilty men, you try to rewrite your history, to forget all the lives the Stark family has destroyed." Simultaneously a judgment of the film's protagonist and of broader American imperialist tendencies as seen by others, he continues: "If you could make God bleed, people would cease to believe in Him. There will be blood in the water, the sharks will come. All I have to do is sit back and watch as the world consumes you." Paralleling the force of global terror, Vanko's indictment of Stark reveals both his desire and the desire of proponents of terrorism to show that the superpower is weak so that others might also attack and bring them down.

Technology and the economics of war

A second theme, vital to the explication of the consequences of the military industrial complex is the notion that it has created 1) An obsession with the technologization and sanitation of killing and 2) An "economics of war" in which there are "big guns" (those who have the power and influence to manipulate world affairs by pushing for a supply sided war economy) and the "pawns of war" (the average soldier, innocent civilians who are at the mercy of the merchants of death). In the opening scene of *Iron Man*, the distinction between the two economies of the powerful and the weak is clearly on display. The soldiers guarding Stark are differentiated by their uniforms and the fact that they are armed to the teeth with the weapons that Stark Industries has profited from over the years. Starks's initial arrogance is overwhelming, and his comfort at the fact that he thinks he is on the right side of war is demonstrated by his casual remark about peace: "Yeah peace, I love peace, I'd be out of a job with peace." At this point the soldiers in the vehicle and the audience themselves are comfortable with this arrogance, perhaps even charmed by it, not only because it is believable but because the idea of a wealthy military industrialist surveying the theatre of war is an image well understood by Americans after almost century of technological warfare. It is in this moment that a roadside bomb explodes and a horrifying confrontation between the sanitized version of us vs. them is immediately complicated for the rest of the film.

This opening scene marks the somewhat heartbreaking beginning of Stark's journey from egotistical heartless war profiteer to superhero. The result of the attack upon the convoy is the revelation that there is a clear economics to war. The pawns of war, the soldiers that laid down their lives to try to protect Stark all end up dead: anonymous, forgotten sacrifices to the war machine, while Stark, the chess master, gets to live, albeit in a damaged form.

The second act of the story unfolds as Tony realizes that, despite his order to shut down the weapons division of Stark Industries, Stark weapons are still being sold and used, causing civilian casualties and deaths. The complicated interplay between Stark's conscience and the reality that, in trying to create a solution, he creates the ultimate weapon (the Iron Man suit) is something that the franchise struggles with through to the end of *Iron Man 3*. The ending of the trilogy sees Tony destroy the Iron Man suit, have the shrapnel and arc reactor removed from his chest, and, in his new purely human form, proclaim that the long lesson of his journey from weapons manufacturer to weaponized human, to vulnerable weaponized human with PTSD has been that it is *he* who is Iron Man, not the suit.

The villain of the first installment is a visual signifier of the corruption of the American weapons trade. Obediah Stane is a bald, cigar-chomping industrialist who is almost a caricature of the economics of war and the profits of death. He has no alliances, no morals, and stands in juxtaposition to Stark, who has called forth those latent ideals through his experiences in his Afghan prison. At first, Stark naively trusts Obi to de-weaponize Stark industries and take the hit in the boardroom. As the film progresses we realize that Stane is so deeply tied to the corruption and profiteering of war that the only trajectory for his character is to destroy himself through his own excess. Stane desires a larger version of the arc reactor to power his own iron suit (Iron Monger), and, toward the end of the film, he gets it.

The final showdown between Obi and Stark is an all-encompassing grudge match between the military industrial complex on the rampage (Stane) and the technologically superior fused human/weapon (Stark). The obsessive need for America to weaponize itself is present in every layer of this scene and speaks to the resurgence in popularity of superheroes in the post 9/11 period. The heroes who have made a comeback and been popular figures in the healing of American wounds post 9/11 have all been complicated by their weaponization.[3]

The complicated battle between Iron Monger and Iron Man pits the remorseless military industrial complex against a human being who, although using sophisticated weapons, has been locked out of his capacity to depersonalize it by his experiences in Afghanistan. Stark has experienced firsthand the human horror of war, and he is no longer capable of coldly running the mechanics of the war machine. The capacity to do so, so present in Stane's Iron Monger, requires the ability to pretend that war is solely about machinery and technology, not human life.[4] In his Iron Man suit, Stark melds the two, ultimately as an agent of peace even as people around him are trying to remake the suit as a weapon of war. Stane's graphic death (frying himself to death in the suit) reaffirms the notion that the result of war mongering is and always must be death. The signifier of Stark's ethical awakening is that in his fight with Stane he chooses to protect Pepper. This becomes a *leitmotif* throughout the film franchise: the notion that every time Stark prioritizes the human capacity to love and make sacrifices for that love, before anything else, he is victorious in his mission.

In *Iron Man 2* the technologization of war and the creation of a literal war machine (Rhodes) is complicated by the fact that said technology falls into the "wrong" hands. Following Whiplash's (Vanko's) attack at the Grand Prix, Tony must seek answers as to how Stark technology got into the hands of a villain, subtly echoing a similar search for answers in the first film. The search for answers in this film, however, explores a number of facets of the aftermath of 9/11 that saw a nation seek to understand what might have motivated such a brutal attack and how to respond to it. Tony's interrogation of Vanko after the attack as mentioned earlier is the initial phase of that inquiry. The previous friendly working relationship between the Starks and Vankos seems to echo the complexities of American geopolitical interaction that armed Osama Bin Laden in an effort to curb Soviet expansion into Afghanistan.[5] Additionally, there is an introduction of espionage into Tony's search for answers, first in the explanation that Anton Vanko was deported for espionage and later in the revelation that Tony's new assistant is really the super-spy Black Widow.

In an early scene, Tony denies the US military access to the Iron Man technology in a testimony in front of Congress, declaring that the technology cannot be created by the nation's enemies. But, once attacked, the military goes into full hawk mode, which eventually results in the seizure of Iron Man tech by Tony's best friend Colonel James Rhodes. This technology is then used against him (again a nod to the proliferation of American arms in the hands of its aggressors) and probed for further development. The immediate military response to being attacked without a concomitant exploration of the potential risks of such a response echo the buildup and execution of Operation Enduring Freedom in response to the 9/11 attacks. In these scenes, audiences are once again introduced to military capitalism, only this time in the form of industrialist Justin Hammer, who, although more bumbling than Obadiah Stane before him, is nonetheless just as greedy and bloodthirsty.

Scenes in the film revealing that the palladium in Tony's chest is slowly killing him add an additional layer to the established allegory about the reliance on weapons and war making in the aftermath of a terrorist attack. Here, his remedy does him harm as a byproduct of his heroics. The technological, weaponized solution is not as immediate a threat as the shrapnel, but this solution, built of Tony's (US) ingenuity, has the side effect of slowly poisoning the body (politic). Tony's arc reactor, built in reaction to the immediate threat of terror, when sustained past the initial threat, serves to poison him. He views this as a death sentence, which sends him into a spiral of his old habits and modes (inconsiderate playboy, party animal). Later, when reminded by his father's film that he is the hope for the future, he taps into that ingenuity to save himself. Like the US's knee jerk reaction to terrorism in which the country did what it thought was necessary to protect itself (The US Patriot Act, wiretapping, torture, etc.), Stark's solution is not sustainable. Tony does finally realize that he can fix himself, only by returning to the idea of the ethical foundation provided by the human part of the human-machine hybrid. By returning to the age-old (American) principles of ingenuity and invention – creating instead of destroying, he is ultimately redeemed. The war machine is defeated, as is the industrialist and politician who had hoped to profit from destruction.

At the heart of the conflicts between Vanko and Stark and between Stark and the military industry (personified in different ways by Hammer and Rhodes) is technology itself. Innovation is a recurring element in the film, and its presence points to American preoccupation with 21st century digital war-making as distinct from the analog wars of the past. This idea is anchored by the Stark Expo, which figures prominently throughout the film. It is first the scene of Tony's spectacle of braggadocio and is the theatre for the final action sequences that pit Iron Man against a remotely controlled War Machine (Rhodes) and later the two friends against Whiplash and an army of drone suits. Mentions of the Expo throughout the film link it to both innovations in human technology outside the sphere of war and within it.[6] But this superior technology and its development are not presented as the improvements that atomic age narratives often presented them exclusively to be. As mentioned earlier, the technology that saves Tony is simultaneously killing him, creating a sense of impending destruction that permeates most of the film. The Iron Man suit is further weaponized and armed to create War Machine taking what had been a symbol of peace and heroics and turning it into a tank. The Stark innovation that intended to better the planet is bastardized and reproduced as Vanko's drones and his Whiplash suit. All of these events seem to point to a societal preoccupation with the advancement of technology and what might happen if the "bad guys" gain control of it. After all, if the presence of Tony in his suit anchored the weapon to a human ethical code, Vanko in a suit harnesses his sociopathy, taking it to bigger, more out of control levels. Much like the threat of biological, chemical, and nuclear weapons falling into the hands of the "bad guys," here we see a villain go mad with power as he gains the technology to wreak havoc on his enemies.

Furthering the preoccupations with the advancement of military technology, in response to and as a deterrent for international terrorism, the fear of cyber terrorism is introduced in this iteration of the Iron Man films in various forms. When Rhodes first becomes War Machine, the scenes that show the beginnings of the transformation of the suit into a powerful weapon of war consistently show Rhodes as the pilot of the suit. By rhetorically linking Rhodes with the War Machine suit, fears the audience might have about its further weaponization are assuaged. After all, here is a "good guy" with powerful weapons to defeat "our" enemies. This is problematized when the War Machine suit is hacked and taken over by Vanko. Speaking to the fears of cyber-attack in our contemporary digital present, the real threat of cyber terrorism is made manifest. In an instant, the weapon of American defense, grounded in human ethics like Iron Man, is removed from that ethical sphere and turned into another mindless weapon of war. Additionally, the drone soldiers controlled remotely by Vanko further deepen the film's concerns with the threat of more covert (cyber) terrorism.

The last two themes in the introductory films mediate upon the pre-technologization of war era and the strain that the military industrial complex (and America's constant involvement in oversees conflicts) has upon the psyche of the nation. In each film there are characters and moments that represent a much simpler time where good was unambiguously good, evil was unambiguously evil, and the weapons and methods of defeating evil were honesty, self-sacrifice, and living a moral life. Nobody more than Yensin (the scientist who is imprisoned in the cave with Tony in Afghanistan and saves his life with the chest arc reactor) signifies the tension between the old *jus ad bellum* and the new stealth, secret, and weaponized methods of contemporary warfare.

The cave scenes in *Iron Man* represent the literal metamorphosis of Stark into Iron Man. When he awakens, he is informed that he is carrying (Stark Industry) shrapnel in his body, which is being held back from piercing his heart by a makeshift electromagnet. The Iron Man suit is, at first, an opportunity to escape. Tony weaponizes his own body in a montage that meditates heavily on 19th-century American industrial strength. As he clanks and smelts the suit into place he is shown as the ultimate inventor, a pseudo-19th-century innovator in a time of robotic manufacturing and mechanized war making. By donning the suit, he attaches the weapon outside to the human inside, symbolically tying technology to human ethics. His manned uniform is now beholden to the ethical quandaries that war brings and stands in juxtaposition to the terrorists and villains trying to recreate unmanned versions, to Vanko and his army of drones in *Iron Man 2* and the creation and explosion of both Iron Patriot and the 42 previous incarnations of the Iron Man suit that Tony builds to distract himself from his lingering PTSD in *Iron Man 3*.

Vital to Stark's initial survival and consequent escape, standing in stark contrast to the arrogant industrialist, is the tragic character of Yensin. Yensin is everything that Stark is not: humble, wise, experienced enough to impart that the love of family comes above everything else, and ultimately doomed. Audiences are given a more detailed look at the character of Yensin later on, in *Iron Man 3*. In that film, Tony is seen meeting Yensin at a conference in Bern, Switzerland, and Yensin is seen operating confidently in the same circles as Stark. It seems he was at least capable and brilliant enough to exist in the same professional circles as Stark, but in *Iron Man* he becomes expendable. Yensin has no agency, other than his brilliance in initially saving Stark's life, which ultimately leads to his own death. This sympathetic figure saves Stark's life, goes on a suicide mission to buy Stark more time to charge up the suit, and dies, bleeding out slowly laid across a pallet of US Grain AID (the ultimate symbol of US idealism in foreign policy, again in the wrong hands). His last words to Stark are: "Don't waste your life," invigorating a sense of decency and responsibility in Tony that causes him to his shut down the weapons division of Stark Industries on his return to the USA. In his return to America we see a completely changed figure. Physically, Tony carries the reminder of his near death and Yensin's sacrifice in his chest. Mentally he is scarred by watching the American troops in his convoy shot to pieces in front of him, and emotionally he struggles with the knowledge that his ingenuity and brilliance are directly responsible for the deaths of countless innocents across the globe.

Throughout the Iron Man franchise and bleeding into the Avengers stories, Stark (more so than any other character) comes to signify the heavy burden that war places upon the American psyche and individuals themselves. In the first film, right before the grudge match between Iron Man and Iron Monger, there is an interesting exchange between Stane and Pepper Potts at Stark HQ when he catches her downloading secret files he is keeping on the Iron Monger project. Obi wistfully ponders the change that he has seen in Stark since he came "out of the cave" and says that the transformation "breaks my heart."[7] Obi feigns sadness about the toll of war while Pepper replies that "(Tony)'s complicated. He has been through a lot." Pepper's insight into Tony is an insight into the American consciousness. Through all the iterations of Iron Man (the three character films, his role in *The Avengers* (2012), and his appearance in *Captain America: Civil War* (2016)), no other character has so painfully represented the ongoing battle within the American psyche about war making, weapons production, revenge, and the use of violence. Stark's lingering trauma begins in Afghanistan, is an ongoing presence in *Iron Man 2*, and reaches a crescendo in the final installation of the franchise where he is seen to be suffering from severe PTSD to the extent that he feels the need to physically change back into his pre-Afghanistan incarnation to begin his own process of healing. The end of the first installment of the Iron Man franchise shows Stark at a press conference, somewhat returned to his previous arrogance contemplating in front of a room full of journalists what it means to have the character of a hero. He talks about his "laundry list of character defects" and "all the mistakes I've made" before admitting that he is Iron Man.

The complexity of Stark's character and his transformation into arguably an even more complex figure by the film's end are indicative of the transformation of superheroes post 9/11. The Iron Man story and particularly the first film carries within in the perfect story arc for an updated meditation on America's role in the weapons trade, its use of force, and the technologization of warfare. By the end of the film Stark, through a rebirth of fire and trauma, has refashioned his war machine into a body of armor, which he alone has the capacity to control. The films that follow explode that assumption and add further layers to the interrogation of American technological superiority and the erroneous assumption that every generation makes: that weapons can be controlled and weapons deployed by the "good guys" are acceptable in the face of expediently dealing with the "bad guys."

If *Iron Man* explores the complexities of the military industrial complex and *Iron Man 2* looks at technological innovation as a weapon of war, *Iron Man 3* is a clear meditation on the media's complicity in the hyperbolic concept of evil. There are three obvious themes (along with multiple smaller explorations) in *Iron Man 3* that are worthy of analysis. The first is the presentation and media complicity regarding the terrorist, the nature of terror, and acts of terrorism. The second theme is the representation of the American military complex, the war machine, and historical and contemporary America foreign policies, and the third, which underpins the first two themes and is woven into the foundation of each scene, is the individual, national, and lingering trauma that was inflicted upon the United States, citizens, and soldiers in the aftermath of the 9/11 attacks and the subsequent wars.

In the eighth minute of the film we are introduced to the terrorist who will plague the United States and Iron Man himself throughout the film. In a video, which stylistically echoes terrorist videos Western audiences are used to seeing coming out of Middle Eastern Terror cells we are introduced to "The Mandarin." In this clip, set to scenes of screaming people, explosions, desert landscapes, and terrorist training camps, The Mandarin recalls past American sins: "In 1864, in Sand Creek, Colorado, the U.S military waited until the friendly Cheyenne braves had all gone hunting; Waited to attack and slaughter the families left behind and, claim their land." Explaining that, in retribution for this and other US foreign policy actions, he has bombed the families of members of the military based in Kuwait while they were out on maneuvers, he calls out the president by name and finishes with a chilling but familiar warning: "You know who I am, You don't know where I am and you will never see me coming." This sequence effectively meshes the very real terrorist threat, post 9/11, with the traditional iconographic "super villain" from the comic book genre.[8] The Mandarin is dressed in a somewhat theatrical costume, exaggerating all the visual characteristics audiences have been exposed to and taught to associate with terrorists and fear. The difference between his "costume" and that of Middle Eastern terrorists Western audiences are used to seeing is that The Mandarin's garb is the presentation of another distinct ethnic tradition but read through the lens of American perceptions. In this film the ethnicity hinted at is Chinese, not so coincidentally a rising power with whom the United States has a necessary but fractious and potentially dangerous alliance, echoing the alliances of the United States' past that came to haunt it in the future. Much like American films that have utilized stylized, "turbaned" Middle Eastern terrorist characters with only a tenuous connection to any sense of authentic ethnic garb, The Mandarin's theatrical pseudo-Chinese costume also evokes a vague association with an enemy "other." Immediately following the introduction of The Mandarin is the American media response to the video that, again, mirrors the now-standard media reaction we associate with global terrorism in the 21st century. The clip replays on national stations, cable news, and the commentary rings with words like "hijacked," "frightening," "high alert," and "fear," pushing the impact of the terrorist video deep into the psyche of Americans and prompting the president to respond.

The second Mandarin video follows after an attack outside Grauman's Chinese Theater, another example of American appropriation and mutation of cultural representations. It begins with The Mandarin educating the audience about the actual origin of the fortune cookie. He claims that it is not, in fact, a Chinese creation but rather an American one, a sign of the American tendency to put forth false representations of cultures, causing self-appointed defenders of those cultures to rise up against America. Promising that "the big one" is coming, The Mandarin shoots a picture of the president between the eyes and warns of his upcoming "graduation." Stark's reaction to the attack, which severely injures his bodyguard, comes through the filter of the media, further underscoring the intrinsic part of the sensationalism of terror that the media perpetuates in the post 9/11 world.

After the attack on Stark's house and The Mandarin's video in which he "executes" a hostage live on television after having the man beg for his life to the president,[9] Stark hunts down The Mandarin and discovers a truth that is as unexpected for the audience as it is jarring. The Mandarin is revealed to be an "actor" whose actual persona is that of a drunken, drug addled, polite loser named Trevor Slattery who has none of the evil characteristics of his alter ego.[10] The revelation of Trevor Slattery is extremely revealing on several fronts. As previously mentioned when comparing the Batman villains, the pre 9/11 genre of super villains tended to be one note characters representing, albeit in a more comically evil way, the dictators and evil characters we have become used to in our real lives. The juxtaposition of the hyperbolic evil figure of The Mandarin, presented to the world as the pinnacle of evil with the comical ruffian Trevor Slattery, evokes these previous comic book villains. What was an expectation of the superhero genre (a larger than life, powerful and charismatic villain that quipped at the hero as he or she tried to escape from a diabolical trap and ultimately used their powers derived from good to triumph) is now much more unsettling. As a society, Western nations are wedded to the notion that there is a clear and definite enemy, that they have recognizable faces, and they are the person embodying the ideas that we hate. Once The Mandarin is revealed to be a fabrication, a manifestation of a more abstract concept of evil begins to take shape. Yet, the populace is still connected to the idea that the best way to get rid of such evil is to react with fatal violence toward the figureheads representing the new manifestation of evil without seriously addressing the fact that when one of them is killed, there are hundreds more ready to take their place. Both the audience and protagonists in *Iron Man 3* are expecting evil and terror to be focused in a single figurehead, and the audience never questions that The Mandarin is behind the terrorism. The creation of The Mandarin challenges traditional genre expectations by using the power of the media to construct the idea of a terrorist whom we blame and want to kill. The audience wants there to be a Mandarin, an enemy responsible for clear acts of evil because faceless terror frightens us more than anything. The killing of Bin Laden did not end the war on terror, and *Iron Man 3*, more than any superhero film since 9/11, specifically directs our attention to the disconnect between how we have traditionally viewed evil and how terrorist organizations have evolved their tactics to account for the fact that when you name a leader you name a target and lose the power to manipulate and terrorize.

Also layered within the main terrorism story arc are constant reminders of the nature of American foreign policy and its perception by the rest of the world. In response to the first terror attack by The Mandarin, the president unveils his plan to fight back in the form of the Iron Patriot. The Iron Patriot, formerly known as War Machine but renamed, draped in the colors of the American flag (a visual reference to Captain America, a previous weapon of the US government), represents the fact that American foreign policy has not really changed post 9/11. Instead, it has been repackaged and injected with a shot of superficial "patriotism." The US did not declare war on a country; it declared war on "terror," and the Iron Patriot represents the shift in presentation. The actions of the Iron Patriot further many of the ideas that were initially explored in *Iron Man 2*, discussed earlier. One such element is the Iron Patriot's deployment to Pakistan, mirroring real life drone attacks in search of terrorists. Although Rhodes is piloting the suit, his arrival at a house full of women echoes American drone attacks on civilian targets. Here, Iron Patriot is able to stop the attack before killing innocents, presenting the potential threat he poses to them as an indictment on American reliance on unmanned technology. While Rhodes is able to assess and stand down, unmanned drones working off of bad intel cannot. Additionally, the theme, previously explored, of American weapons being used against the US by its enemies is again present, this time in the form of Iron Patriot being used as a Trojan horse. When in the wrong hands, an American creation can be used as a weapon to destroy its interests.

The final subplot is an interesting take on the fragility of Tony Stark since the attack on New York City, which he fought with the help of The Avengers.

Many have noted that *The Avengers* film was an obvious recreation of the events of 9/11 and served as a cathartic experience for audiences in the US who watched and re-watched it in the millions.[11] In the aftermath of the attack at the beginning of *Iron Man 3*, we are aware that Tony Stark is experiencing the symptoms of PTSD, a disorder that the American public has become ever more familiar with as their soldiers return from Middle Eastern wars, affected by it in the thousands. Early in the film Stark, who hasn't slept for more than 73 hours, says: "Nothing has been the same since New York." As his lack of sleep begins to affect him physically he has several anxiety attacks, one induced directly after the mention of the New York attacks, followed by an incident in which he (in an altered psychological state) calls forth the Iron Man suit in bed and attacks Pepper Potts.[12] In his suffering, Tony Stark/Iron Man acts as the national consciousness. It is left up to him to both find and kill The Mandarin and take healing steps, which will reflect in his actions and have a cathartic impact on ordinary American citizens.

In the denouement of the film we are confronted with the unexpected decision of Stark to undergo surgery to remove the shrapnel (obtained during the attack in Afghanistan) from his chest and remove his arc reactor (the technology that has thus far been keeping him alive). In this scene he heals his war wounds physically. The psychological healing only comes in the scenes that directly follow when he blows up his Iron Man suits and chooses to prioritize love over war. This presents the audience with a confirming "Hollywood" ending in which the protagonist reminds us of our human strength to choose love over hatred, weapons, and conflict that serves to remind us that the idealistic, if unrealistic, way to beat terrorism is to choose to love, to be human, and to gather strength in the human ideals that we presume the terrorists do not share. In the final scene Stark meditates ion the destruction of his armor: "My armor was never a distraction or a hobby, it was a cocoon and now I'm a changed man. I am Iron Man." In this scene Stark confirms that it was not the suit that made him Iron Man the superhero, but rather it was the ideals and the core values for which he stood that gave him his power as a cultural icon and a protector of America.

Iron Man 3 is one of the more complex superhero films from the post 9/11 series. Tony Stark evolves from the first film, turns his back on the military industrial complex he himself helped to create, and becomes a force for good. *Iron Man 3* attempts to unravel the particular complexities of the war against terror we have been waging for 15 years with explicit references to weapons technology, the American war machine, and the manner in which the media is complicit in sensationalizing terror.

In the Iron Man films, we find a fascinating and revealing exploration of technology and terror in the post 9/11 period. In each film, the villain that Iron Man faces is not a supervillain alone but rather a military industrialist personifying the system of greed on the backs and lives of others. In these films the industry itself and the capitalism on which it is built are reexamined and questioned, and in doing so, each film unpacks a concept or preoccupation that is the hallmark of a post 9/11 world. In *Iron Man*, the industrialist Stane literally becomes the Iron Monger at the end of the film. He is both antagonist and the supporter of terrorism in this way. In Stane, audiences can see how greed can contribute to (and sometimes even become) the real threat. In *Iron Man 2*, The industrialist Hammer's greed supports Whiplash's (Vanko) revenge. But as a criticism of the uncertainty of technology and the ease by which it can slip into the wrong hands, Hammer's creations are used against him, and he is defeated. Finally, in *Iron Man 3*, the industrialist Killian goes to great lengths to create a fake terror network to mask the development of yet another weaponized scientific development. In each instance, audiences must question the motives and the actions of these antagonists and in doing so come to question recent past events on the global stage. As is the case with most of the films studied in this book, there are no longer clear-cut answers to the myriad questions that arise through examination of these films. Good guys can get hijacked and become bad or are threatened by their own mortality, psychology, or physiology, and bad guys seeking revenge might gain control of the technology created for "good" or might be complete fabrications of media hype. The questions raised, although not answered fully, are an essential part of our post 9/11 consciousness and are able to be processed and better understood through the iterative narrative of a billionaire in a suit. Tony famously ends *Iron Man 1* and *3* by saying "I am Iron Man." Tony's declaration is not only his own but that of the American people. As audiences witness him struggle with the issues explored here, the end result is not only Tony's "I am Iron Man" but the collective "We are Iron Man."

Notes

1 Joseph Campbell states that myths and stories from around the world and throughout history follow a basic, circular pattern in which the hero faces the same journey, same challenges and is restructured in the same (newly named) form to reflect the expectations of the society that produces their story.

2 The brief appearance of the 10 Rings in *Iron Man 2* weaves the organization into all of the Iron Man films and is significant in that is communicates a network of interconnected terror continuously plotting attacks.

3 Hulk is a giant atom bomb; Captain America is American values injected with super soldier serum, which forces him into a constant conflict between his ideals and his strength. Hawkeye and Black Widow are psychologically weaponized people who struggle with the "red in their ledger," and Tony Stark is an unambiguous representation of a sophisticated weapons system that allows us to depersonalize death, until we realize that the collateral damage is still existent and vast.

4 This dichotomy will be explored in more detail in *Iron Man 2* when Hammer seeks to create Iron Man suits that have no human pilot in them, further emphasizing the need of those in charge of the military industrial complex to ignore the human cost of war in favor of pure mechanization.

5 While the Soviet/Afghan conflict is implied here, it is distinct from the diegetic cooperation between Anton Vanko and Howard Stark, given that, instead of arming the Afghans to keep the Russians at bay, a Soviet scientist is recruited to help fight his own countrymen, and then, later, his son is jailed for selling plutonium to Pakistan once again pointing to

the complexity and interchange of trading weapons with "frenemy" alliances. Although the specifics are distinct, the arming and scientific support of one power against another in a regional conflict link these plot elements to the global terror network both responsible for and, later, a product of, the 9/11 attacks.

6 Howard Stark's film introducing the Expo is evocative of Walt Disney explaining his dream of a technological future to American television audiences, and prominent real life innovators in the realm of technology Elon Musk and Larry Ellison (CEO of Oracle) make cameos.

7 Stane's reference to Tony's transformation once he has "come out of the cave" could also be understood as a connection to Aristotle's cave allegory. After living in a world that ignored the realities of war and the death that his technology would bring, Tony emerges both literally and figuratively from the cave, with his eyes wide open to the harsh reality of his industry.

8 A more direct connection between the fictitious terrorist group 10 Rings and the real Al Qaeda can be seen in the short film *All Hail the King*, which serves as a sort of epilogue to *Iron Man 3*, when Justin Hammer describes Trevor Slattery (The Mandarin) as the result "if Bin Laden and Benny Hill had a baby."

9 In a series of terrorist videos since 2001, hostages have directly addressed the leaders of their various nations, issuing the terrorist demands (which are usually money, the release of terrorists in custody, or the removal of their militaries from the Middle East). When the leaders do not capitulate, the hostage is forced to blame their leader and their country for their death before they are horrifically executed. This again labors on the point that the whole endeavor of terrorism is to use very few resources to terrify a great number of people. It shows the reach that terrorists have when they have the capacity to demand the attention of world leaders and underscores the media as the conduit between and mechanism of the connection between terrorists and world leaders that directly plays into our fears about the capacity for one person or a small group to subvert the democratic process.

10 It is also likely not accidental that the man behind The Mandarin shares initials with Tony Stark. This symbolically links the two characters and puts them in direct contrast to one another. Down and out, unsuccessful, boozy, wannabe playboy Slattery is molded by shadowy powers into The Mandarin for evil, while billionaire playboy Stark creates Iron Man himself and eventually comes to discursively fuse the two identities (Stark/Iron Man) into one heroic figure while the figure of The Mandarin collapses when the truth is revealed about his origins.

11 For a more detailed analysis, see Hagley and Harrison (2014).

12 One of the most recognizable characteristics of returning Iraq and Afghanistan veterans with PTSD that has been played out in several television shows (*Homeland*, *Grey's Anatomy*) are night terrors in which they attack their sleeping partners in their altered states. It is a motif, which American audiences immediately recognize as a signal of combat related PTSD from this repeated media representation as such.

Bibliography

Campbell, Joseph. *The Hero with a Thousand Faces.* New York: Pantheon Books, 1949.

Council on Foreign Relations Report, January 14, 2014. www.cfr.org/defense-budget/trends-us-military-spending/p28855

Eisenhower, Dwight D. "Farewell Address." [DDE's Papers as President, Speech Series, Box 38, Final TV Talk (1); NAID #594599] Dwight D. Eisenhower Presidential Library, Museum, and Presidential Home, Abilene Kansas. www.eisenhowerlibrary.gov/sites/default/files/research/online-documents/farewell-address/reading-copy.pdf.

Epstein, Catherine C. *Torpedo: Inventing the Military Industrial Complex in the United States and Great Britain.* Cambridge, MA: Harvard University Press, 2014.

Gentzkow, Matthew and Jesse M. Shapiro. "What Drives Media Slant? Evidence from U.S. Daily Newspapers." *Econometrica*, Vol. 78, No. 1, 2010, pp 35–71.

Hagley, Annika and Michael Harrison. "Fighting the Battles We Never Could: *The Avengers* and Post-September 11 American Political Identities." *PS: Political Science and Politics*, Vol. 47, No. 1, 2014. pp. 120–124.

Houston, Brant. "The Future of Investigative Journalism." *Daedalus*, Vol. 139, No. 2, 2010. pp. 45–56.

Iron Man. Dir. Jon Favreau. Marvel Studios, 2008.

Iron Man 2. Dir. Jon Favreau. Marvel Studios, 2010.

Iron Man 3. Dir. Shane Black. Marvel Studios, 2013.

Lee, Stan. *Interview – The Invincible Iron Man* (Ultimate two disc edition) *Iron Man* DVD. Paramount Pictures. 2008.

McCartney, James. *America's War Machine: Vested Interests, Endless Conflicts*. New York: St. Martin's Press, 2015.

Smith, Kyle. "The Stunning Tale of Naïve Weakness that Led to the Iran Deal." *New York Post*, 2016.

4 Post 9/11 and the reappearing women

Wonder Woman

Why Wonder Woman? Why now?

One of the most significant aspects of the post 9/11 superhero resurgence was the fact that it initially centered around patriarchal, male and militaristic impulses. In the rush to return America to its "traditional" values, the voices, contributions, and artistic inputs of those who did not represent such impulses were squashed. Post 9/11 popular culture suffered from a definitive lack of diversity in terms of narrative, characters, and the means of production itself. Although the refocus of American values returned to the mythological and misogynistic for nearly 15 years, when the stranglehold *was* broken it was, in part, by two astonishing movies, *Wonder Woman* and *Black Panther*, each offering a true alternative within the genre regarding the strength of humanity and love.

The Wonder Woman movie was given space to develop by the resurrection of the superhero genre post 9/11 but offered a radical departure from the hyper masculine, militaristic narratives of those films. At its heart it is a story about love: the love of a mother for her daughter, the love of a community of women for one another, the love of a woman and a man, the love of comrades, and the kind of love it takes to offer healing instead of destruction in the face of fear. It worked because Wonder Woman was one of the most recognizable faces of feminism in the world and, like Captain America, had been through several changes and shifts since her creation, which ideally positioned her to be rebooted as a moral authority on the impulses of war. This version of Wonder Woman was empowering and amplified Diana as capable, balanced, endearing, and as a non-hyper-sexualized warrior who was capable of saving the world, not by enacting masculinity but by offering a unique alternative to its worst characteristics.

Wonder Woman weaves a narrative of femininity, masculinity, heroism, kindness, and love, all contained within a balance that clearly refutes the impulses of war. The denouement of the action concentrates on the fact that, as a woman, Diana (even in her warrior status) is driven primarily by love. That love, in balance with her strength and ability to wreak destruction on those around her if she so chooses, offers a tantalizingly different vision of power when it is wielded by a benevolent, female, force. Like T'Challa, Wonder Woman is one of the very few characters in the super heroic stable who is able to offer a serious contemplation of American patriarchal impulses as they are confronted by alternative and challenging discourses. Her ability to act as a conduit between her audience and a deeper examination of American ideals and practice is embedded in her unique creation. The challenges and changes she underwent over the six decades since her creation and, ultimately, in her position as one of the most recognizable symbols of feminism and female strength in the world, lay the foundations for her spectacular post 9/11 revival. The vision of 2017 Wonder Woman and all she stood for could only be realized because the impulses of the nation post 9/11 had reached a tired, war worn zenith, and for the first time in 17 years, female voices were finally given the space to remerge within society and then within the pop culture machine that reflects it. Patty Jenkins' version of Wonder Woman confronted the masculine centered post 9/11 narrative, blew it apart, and showed an alternative course of action in which love was the guiding force.

In all of her iterations, Wonder Woman retained the unique disposition of being a female, empowered with strengths that "normal" men and women could never possess. Because she was a woman, the manner in which she wielded her power and the presentation of her characteristics has always been loaded and contested ground. As Wonder Woman moved through the decades she became a figure upon which societal expectations and constrictions were written. She was a figure who at times was deliberately used in the hands of progressive feminist writers as a loving embodiment of the struggles within the women's rights movement and a figure who (in her sometimes loose and sometimes strong connection to America) represented an alternative vision of national strength, the use of force, and the power of mercy and rehabilitation. Post 9/11, Wonder Woman suffered the same fate as women across America who were marginalized in their professional capacity, reduced to "the rescued" in the never-ending masculine saga of retribution, or confined to the domestic front to guard the family and home while the warrior men were at war. The success of her 2017 film is anchored in her unique creation and constantly evolving visions of her throughout the decades. It is mostly anchored in the notion that the alternative vision of a just society that she has never abandoned was a narrative that was desperately needed. Sixteen years of war, misery, economic constriction, and hypermasculinity had exhausted an audience (some of whom had not been born at the time of the attack and had little appreciation for the complexities of the national psyche after it). Just as *Black Panther* was able to break free from the constraints of the white hegemonic American power structure, *Wonder Woman* was similarly situated as a revolutionary presentation of what might have been if only America had chosen love, mercy, and justice above hatred, vengeance, and the annihilation of not just its enemies but the lofty ideals upon which it was founded.

Women in post 9/11 America

The voices and roles of women post 9/11 were subject to a slow and complicated recasting and removal, which had a chilling effect on feminist discourse and the representation of women in popular culture. In her insightful examination of gender in post 9/11 America, Susan Faludi states: "You didn't have to be a feminist to feel the purge. Soon after the World Trade Center vaporized into two biblical plumes of smoke, another vanishing act occurred on television sets and newspaper pages across the country. Women began disappearing"(Faludi, 2007, p. 44). In the first instance they were relegated to victims, and their victim status was focused upon far more than men who outnumbered them in death on the day itself three to one. In every guise, their purpose was to reinforce the masculine warrior status of rescuers (men) and the feminine vulnerability of wives, mothers, and rescuees (women). Faludi hones in on the visual narrative of the day itself, including pictures of heroic men looming over helpless women and offering them a reassuring hand to lead them away from the rubble of the twin towers. Descriptions of the unfolding drama on Flight 93 was laser focused on the expectation that it would have been the men aboard the doomed plane that made the decision to fight back. This recreation of unverified heroism was invented and reinforced by the imaginations and desires of helpless Americans, desperate for a story of masculine salvation. Female flight attendants, one trained in hand to hand combat, were ignored, or suggestions were made that they "may" have helped the heroic men by boiling water to throw at the hijackers (Faludi, 2007, p. 74).

Describing a slow unfolding of expectations around widowhood and motherhood, Faludi suggests that the media dwelt obsessively upon a particular kind of widow, one who deferred to the heroic status of their husbands, stayed at home with their bereaved children, and supported the government's efforts to bring the terrorists responsible for the attacks to justice. What lacked in the media coverage was attention to the fact that a much more common story involved women returning to work and wives recovering from their trauma enough to start new relationships. Highlighting a study showing that op-eds by women reduced significantly in number following the attacks and the number of female talking heads on news programs suffered the same fate, Faludi (2007) concludes that: "various impulses {that} surfaced after 9/11 – the denigration of capable women, the magnification of manly men, the heightened call for domesticity, (and) the search for and sanctification of helpless girls" (p. 18) was, perhaps, a subconscious cultural "desire to rein in a liberated female population"(p. 25).

As the erasure of female and minority voices continued in America, the news, music, and pop cultural landscapes reflected the change and shifted gears to produce pro-American, masculine narratives that remained popular for an entire decade. When breathing space emerged from the remasculinization of American culture, women reasserted themselves in meaningful ways.

The "Me Too" movement served as a rallying cry partly for the notion that a culture of toxic masculinity creates a counterculture for women in which they are at best marginalized and at worst physically and sexually assaulted. The record numbers of women running for political office following the election of Donald Trump showed a defiance in the face of another attempt to return America to a white, patriarchal system, and the global marches the day after Trump's inauguration sent a message that women were angered by the disrespect, danger, and destruction of the male-led post 9/11 world.

History of female heroes and the creation of the Amazon Princess

Any discussion of Wonder Woman's creation must begin with an examination of the nature and positioning of female heroes generally within the super heroic canon and focus upon the issues that confront them as they try to exist and wield power in a hyper masculine pop culture space. Female heroes generally existed alongside male heroes in Greek, Norse, and Roman mythology even when the focus was primarily on the behavior and narratives of the male gods. Female action heroes have changed significantly over time and presented both analysts and audiences with interesting conundrums within which to view questions of female existence and experiences. Initially, female characters in comics were there to date the male heroes, be saved by the male heroes, or to serve as a blunt narrative to show how hard it was for anyone (especially a woman) to understand the sacrifices superheroes were forced to endure to fulfil their missions. As Alison Mandaville points out in a seminal work regarding female characters in super heroic texts, women also, disturbingly, existed as a plot device in which graphic and intense violence was inflicted upon them as a matter of expectation (Mandaville, 2014).

The space and commercial desire for female action heroes reached its zenith in the 1990s, which saw a slew of female heroes like Xena, Buffy, Barb Wire, Sarah Connor, and G.I. Jane grace television and movie screens all over the world. According to Sherrie Inness, the prevalence and increasing numbers of female action heroes coincided with a societal shift in expectations for women, including an increasing acceptance that they could fulfill many employment roles as successfully as men and be a meaningful presence in the workforce and society at large (Inness, 2004, p. 3).

Viewing the pro-feminist representations of female action heroes in the 1990s may have led to the conclusion that a true watershed moment had been reached in societal acceptance of women with power, serving in traditionally male heroic roles. While it was true that the numbers of female heroes were significantly increasing, it is also true that problematic issues within their representation continued to exist and further perpetuate narrow stereotypes of women whilst failing to account for the whole spectrum of female difference and strength that existed in reality.

One of the most obvious concerns was the physicality of female heroes. Early incarnations of female comic and action heroes were drawn as either hypersexualized or "ideal physical myth(s) of contemporary Western femininity" (Natale, 2013, p. 81). Drawing female strength exclusively for the Western male gaze problematized the notion of female strength. The perfect physical forms that female heroes took served only to perpetuate body shaming and encourage insecurities within women who did not fit the impossible profile of perfection (most women). This doubly disenfranchised women of color and non-binary females. In seeking to present women as heroic, what was mostly achieved was the reinforcement of societal expectations about the female form on one hand and the contouring "representation of women as victims" (Pennell and Behm-Morawitz, 2015, p. 218). It is clear that the representation of women in pop culture has enormous capacity to "become normative and influence real world perceptions" (Pennell and Behm-Morawitz, 2015, p. 270), so, viewing the experiment with female action heroes through the eyes of girls and women who were then forced to accommodate another unrealistic expectation of their strength, femininity, and sexuality, it is no surprise that the existence of such heroes generally led to: "lower body self-esteem from female viewers"(Pennell and Behm-Morawitz, 2015, p. 219).

Further evidence of the destructive presence of female superheroes (drawn by men) is revealed in aspects of their characters beyond the physical. In a study of super heroic female characters, Baker and Raney (2007) found significantly fewer female heroes than male ones. Heroes of color were even less likely, and female heroes of color were basically nonexistent. They also pointed to the fact that the portrayal of female characters perpetuated stereotypes such as women worrying about their physical appearance and being more emotional than their male counterparts. A further concerning signal, given by the presence of twice as many mentors for female heroes than males, was that women with power were not to be unleashed onto the world without some calming and guiding male presence to ensure they did not deploy their powers in an emotional manner (Baker and Raney, 2007). Such depictions, designed to empower women and girls, are shown to do quite the opposite. The presence of women in superhero films are so few and far between that the ones who do exist take on extra significance and draw extra attention to the way they are presented and behave. Given that superheroes are "products and embodiments of their cultures" (Shugart, 2009), the amplification of stereotypes, concerns with physicality, and the generally weak natured state of even superpowered women "tended to perpetuate rather than challenge conventional discourses of masculine and white privilege" (Shugart, 2009, p. 99).

Another key tension in the representation of female action heroes is the accusation from some critics that, rather than developing a sense of power derived from the distinct differences between men and women and creating a multifaceted presentation of the various forms of female strength, female action heroes are simply, "enacting masculinity" (Brown, 2004, p. 49). In her book *Tough Girls*, Sherrie A. Inness (1998) argues that, because comic books are created by men, principally to be indulged in by boys, certain preferences are, "catered to, resulting in many woman characters who are still little more than overly endowed male fantasies who would be right at home in the Hugh Hefner mansion"(p. 142). She further states that, even "bad girl" comics, which were drawn consciously to try and liberate women from the previously stifling incarnations of heroism, still relied upon women as "sex objects for male gratification"(p. 146). In rebuke, Jeffrey A. Brown (2004) takes issue with critics who focus on the enacting of masculinity of female heroes without paying attention to the qualities he views as truly "transgressive." Using several examples, including G.I. Jane and Ripley from the *Alien* series, Brown hones in on the idea that female action heroes are more complex than a simple enacting of the masculine binary and states, "The alternative I wish to suggest here is that the tough action heroine is a transgressive figure not because she operates outside of gender restrictions (like Ripley) but because she straddles both sides of the psychoanalytical gender divide"(p. 49). Here, Brown, perhaps unconsciously, touches upon one of the reasons why *Wonder Woman* (2017) was so well constructed and so well received. Diana was not simply enacting masculinity in a Hollywood blockbuster. The character was extremely well developed in terms of all aspects of her femininity, her power, her mercy, and at certain points in the sequence of action, she deploys some or all of these traits to great effect. Unlike the female action heroes of the 1990s, in this instance, filmmakers managed to create a character who was both transgressive yet believable *because* of her gender, not in spite of it.

Wonder Woman: then and now

Known for resurrecting Wonder Woman for the front cover of radical feminist magazine *Ms.*, Gloria Steinem (1995) recalled a series of compelling reasons as to why she chose the fictional Amazonian to represent the progress and the hopes of the then second wave feminist movement. Situating her identification with the superheroine within the memory of the time she got her hands on her first copy of a Wonder Woman comic, she describes feeling empowered for the first time in her life. Recognizing the fact that female characters, up until that point, had left little girls with the idea that, "Even when her body is as big as her spirit, she will still be helping with minor tasks, appreciating the accomplishments of others, and waiting to be rescued," Steinem points to a central sexism in comic book commerce that highlighted the lesser status of even the most powerful female superhero (p. 6). Describing a scenario in which the swapping of one *Wonder Woman* comic demanded three times the male centered titles in return, she touched upon the realization that, early in all their lives, little girls are taught that they are less valuable than men (p. 11).

The most striking and heartbreaking aspect of Steinem's *Introduction* is when she discusses the expectation of shame and violence that little girls develop as they approach adulthood in a world where many expect to be degraded, assaulted, and humiliated on a regular basis. In a society where women are routinely told to walk in pairs, catcalled, told to avoid dressing like a "slut," and expect that men will be unable to control themselves to the extent that their sexual assault of women was a societal expectation, Wonder Woman represented a possibility of strength and power that had been previously unavailable to girls and women in America. Steinem adored the first incarnation of the Amazonian goddess, railed against the degradation of her powers over time at the hands of male writers attempting "feminist" narratives, resurrected her in all her glory on the front cover of *Ms. Magazine*, and demanded that she be restored to her previous female centric orientation. Steinem's intervention was successful and led to D.C. turning over creative control of Wonder Woman to women, queer men, and people of color – but not before she had been through several stages of development in which, like women everywhere, she was degraded, stripped of her powers, humiliated before her male counterparts, viewed as less than because of her femininity, and presented in confused, bipolar narratives that espoused feminist ideals but sorely misunderstood them.

Wonder Woman first appeared in Dec. 1941 and was created by psychologist William Moulton Marston at the beginning of American involvement in World War II. Delineating Marston's "feminist agenda," Finn (2014) details the main aspects of her creation as being driven by Marston's genuine belief, anchored in his study of how human beings reacted to certain stimuli, that women were fundamentally motivated by love. Marston's Wonder Woman was a combination of physical strength, morality, femininity, and love. She offered, for the first time in American comics history, a role model for young girls and women like Gloria Steinem who yearned to be free of the crushing societal expectations she did not yet understand. She also showed young boys and men that a woman could be possessed of super heroic powers, strength, and virtue. Early iterations of the comic series reveal Marston's intended narrative to be pro-women, progressive, and incredibly liberal for the time (Finn, 2014, p. 11). At times, Marston's narrative tended toward an anti-feminist message in terms of his portrayal and representation of men as driven by "destructive impulses that fostered selfishness and greed,"(Finn, 2014, p. 11) and his continual reference to the fact that the women in his story were guided by the goddess of Love while the men were consumed by the whims of the god of War. Frederic Wertham (1953) was quick to hone in on this aspect of the *Wonder Woman* narrative in his book *Seduction of the Innocent* and accused Marston of creating a character that degraded men and created a: "frightening morbid ideal" for little girls (p 193). Wertham dwelt obsessively on female relationships within *Wonder Woman* as sexually coded (lesbian) and destructive to a properly functioning society.

The interesting tension at the center of Wonder Woman's creation was played out in the domestic and international sphere of World War II and its aftermath. A well-documented aspect of the war was the paradoxical domestic liberation it provided for women in the United States and Europe who stepped up to fulfill roles left by a generation of absent men in the industrial and manufacturing sector. Her existence and popularity (as well as the criticism and ire she drew from Wertham) would not, perhaps, have been so powerful were it not for that fact that, owing to the contemporary women's war effort her "masculine traits were seen as appropriate for the time"(Knaff, 2014). Another tension, one that played out in all Golden Age comics, was that, despite the presentation of super heroic characters as humans whose morality and sense of duty was amplified to the extreme, most of the narratives were thoughtlessly racist and continued to depict racial and gender stereotypes in ways that damaged their transformative potential. The central issue within the *Wonder Woman* stories was that Wonder Woman was stunningly beautiful, physically impossible, and artistically rendered to appeal to the male gaze. She was also created by a man who had decided that the strength of women lay in their kindness, love, and humanity, thus reducing the scope of what a woman could be. If women did not fit Marston's expectations of "love leadership," there was no other avenue in which the spectrum of femininity could be explored, presented, and shown as a viable alternative to the expectations that Marston had created. In terms of feminism, Wonder Woman was the most empowered female character who had been created at that time. She was also "not free to deviate too far from the standards of womanhood established by the dominant, white middle class culture"(Finn, 2014, p. 16).

As with all major upheavals and moments of progressive politics that liberate minoritized groups within the American population, a backlash and reestablishment of pre-World War II ideals was quickly imposed when the soldiers came home and the American government turned its attention to the increasing Soviet threat of the 1950s. The original iteration of *Wonder Woman*: strong, self-possessed, beautiful, merciful, and dangerous, could not hope to thrive in a new cultural landscape that emphasized a return of women to the domestic sphere; the elevation of men back to heads of the household, workers, and leaders; and the home front as the most important place for women to contribute to the safety and prosperity of the nation.

The change was reflected in the post-World War II *Wonder Woman* comics that switched focus away from profiles of "Wonder Women of history" to focus on "marriage customs around the world" (This, 2014, p. 37). The post creation fate of Wonder Woman was to suffer. As all American women who had been somewhat liberated from domestic drudgery during the war, Wonder Woman was to have unbearable pressure imposed upon her choice of happiness: "World War II created the vision of Wonder Woman and strong, independent women. Wertham contained her and so did post war writers who introduced tension between career, marriage, and family" (This, 2014, p. 40).

The Cold War iteration of *Wonder Woman* in which her feminist origins, independence, and physical strength sat at odds with the overwhelming message that recovery from World War II was dependent on women returning to the domestic sphere would not retain commercial success for long. With the women's liberation movement gaining momentum in America and other developed Western nations, feminist readers (who had viewed Wonder Woman in the same way as Gloria Steinem in her creation) were upset with the 1950s and early 1960s *Wonder Woman* stories. At a time where "Women's movement activists were calling for equality of opportunity and respect for the capacities of all people, men and women, to lead, to follow, and to participate in all levels of society" (Latouche, 2014, p. 82), the morphing of the original Wonder Woman from her Golden Age presence into a tortured, confused, and watered down version of her former glory was sharply criticized by readers. In response, writers tried in earnest to move toward a less stultified narrative for both Wonder Woman and Diana Prince. Moving slowly away from her Cold War casting, the writers refocused *Wonder Woman* on her initial mission and showed several scenes where, "She and Steve Trevor have nightmares about being married and how bad it is" (Velcour, 2014, p. 70).

From the late 1960s onwards, writers saw the increasing power of the women's movement but utterly failed to understand and represent it faithfully. *Wonder Woman* was shown to have surrendered her powers and entered life as an ordinary citizen, even running a mod boutique. Her decision to relinquish that which made her powerful was driven by a desire to help Steve Trevor, and, as a consequence, was out of step with the prevailing feminist sentiments of the times.

In 1972 D.C. created a one-off "women's lib" issue of the *Wonder Woman* story. One of the most controversial aspects of the new narrative, other than it being written and drawn exclusively by men, was that Wonder Woman was stripped of her costume and her powers in order to reduce her to "normality." Criticism was brushed off by the male production team, and they justified their vision of Wonder Woman in this iteration by explaining that it showed that her "real" power existed because she was a "modern feminist" (Latouche, 2014, p. 82). Jason Latouche (2014) describes the updated women's lib Wonder Woman as being presented as: "submissive to almost every man she meets." On top of the insult of her submissiveness, she is mentored by a man who is cruel and verbally abusive to her and is prone to "extreme displays of emotion" (p. 86). He further suggests central differences in the way that male superheroes were characterized when they were given more human qualities as: "explaining their core strengths and sense of purpose" as opposed to the presentation/humanizing of Wonder Woman as: "containing only the most superficial of empowering characteristics" (p. 87). Here was a superpowered woman, previously celebrated by feminists and empowered with all the strength of a male superhero with a layer of female wisdom on top, reduced to a dithering character, dominated by the men around her, devoid of her superpowers and drawn with increasing reliance upon her physical beauty and helplessness, all to engage male readers. That this happened at a time when women were actively seeking equality in increasingly imaginative and political ways seemed like a double insult to the Golden Age legacy.

Regaining her powers in 1974 was a step in the right direction as far as feminist critics were concerned but continued to highlight and exacerbate tensions between expectations that people had for the character and the ongoing inability of male writers to situate her as a convincing feminist with a consistent set of pro-feminist values. In reestablishing her power, Martin Pasko returned some of her Golden Age dignity. He also undercut it by presenting her feeling unworthy of her powers and created a storyline in which she undergoes the "twelve labors" in order to prove to the rest of the Justice League of America that she can be trusted with membership. Joseph Darowski (2014) describes the twelve labors storyline as a "creepy male framed story"(p 133) in which the male characters spy on Wonder Woman and, by interceding in her tasks, undercut her agency ensuring that, even in completing her Herculean challenge, she is reduced in the eyes of the audience.

The 1980s presented tough terrain for superheroes to operate within, and as a result many of the stories lacked correlation with real life politi-cal and social events or reprinted stories about the prevailing cultural land-scape of America at the time. Both Marvel and D.C. characters were reduced, revamped, rebooted, and mostly engaged in confusing, "other dimension" storylines (Wonder Woman) or shown to be integrated into non-super heroic society by working as art teachers in liberal arts colleges (Steve Rogers).

Toward the end of the decade, Wonder Woman was rescued by a reboot that placed creative control in the hands of George Perez. Perez was drafted in a deliberate "attempt to draw in female readers" after the disastrous slump in sales of the 1980s (Emad, 2006, p. 969). Perez significantly altered both the back story, supporting characters, and the forward trajectory of the *Wonder Woman* narrative and deliberately foregrounded female unity, strength, and independence. While staying true to the very basic storylines, Perez deviated from gender expectations and explicitly dwelt upon issues such as violence against women. During Perez's run, Themyscira itself was home to "reincar-nations of battered women who were killed by their abusers" (Emad, 2006, p. 971). Perez also altered the visual of Wonder Woman and set the physical tone for how she was to be eventually presented in the 2017 movie. Instead of focusing on hypersexualizing the Amazonians, Perez created a vision in which Wonder Woman is appropriately attired for battle and reveals a: "toned and muscular body" (Emad, 2006, p. 974). According to Emad, Perez also separated Wonder Woman from explicitly war-driven American foreign policy narratives and presented her instead as "an ambassador from a superior culture" (Emad, 2006, p. 973). Perez's tenure and experimenta-tion and his interpretation and presentation of women and women's issues was a radical departure from the previous decades for *Wonder Woman*, and his audience approved. His deliberate attempt to redirect the trajectory of the Wonder Woman character away from previous decades in which she had been weakened whilst retaining some of her Golden Age appeal was a critical and commercial success. Throughout his tenure, Perez "consistently broke sales records," largely because women were buying into the character again and increasing their participation as consumers of the franchise (Emad, 2006, p. 970).

Several more attempts to rescue Wonder Woman from the drudgery of female servitude were made in the decades following Perez's groundbreaking work. In 1992, D.C. hired Samuel R. Delaney, a noted writer and critic specializing in sexuality, to write a "multiple issue feminist story arc for Wonder Woman" (Bamberger, 2014, p. 117). This run saw her experimenting with women's liberation, uniting with other women to explore issues of feminism, and being fully restored in her capacity to fight for herself after years of abuse from I. Ching. In addressing some of the offenses committed against Wonder Women in the allegedly "Women's Lib" issues of 1972 and reversing the misguided path of those storylines, Delaney set the foundations for even more radical story arcs that followed when creative control was finally given over to female creative writers and production teams. Gail Simone, a comics writer who cut her teeth on *Deadpool* and *Agent X*, became the longest-serving female writer to work on the *Wonder Woman* series and further shaped the character along with Perez in ways that significantly influenced the 2017 *Wonder Woman* film.

Starting from the presupposition that Wonder Woman was an important figure in the feminist movement, Simone used her version of the character to challenge both the shortsighted previous renderings of the story and aspects of the first and second waves of the feminist movement. Having won the battle for basic rights in the first and second wave, the third wave turned its lens upon the internal tensions within the feminist collective. Recognizing that early forms of feminism had not been inclusive of all women, the third wave: "[was] anchored in {a} desire for inclusion {and} deep investment in cultural production as a site of change"(Mandaville, 2014, p. 208). Alison Mandaville (2014) argues that Simone's version of *Wonder Woman* was revolutionary in the sense that it reclaimed the means of production away from men and the male gaze, focused on the notion that a female character and female relationships did not have to be relegated to the sidelines in order for a comic to be commercially successful, and showed female characters as leaders in all spheres, domestic and international (p. 216). It was upon Simone's foundations that Patty Jenkins was able to lay the building blocks of a feminist character finally free from the constrictions of a male dominated, conflict obsessed society and, finally, wield the character within a truly post third wave feminist pop culture production.

Wonder Woman (2017)

It is interesting that two of the most potent symbols of American patriotism, Captain America and Wonder Woman, serve as bookends to the movies that specifically address the post 9/11 American cultural landscape. Cap is rebooted with his World War II ideals and motivations intact and is shown to retain those values even as the world around him becomes less moral and more complicated. Wonder Woman seems to suggest that the response to 9/11 and the consequent wars in which the nation became embroiled could have been handled in a completely different manner and with much less loss of life and dignity.

By the end of *Infinity War*, Captain America has slowly been awakened to the fact that his nation has not always behaved in accordance with his moral imperatives and continues to sow the seeds of a great deal of pain and misery in the world. Cap continues in his mission because he believes in the human proclivity toward justice and kindness. Wonder Woman begins her story by stating that she has already learned that lesson a long time ago in the battle-fields of World War I (the war to end all wars) that was simply the beginning of never ending human conflict.

Wonder Woman's opening speech dwells upon the inherent beauty of humanity alongside its tendency toward inhumanity and evil. In recognizing that humans represent both sides of the moral coin, she situates herself not in the service of a nation or a strict set of moral codes but in the belief that the tendency toward love will prevail in most cases. Immediately dispatching with the explicit ties between Wonder Woman and a nationalistic, patriotic, American-centered narrative is vital in establishing to the audience that this Wonder Woman is not tied to the agenda of a nation and, most specifically, has no allegiance to the post 9/11 American narrative and consequence course of action.

Establishing Diana's homeland

In a sequence of action that smashes the Bechdel test,[1] Themyscira is presented to the audience in a manner that inverts the expected patriarchal order, foregrounds the notion of women as warriors, and presents a truly unexpected vison of an empowered female society. In this one scene, every woman on the island is shown fulfilling a role, some of which would ordinarily be reserved solely for males in a traditional society. In a pastiche of all the roles that the women on Paradise Island occupy we see child carers, mothers, aunts, warriors, tutors, and Senators. Equally important to this spectrum of femininity is the fact that it is diverse in terms of body type and race and shows non-white women in possession of political, physical, and intellectual agency alongside their white counterparts. The decision to address the lack of diversity in the origin story head on and recreate it to present an inclusive, female utopia was necessary given that the essence of the Wonder Woman film was the version created by Simone and Perez, which dealt with intersectional feminism and explored the revolutionary ideas that came about within the evolution of the movement. Accusations of non-feminism levelled at the narrative of the Wonder Woman film centered on the casting of Gal Gadot and was complicated by the fact that she is an Israeli citizen who has stood firmly on the side of her nation in what has been viewed in more radical feminist discourse as the continued oppression and deliberate annihilation of Palestinians (NerdyPoC).

The physicality of the women of Themyscira is as important as the different roles they are shown to be occupying. The first aspect of note is that the costumes are not created for the male gaze. They are the uniforms of fully functional warriors and work in concert with an intentional visual of what can be achieved with your body when you are lithe and agile enough to slide down a horse and pick up a shield from the ground but strong enough to prevail in close quarters combat. These images announce the fact that these warriors will not be male analogues enacting the powers usually reserved for men; they are female warriors, appropriately dressed to engage in vicious fighting and good at it because they are women, not in spite of that fact.

Diana is, at first, banned from training, and her desire to be strong leads her to a familiar conundrum that resonates with many women. She works harder to prove herself capable, and she must train longer and harder than all the other Amazons just to be considered as worthy as them. As her mother tries to protect her and keep her close to the home fires, Diana breaks free because of sheer hard work, something we do not generally see in the battle training of male superheroes who are usually struck by some incident or take a secret potion to gain their immense powers. Even in the attainment of her powers as a superhero, Wonder Woman's route is distinct from her male counterparts; a signal to the audience that a woman may wield such power but only if she works to attain it in the first place and is then shown to be worthy, merciful, and judicious enough (more so than men) to keep it.

Clear from both Hippolyta's reluctance to allow Diana to train with the Amazons and the constant reinforcement of the message through Amazonian stories is the belief that "War is nothing to hope for." A distinction between the cadre of female warriors on the island and those in the rest of the world who train for war is that this group of women views conflict as both undesirable and an absolute last resort to protect innocents who are caught up in it. As Hippolyta tells the story of how the Amazons came to be, the warrior/ pacifist identity is further molded. Hippolyta tells a story that is parallel to the intentions of William Moulton Marston in the sense that men (both the gods who created then corrupted them and the earthly manifestation of them) are responsible for the suffering in the world. In this version of the gods, Ares is revealed to be the one who deliberately sows the seeds of discord among mankind and leads them to fight. Although this may exonerate mankind a little (if they are only acting at the whim of a higher power), it is clear from the narrative that each man makes his choice, so they are not completely influenced by Ares' nefarious actions. This distinction is vital for the denouement of the action when Wonder Woman realizes that the fine line between Ares' warmongering and mankind's ability to resist it comes only from their capacity for love. The end of the film does not solve the conflict between mankind's propensity for destruction and its capacity for humanity, but it does make Diana realize that the difference lies in a choice each person makes, allowing her to see that the balance between good and evil is more complex than she first imagines, a realization that changes her mission forever.

Complicating the feminist superhero

In terms of costume and the presentation of the female body, *Wonder Woman* is firmly anchored in the third wave feminist vision of the character. The Queen of the Amazons, Hippolyta, is shown in what is essentially the original Wonder Woman costume but in white with gold accents. This signifies her regality, purity, and the neutrality of the Amazons. In her initial incarnation, Wonder Woman proudly dons an almost garish version of the American flag, showing that she is aligned with American ideals. In the movie, her costume is a significantly more muted version of the Golden Age version. It is clear that the reboot does not intend to visually cue her as an unquestioning agent of American ideals but as an independent agent, born in a land that has never been subject to outside interference and driven by her own sense of what is morally right. The only signifier imbued with an expectation of behavior that Diana possesses as part of her costume is Antiope's headdress. When Hippolyta gifts it to her as she leaves the island, it is understood that Antiope was Themyscira's greatest warrior and that Diana must live up to her example in her endeavors. Here, the Golden Age allegiance to America is replaced by a symbol of the ultimate degree of female strength, courage, and wisdom.

Diana's arrival in stuffy Edwardian England serves as a means of meditating on the evolution of expectations of women in society and how we can read those expectations through the clothing that has been available to them. Her unashamed clothing contrasts greatly with the dark, gloomy Edwardian uptightness, and the montage of her trying various outfits is telling in terms of how she views costume choice (functional and freeing) in contrast with how others around her view what is appropriate for women (suffocating and diminishing). Diana is ultimately concerned with the functionality of each choice of clothing and asks of each restrictive outfit, "How can a woman fight in this?" An archetypal montage follows in which Etta Candy attempts to help Diana find a costume that will allow her to fit in whilst Diana is trying to find the most utilitarian costume that will allow her to engage in combat. Having selected a masculine tweed suit as her combat-friendly choice of clothing, Steve Trevor is still unsatisfied with Diana's "normal" outfit and selects a pair of spectacles for her, which he believes make her less conspicuous. Etta Candy underscores the ridiculous inversion of the "nerd" trope in this scene by commenting: "Oh yes, put glasses on her and suddenly she's not the most beautiful woman you've ever seen." The notion that the addition of a pair of glasses is quintessential to the secret guise of a superhero is long established and begins with Superman. The addition of glasses was essential in preserving the secret identity of all heroes in the Golden, Silver, and Bronze eras. In this instance (post 9/11) superhero identities don't even matter. Steve Trevor is attempting to help Diana forge a dual identity as a plain Jane. Diana is resisting and, having chosen her outfit and donned the spectacles, emerges with a sword, collapsing the secret identity in on itself. Diana's glasses get destroyed in the fight scene that follows, so the symbolic containment of her warrior nature and femininity is destroyed almost as soon as it is thrust upon her.

In her interaction with the men in the war cabinet, Diana reveals her lack of deference to the patriarchal power structure, failing to even notice the shock and discomfort of the men gathered to the very presence of a woman in their midst, least of all one who wants to talk and be listened to. The presence of a woman in the coded male space renders most of the gathered men speechless, and Steve Trevor is left to try to physically remove Diana from the room (to no avail). Within this interaction there is explicit reference to the female centered/warrior type of warfare that Diana and her Amazons are steeped in and the cold, industrial, emotionally removed warfare that the men in the room are presently directing. Indicting the cowardice of the generals (and given that war had not changed, the cowardice of real-life cotemporary politicians) in response to the cold emotionless notion that "That's what they do. Soldiers die," Diana is disgusted and launches an invective of the way in which she believes wars should be waged: "Everybody fights . . . if you don't have a personal stake you don't care." Clear in this scene is a sense of what lies behind the two distinct attitudes toward war. From the minute Steve Trevor inadvertently brings German soldiers to Themyscira, he introduces an enemy, using the cold, cruel, penetrative weapons of mankind to fight against the Amazons who fight in close quarters, facing their opponents. In the hard juxtaposition of smog ridden London where the cowardly generals hide in cabinet rooms as they direct thousands of soldiers and innocent people to their deaths daily, Diana's vision of justice and her naivety about the intentions of men are tested for the first time.

Action heroines and "bad girl" bodies

In taking on the task of bringing Wonder Woman to a 2017 audience who were more versed in the discourse surrounding female bodies and the male gaze, the director was significantly challenged by a history of female action heroes laden with hypersexuality and drawn explicitly *for* the male gaze. The manner in which Wonder Woman was presented in her bodily whole was one of the most vital aspects of the success in desexualizing the character for modern times and focusing on the qualities that made her a warrior rather than a sex symbol. Interestingly, Patty Jenkins turned to existing genre conventions in the presentation of battle-ready male bodies and modified them slightly to redirect the focus of the viewer away from the sexual/bodily and toward the warrior/bodily.

In perhaps what is the most iconic moment of action, Diana ignores warnings that she will get herself killed and for the sake of the innocents caught between the warring sides, crosses no man's land from one side to the other, deflecting a hail of bullets and bombs with her bracelets and agility. In another deliberate inversion of the expected superhero film trope, the camera pans to disconnected parts of Wonder Woman's whole and holds the focus on each long enough to show that the intended gaze is directed at that which makes her a warrior (her armor) and nothing that accentuates her body or her sexuality. The attention goes from shield to armor to boots to rope to wraps and eventually all of her. There is no close up, no subversion into the male gaze. In this moment it is, importantly, not an impossible body waiting to be objectified on display but a mosaic of female power, deflecting all the fire and signifying the unpaid work of women so that the men can cross behind her. In this scene she is not hypersexualized; rather she is magnificent in the visual combination of her body, power, and costume. Within this scene, Wonder Woman traverses the spectrum of femininity imagined possible. In the beginning she is devastated by the misery and desolation of the innocents and shows a pure manifestation of empathy and altruism when the men around her have none. Diana exhibits true pain at the collateral damage of war, presumably because of her connection to the lives around her. She can conceive of warriors killing warriors, but the idea that somebody would kill a mother and child or an old lady in the middle of a battle is something she has never even thought of, so she finds it truly devastating. In the middle of the scene she turns that emotion into action and crosses no man's land. At the end of the scene, she returns to her regular state of being without commenting on or acknowledging the power, courage, and sacrifice she has just made. As the people of the liberated village gather around to give their thanks, it is she (not the men) who is cheered and worshipped, with the men in so much awe that they show great deference and respect toward her.

Alongside the considered presentation of her physicality, there are several other important signifiers of the unusual place that Wonder Woman holds within what is essentially a movie about war. First, several masculine/feminine tropes are deliberately inverted or adjusted to accommodate the fact that this iteration of Wonder Woman is most closely aligned with third wave feminist ideals. It is established early in the pastiche of Themyscira and Diana's continuing interactions with those around her that she was raised free from any male influence and is therefore naturally inclined to react and empathize with women more strongly than she is with men. Her relationship with Etta Candy is one of immediate trust on the part of Diana, who gives her the God Killer instead of Steve Trevor, who is more bodily but less trustworthy to Diana. In turn, she empowers Etta, who already shows predilections toward suffragettism both in her costume and her comments, to take more of a leadership role of the team.

Diana's interactions with the psychologically damaged "gang" that Trevor gathers to accompany them to the front serves the dual purpose of educating her about the complexity of the history of mankind as well as restoring enough humanity in each of them that, when called to choose between apathy/action and war/peace, they position themselves on the side of love. In Turtle we see a man so tortured by war and suffering from PTSD that he has lost the capacity to function without alcohol, has night terrors, and cannot fulfill his role as a sniper when he is needed. In Sammy, we see an outcast by virtue of his ethnicity, whose only desire was to be an actor, sadly explaining to Diana that his dream will never come true because he doesn't belong. The presence of the Chief in the lineup is an interesting and unusual narrative tool, used to teach Diana that her binary view of good and evil is something that she needs to revisit. Until the point that the Chief informs her that it was Steve Trevor's people who killed his people, she is convinced that the Americans and the British are the good guys and the Germans are under the thrall of the God of War. As a neutral actor who is only against Ares and for the protection of innocents, it is in this interlude that she starts to understand that the good guys are not always good and the bad guys have more agency than she first believed. The gang begins the narrative compelled only by the promise of being paid and the commercial potential of aspects of the war. They end the narrative by stepping up into the necessary roles to prevent chemical weapons from being unleashed because of Diana's leadership. Her extraordinary feats in no man's land, her emotional reaction to the death of innocents, and her continued insistence that humans are worthy of saving compel each of these misfits out of their shell-shocked and apathetic states and into individual decisions to embrace courage, sacrifice, and humanity itself.

Her relationship with Steve Trevor is both central to the action and a metaphor for the difference between man's propensity for war and the Amazonian notion of love leadership. Although Steve Trevor is a physically strong and an intellectually capable man, he is realistically humbled by Diana's extraordinary powers and respects her immediately and completely. This mutual respect is highlighted in the sex scene between the two. They are both shown to have agency, both make a consensual decision to engage one another, and they are seen to be reaching for one another at the same time. In a time period where an audience would expect to see the man make the first move and sweep the uncertain woman off her feet, even this small, unexpected gesture reveals the progressive feminist message of the movie.

While Trevor is an embodiment of the proactive American intervention in the war that was propelled by the desire to squash the Germans and create a new world order, his motives are more centered in American ideals of standing up when something is unjust and trying to help people who are helpless. It is the addition of Trevor's story about his father teaching him right from wrong that allows Diana to first see nuance in the human psyche and further allows their relationship to flourish, culminating in him sacrificing his life for the greater good and crystallizing for Diana what it is she believes in enough that she is able to prevail against Ares. One of the most dominant and powerful themes of the final scenes of Wonder Woman is the unabashed message that humans may be complicated and prone to hatred, but there is an alternative that they are also capable of. Amazons were created as a response to hatred, and Diana comes born of that love to restore peace to the earth. When she states that Amazons are "the bridge to a greater understanding between all men" she is saying that they are the literal manifestation of international-ism and cooperation. Speaking all languages ensures that there are no barriers in their way, and, when they lead by the example they were created for and humans respond in kind, they can end wars.

The other interactions that are important to the development of Diana's understanding of humankind are with her enemies. First, we have Luden-dorff, who seems to check all the boxes of mindless evil enough that, until the last scenes of the movie, Diana believes that he is Ares, the God of War. A crazed, chemical sniffing Nazi whose plans for destruction and victory out-pace even those of Hitler himself, Ludendorff is a perfect foil for Diana as long as her belief is that Ares is solely responsible for the corruption of man-kind. His plan to win the war sees him team up with a chemical warfare sci-entist to create a gas that will kill millions of people and force the surrender of the Allies. There is little depth to Ludendorff's character, no back story that reveals why he may have become evil, and, like Diana's expectation of Ares, he seems simply to thrive on death and destruction. Ludendorff teams up with Dr. Maru, a toxin specialist who delivers his poison to him for use against innocents. Pointing again to a spectrum of femininity, Maru is interesting in that she is the virtual opposite of Diana's humanity. Disfigured to the point that she has to wear a mask to cover half of her face, she is an inversion of every expectation of femininity that the audience has. Unlike Diana, who is raised in a tropical paradise, Maru reveals no backstory and is first seen operating in the cold and sterile chemical lab within German headquarters. Where Diana is mythical and tied to religious tradition, Maru shows nothing but allegiance to Ludendorff and an almost sexual pleasure in the creation of her weapons of mass destruction. The development of the character is com-plicated toward the end of the film when we see that she is more than just completely evil. In the scene at the ball in the castle, Steve Trevor attempts to appeal to her vanity by praising her work. At first she is intrigued by him, but she quickly realizes that he is focused on Diana and walks away in disgust. At the end of the movie, she is revealed, cowering and pathetic in front of Diana who chooses to spare her life. It seems that Maru made choices about the evil she would be part of, but with the loss of Ludendorff, she shows weakness for the first time. Diana's mercy is important in this scene for two reasons. First, it reinforces the notion of rehabilitation that she truly believes in and presents her with the very real opportunity to choose between vengeance and love, a choice that is vital to the consistency of her character and the message of the final scene of action.

The culmination of the story is a death match in which the compulsion to destroy (male) and the compulsion to protect (female) are in mortal combat with one another. Ares uses every tactic he has to try to persuade Diana that humans are not worthy of her protection, including physically attacking and restraining her using his metal armor and slabs of concrete. He also tries to convince Diana that human beings are only capable of "great hatred and horrors." The single most important part of this scene is when Steve Trevor chooses to sacrifice his life to guide the chemical weapons away from civilians and soldiers on the battlefield. Trevor's actions are almost identical to those undertaken by Captain America in the final scenes of *The First Avenger*, the vital difference, of course, being that Steve Trevor sacrifices himself because he truly believes that the values that Wonder Woman serves are better suited to peace than anything he is able to offer. As Ares revisits the reasons he hates all humans, he makes the mistake of including Diana's sacrificed love in his diatribe: "Mankind did this! Ugly, filled with hatred, weak; just like your Captain Trevor." It is the mention of his name that pulls Diana back to reality, and she has a flashback in which she hears what he said to her before he piloted his plane to his death: "I have to go. It has to be me. I can save today. You can save the world." Unmissable in this statement is the inversion of the gender trope that has existed in superhero comics and movies since World War II: that men are the heroes. Steve hands off the mission of a past bloody entrenched war, caused and directed by men, to a woman who symbolizes diplomacy, peace, and the protection of the innocent. At this moment, Diana finally recognizes the root of the complexity she has spent the whole movie wrestling with: that mankind *is* ugly; they torture, kill, and exhibit great selfishness in their guardianship of the earth as well as being capable of self-sacrifice and empathy and motivated in large part by love. Steve's choice shows Diana that love is the quality within mankind that she is also motivated by. When Steve tells her "I love you," she finds the power to erupt out of her being and defeat Ares. His actual demise comes when Diana destroys him with a power source that is coming right out of her chest. Her mercy does not extend to Ares. As the being responsible for the immense suffering of innocents, Diana kills him. It is a truly groundbreaking cinematic moment to watch the world's most recognized female superhero vanquish her enemy while the focus remains so intently on the fact that her actions are motivated by a force entirely different than her male counterparts. Leaving the audience with a sense that Diana's values, so sorely absent in the aftermath of 9/11, always offered an alternative way to fight one's enemies, we are forced to question the entire narrative of the post 9/11 masculine war machine as one that deserved our support.

Conclusion

In an essay entitled "This Ain't Gender Studies Sweetheart," Carole Stabile perfectly crystallizes the post 9/11 tendencies for the marginalization of women in popular culture, life, and political action: "The affective pull of female vulnerability, moreover, and this is particularly heightened in the narratives that have emerged since September 11th, is used as a grounds for the protectors violence and to legitimize their acts of torture and extreme violence" (Stabile, 2009, p. 87). While it is true that the resurrection of male superheroes post 9/11 acted first as a balm to a wounded nation and second as a vehicle for more radical discourses to emerge (ones that questioned the actions of the US government), it is also true that, until the release of the Wonder Woman film, they played somewhat into the militaristic expectation of American violence and vengeance. American culture following the 9/11 attacks forced women and minorities to the sidelines and front and centered a dominant narrative of maleness, whiteness, and military might. Susan Faludi suggests that in creating such a myth of what America was "We made the world and ourselves less secure" (Faludi, 2007, p. 385). By recreating a narrative of a battle between good and evil (based in historical reality) and complicated by the admission that no one country is "more good" than others, the reboot of Wonder Woman shone a searing and painful spotlight on the fact that alternative, non-violent, non-vengeful courses of action *were* available in the days and years following 9/11. The fact that they were ignored, not taken seriously, and dismissed out of hand, pointed the nation toward ongoing conflict as a way of life; a life that has consumed America for the last 18 years.

By anchoring the 2017 Wonder Woman firmly within her Golden Age character traits and layering her with third wave feminist discourses of peace and violence, Patty Jenkins created a truly revolutionary superheroine movie. Diana remained: "a creature bred for war who works for peace" but opened up the door for future forays into representations of female power on the big screen (Gabriel and Berns, 2009, p. 195). Expectations for the *Wonder Woman* film were high, and the production team was facing extra scrutiny because of Wonder Woman's unique place as the only truly recognizable representation of female super heroic power. What the reboot of *Wonder Woman* does not do is move past the initial third wave sentiments into a real contemplation of feminine solidarity and intersectionality, but as the expectation for her capacity to push the existing boundaries of feminist discourse onto the big screen grows, critics may yet get their vision of a post third wave feminist character laced with mainstream appeal and blockbuster commercial power.

Note

1 The Bechdel test is a framework described by comics artist Alison Bechdel as a way of determining if female characters in a work of fiction have their own agency and importance in the narrative of the story. Among the various "tests" are such questions as "Do two women have a conversation that does not have to do with men?"

Bibliography

Baker, Kaysee and Arthur A. Raney. "Equally Super? Gender Role Stereotyping of Superheroes in Children's Animated Programs." *Mass Communication and Society*, Vol. 10, No. 1, 2007. pp. 25–41.

Bamberger, W.C. "The Near Awakening of Diana Prince." In *The Ages of Wonder Woman: Essays on the Amazon Princess in Changing Times*. Ed. Joseph Darowski. Jefferson, NC: McFarland, 2014. pp. 117–125.

Brown, Jeffrey. "Gender, Sexuality and Toughness: The Bad Girls of Action Films and Comic Books." In *Dangerous Curves: Action Heroines, Gender, Fetishism, and Popular Culture*. Jackson, MS: University Press of Mississippi, 2004. pp. 47–74.

Darowski, Joseph. "I No Longer Deserve to Belong: The Justice League, Wonder Woman and the Teve Labors." In *The Ages of Wonder Woman: Essays on the Amazon Princess in Changing Times*. Ed. Joseph Darowski. Jefferson, NC: McFarland, 2014. pp. 126–135.

Emad, Mitra. "Reading Wonder Woman's Body: Mythologies of Gender and Nation." *The Journal of Popular Culture*, Vol. 39, No. 6, 2006. pp. 954–984.

Faludi, Susan. *The Terror Dream: Myth and Misogyny in an Insecure America*. New York: Picador, 2007.

Finn, Michelle R. "William Marston's Feminist Agenda." In *The Ages of Wonder Woman: Essays on the Amazon Princess in Changing Times*. Ed. Joseph Darowski. Jefferson, NC: McFarland, 2014. pp. 7–21.

Gabriel, Fernando and Pagnoni Berns. "War Foreign Policy and the Media: The Rucker Years." *The Ages of Wonder Woman: Essays on the Amazon Princess in Changing Times*. Ed. Joseph J. Darowski. Jefferson, NC: McFarland, 2009. pp. 194–204.

Innes, Sherrie A. *Tough Girls: Women Warriors and Wonder Women in Popular Culture*. Philadelphia, PA: University of Pennsylvania Press, 1998. pp. 138–159.

Inness, Sherrie A. "Boxing Gloves and Bustiers: New Images of Tough Women." In *Action Chicks: New Images of Tough Women in Popular Culture*. New York: Palgrave, 2004. pp. 1–20.

Knaff, Donna B. "A Most Thrilling Struggle: Wonder Woman as a Wartime and Post War Feminist." In *The Ages of Wonder Woman: Essays on the Amazon Princess in Changing Times*. Ed. Joseph Darowski. Jefferson, NC: McFarland, 2014. pp. 22–29.

Latouche, Jason. "What a Woman Wonders? This Is Feminism?" In *The Ages of Wonder Woman: Essays on the Amazon Princess in Changing Times*. Ed. Joseph Darowski. Jefferson, NC: McFarland, 2014. pp. 79–89.

Mandaville, Allison. "Out of the Refrigerator: Gail Simone's Wonder Woman 2008–2010." *The Ages of Wonder Woman: Essays on the Amazon Princess in Changing Times*. Eds. Joseph J. Darowski. Jefferson, NC: McFarland, 2014. pp. 205–222.

Natale, Edward A. "An Analysis of Embodiment Among Six Superheroes in D.C. Comics." *Social Thought and Research*, Vol. 32, 2013, pp 71–106.

NerdyPoC. https://medium.com/@nerdypoc/gal-gadot-isnt-wonder-woman-23ce51d30859

Pennell, Hilary and Elizabeth Behm-Morawitz. 2015. "The Empowering (super) Heroine? The Effects of Sexualized Female Characters in Superhero Films on Women." *Sex Roles*. Springer 2015. pp. 211–220.

Shugart, Helen. "Super Marginal." *Communication and Critical Cultural Studies*, Vol. 6, No. 1, 2009. pp. 98–102.

Stabile, Carole A. "Sweetheart, This Ain't Gender Studies: Sexism and Superheroes." *Communication and Critical Cultural Studies*, Vol. 6, No. 1, 2009. pp. 86–92.

Steinem, Gloria. "Introduction." In *Wonder Woman: Featuring Over Five Decades of Great Covers*. Eds. Amy Handy and Steven Korte. New York: Abbeville Press, 1995. pp. 5–19.

This, Craig. "Containing Wonder Woman: Frederic Wertham's Battle Against the Mighty Amazon." In *The Ages of Wonder Woman: Essays on the Amazon Princess in Changing Times*. Ed. Joseph Darowski. Jefferson, NC: McFarland, 2014. pp. 30–41.

Velcour, Francine. "Wonder Woman's Lib: Feminism and the 'New' Amazing Amazon." In *The Ages of Wonder Woman: Essays on the Amazon Princess in Changing Times*. Ed. Joseph Darowski. Jefferson, NC: McFarland, 2014. pp. 90–116.

Wertham, Frederic. *Seduction of the Innocent*. New York: Rinehart and Company, 1953.

Wonder Woman. Dir. Patty Jenkins. Warner Brothers, 2017.

5 A miracle of counter resistance

Post 9/11 racial narratives in Black Panther

The release of *Black Panther* in February of 2018 came at a critical time in American racial history. Debate about its impact was centered around a discourse of critical race theory that was both more complicated and more widely understood by the audience than ever before. This was compounded by the fact that the representation of "blackness" in American popular culture has always been a painful and contested arena in which the dominant racial group in America (White Europeans) have both constructed then reinforced their vision of what it means to be black, with little to no input from African Americans themselves.

The *Black Panther* film and many other artistic and social expressions of the agony of black America were always likely after the events of 9/11. For 17 years America processed its trauma by turning to patriotism, symbolism, and ultimately nationalism, all of which leaked into the post-reconstruction scars of American history and wetted them enough to open a floodgate through which black Americans continued to suffer. Black America was ignored, marginalized, and given lip service to during the War on Terror and, while the election of Barack Obama served as a temporary balm to the American racial trauma, the very fact that the reconstruction of America post 9/11 was deliberately imagined by predominately white, conservative politicians and was, in essence, divisive and racist (you're with us or you're with them) was increasingly provocative toward people of color and immigrants.

The declaration of a Global War on Terror, combined with the positioning of whiteness as the healthy "norm" in American society added another layer to the American racial story in the days and months following the 9/11 attacks. The casting of "otherness" as the enemy with repeated statements that American citizens could only exist on the side of justice if they wholeheartedly supported the wars in the Middle East was deliberately designed to bolster patriotism (even in the event that it turned into nationalism) and suppress voices who questioned the established story of American innocence.

It is unsurprising that calls to patriotism and vengeance did not sit comfortably with a demographic of Americans who were reexperiencing the "deeply set American tendencies towards fear of others" (Garneau and Foley, 2014, p. 178). Black opposition to the invasion of Iraq showed that "While

78% of whites favor the war, just 29% of blacks do, for a gap of 49 points. Nearly 7 in 10 blacks, 68%, oppose the war" (Jones, 2003). The poll results supported the notion that black Americans had never shown an easily triggered propensity to either rally round the flag or invade other countries in the service of vengeance for the white power structure. Writing for *The Guardian*, author Walter Mosely (2002) attempted to provide some context to the lack of black support for post 9/11 American incursions into other countries. Describing a disconnect with white Americans who unquestioningly rallied around their government, armed forces, and flag, Mosely discussed the "rage" that black Americans live with every day as a "rage" against America. White American innocence narratives were at a loss to explain why anyone would be compelled to attack the United States; people of color, going about their lives in a racialized American system, were not. Warning that white America was "inured to its own prejudices," Mosely foreshadowed the coming racial tension of the 2000s: "You cannot ignore rage. It does not go away. It only goes away when the causes of that rage are addressed"(Mosely, 2002).

Instead of being addressed, the covert and overt racism of post 9/11 America gathered pace and began to envelop communities of immigrants and ethnic groups beyond black America. Despite President Bush's careful delineation of the difference between terrorists and Arabs, Arab and South Asian Americans "got a taste of what it was to be a black American" (Chedade, 2002). In a detailed exploration of bias incidents and changes in the legal system post 9/11, Muneer I. Ahmad (2004) describes a significant increase in violent attacks against Arabs and South Asians, which he views as accompanied by and therefore encouraged and normalized by "a quickly developed and broadly applied policy of racial profiling of these communities" (p. 1267).

In the absence of attention paid to black victims of 9/11 and the erupting racism toward Arabs and South Asians that followed, the notion of an "authentic" American identity was crystallized as white, masculine, and militaristic. The rights of citizens of color and immigrants were eroded further in the prosecution of the Global War on Terror. In terms of popular culture, the vacuum created in the aftermath of the 24/7 weeks of disaster coverage was quickly filled with productions that further reified the innocence, normality, and democracy of white America. As the: "shift is racial profiling from black while driving to Muslim while walking" came full circle, the degradation of communities of color continued but without the creative outlet and pop culture presence that has existed, albeit in sparse amounts, in the past (Ross, 2005, p. 237). Thomas Ross describes the landscape for Americans of color as one in which: "the violence and deaths continued, but 9/11 sucked the air out of the room and nothing else mattered" (Ross, 2005, p. 237).

When Barack Obama was inaugurated as America's 44th president with a backdrop of generally high approval ratings across the American political spectrum, some may have been forgiven for daring to believe that the nation had moved significantly past its history of racism and attendant discrimination against minorities (Presidential Approval Ratings). It was almost impossible to conceive of the dueling notion that a black man was elected to preside over a nation in which racism was deeply and socially ingrained within many of its citizens. Obama's honeymoon period was cut short almost immediately by the backlash and opposition that grew around the idea that he was (although acting in complete accordance with his campaign promises and the general position of many democratic candidates) "dishonoring" the nation and creating division. With the rise of opposition on the right, the founding of the Tea Party and Glenn Beck's "Rally to Restore Honor" held in Washington D.C. just seven months after Obama's inauguration, the feelings of some Republicans at their failure to retain the White House boiled over into a toxic mix of anger, indignity, and paranoia toward their new president. The worst extremes of such behavior manifested within the "birther" movement and the increasingly vocal suspicion that Obama was a "secret Muslim."[1] The notion of a secret Muslim president was particularly alarming to those Americans who, still smarting from the humiliation and pain of 9/11, seemed to sincerely believe that Obama's presidency was the next action of a plan for a radical Islamic takeover of America.[2] For the next eight years, Obama plodded on with his agenda, facing a constant barrage of criticism, insults, and suspicion about his intentions, alongside the constant questioning of his patriotism. Several high-profile incidents of racial bias leading to the deaths of unarmed black men forced the president to comment upon the lurking racism within the American psyche. His words were regarded as not strong enough by the left and as an attack upon white Americans and law enforcement by some conservatives. Obama walked an impossible tightrope with race relations in America, complicated further by the fact that he was subject to both subtle and overt incidences of racism throughout his presidency and was acutely aware of the fact that any comments viewed as an attack upon police officers would trigger a backlash against his presidency, the Democratic party, and black Americans themselves. Obama was ultimately unable to be the catalyst for a thoughtful, self-reflective discussion about race relations in America. Historical tension combined with the post 9/11 suppression of minority voices and the growing realization that Obama's election had not sealed the racial wounds America had been carrying. It had instead ripped the wound wide open, culminating in the creation of the "Black Lives Matter" movement who protested around the country regarding police officers' deadly interactions with the black community.

At a time of heightened sensitivity toward racial difference, Donald J. Trump rode the coattails of white nationalism, birtherism, and a promise of "America First" into the American presidency. Trump's vision of the America he wanted to put first and the tone-deaf manner in which he addressed issues of race, poverty, and immigration was a classic case of "othering." As he toured the country blaming everyone but America for the state that America was in (which he viewed as terrible), he spewed forth invective after invective about "rapist" Mexicans, "terrorist" Muslims, "the blacks," and "illegals" in an attempt to solidify a base of white, working-class support. Many arguments have been made about the racism surrounding the election of 2016, including that it was economic concerns that drove white working-class voters away from the Democratic party and into the arms of Trump. Some may have merit, but, as study after study has shown, the average Trump supporter's feelings about immigrants and "others" were strongly negative on the whole, so it did not take the Trump campaign much effort to prime a humiliated population in jingoistic terms and lay a fairytale agenda at their feet promising to restore them to their previous place of employment and dignity by getting rid of the "others" who he stated had taken those jobs and that entitlement to the American dream (Bobo, 2017).

The racial discourse flowing from the White House down, through the states, municipalities, and towns of America was, once again, indicative of a deep divide within the country. It was clear that there was a complete and utter lack of capacity for most Americans to understand the nuances of a conversation about the treatment of black citizens in which they did not feel complicit. What followed was a rejection of black forms of expression from peaceful protest to the now infamous Childish Gambino music video *This is America*, all of which were met with howls of white outrage. The refusal of a majority of white Americans to engage in self-reflection and empathy about race played out in this rejection of black expression. Many voiced opinions echoing sentiments during the civil rights movement: "If they didn't do x, y, or z, I might listen." The fact remains that there has never been a form of black protest that has been acceptable to the rest of American society, and black American art, films, TV shows, and music have always been viewed with suspicion and anger.

At the zenith of the post 9/11, post Obama, post Ferguson, post Trayvon Martin, post white supremacist rallies in America, *Black Panther* (2018) premiered. It came as an immense surprise to most that it was both commercially successful (destroying box office records and dispensing with the notion that white Americans would not consume black produced pop culture). The second surprise was the quality of the content itself. The superhero genre is formulaic, white centric, conservative, and pro-America. The black production team and black American director managed to create a blockbuster than wove the African and American story together and stayed true to the general conventions of the genre at the same time as confronting audiences with intensely problematic scenarios of racism, isolationism, colonialism, and black power.

How this came to be can largely be explained by the pre 9/11 cultural landscape with regard to race relations in the United States. Given the temporal recency and brutality of the American story, American popular culture has always carried within it an incredibly tense relationship with race. Beginning early with the identification and vilification of non-whites in movies, revues, and songs, American pop culture moved through several stages of attempting to mediate the issue of race. None have been particularly effective, partly because the initial wound was so deeply set and partly because there has always been a continuing and passionate resistance to empowering non-white artists, storytellers, actors, and narratives.

African Americans in pop culture

An obvious point of discussion when considering race and popular culture is that, until very recently, representation of non-white experiences were significantly limited, stereotyped, and created, whether consciously or not, to reinforce the narrative of white American innocence and black American threat. The sheer range of characters in all aspects of popular culture who represent the white experience dwarfed representations of non-white narratives. Jamil Smith (2018) points out in his article for *Time Magazine* on the revolutionary power of *Black Panther*, "Those of us who are not white have considerably more trouble not only finding representation of ourselves in mass media and other arenas of public life, but also finding representation that indicates that our humanity is multifaceted." For every white doctor, teacher, police officer, firefighter, mother, father, child, president, leader, or soldier, represented in hundreds of complicated and human ways, there has always been a counter portrayal of black, jive talkin', criminal, deadbeat dad, welfare queen, gang member, and drug dealers to represent the fears of white Americans about the presence of non-whites within their country.

In constructing the "black threat" in popular culture, black Americans (particularly young men) are presented as dangerous menaces to the social order. Tyree and Jacobs (2014) discuss the consequences of the obsessive Hollywood "binary construction of black manhood" as being a lack of attention given to the notion that black males have "political depth and humanity" and that they have made a "very significant contribution to the culture and progress of this [American] Nation" (p. 8). A real challenge faced in telling non-dominant narratives is that the ownership and construction of black identity has "largely been shaped in the West"(Biakolo, 2018). Kovie Biakolo summarizes the central problem in the creation of black identity in popular culture as existing because blackness itself was shaped first by "the racist ideologies primarily advanced by Europeans and Americans, and then, through subsequent resistance to these ideas, by African-descended people in the West, notably black Americans." If blackness in America exists in the form of a call (racism and slavery) and a response (emancipation and the continuing struggle to assert one's humanity and rights), then the pop culture playing field is forever and always stacked against the elevation of authentic black American experiences. In the face of seemingly insurmountable resistance and a monolithic American pop culture machine, it could be considered a miracle of counter-resistance that there are any non-white reference points to contemplate at all. That the black American experience has found minute pockets of air to create itself away from the hegemonic system of white supremacy is testament, perhaps, to the power of storytelling and its capacity to reduce "alienation for members of excluded groups" (Delgado and Stefacic, 2012, p. 51).

The commercial and critical success of the *Black Panther* film is a complicated phenomenon to untangle. While many critical race scholars correctly identified problematic ties between the white dominated means of film production (Disney) and the black produced and centered product, most viewed the film as an important breakwater in the ongoing racial discourse of America. Jamil Smith (2018) identified *Black Panther* as the most "splendidly black" blockbuster Hollywood had ever produced. Smith's notion of the film as revolutionary rested further on the fact that the empowered black production team and cast was able to offer much more depth than the average superhero film: "Its themes challenge institutional biases; its characters take unsubtle digs at oppressors and its narrative includes prismatic perspectives on black life and tradition."

Other critics, while appreciative of the non-white centeredness of the film, were more circumspect in their praise. Rebecca Wanzo (2018) suggested that Black Panther was "not the most progressive film imaginable but [it is] more than many had hoped for." Noting that the character of Black Panther began as a "white fantasy of blackness," she points to a vitally important thorn in the side of the black super heroic endeavor. Signaling the obvious truth that the superhero genre is both inherently racist and conservative, she delineates an entrenched problem in terms of how quick we are to celebrate positive presentations of black characters at the expense of questioning their origin as initial attempts to maintain the racial status quo. In addressing that central conundrum, it is important to explore the history of the representation of race within the superhero genre, discuss the evolution of attitudes from the 1960s to today, and situate the Black Panther himself within the canon of literature from which he was born. In understanding the significant underlying struggle that black superheroes have faced in genesis and evolution, we are better placed to analyze the blockbuster version of the character in terms of his meaning and impact in a post-civil rights but still deeply racial American society.

The history of black superheroes

In dealing with a genre that was established early as white-centric and American, the challenge to the creation of authentic black superheroes was doubly hamstrung. The obviously Aryan ideal that was being molded in the likes of Superman, Captain America, Batman, and others combined with a prevailing sense that anyone who did not fit the white immigrant stereotype of "Americanness" was to be viewed with suspicion.

Initially, representation of minority superheroes suffered from lack. The only non-white characters drawn in the major comics and serials of the time were grossly stereotyped caricatures of the worst kind. Every single major comic from the 1940s to the 1960s displayed extreme racism in the representation of minority characters – some, like Captain America, at the same time as espousing equality, freedom, and the American dream. Describing comic books of the World War II era, Bradford Wright (2001) notes that they were generally: "High minded and hateful" (p. 55). They pushed storylines in which the adored white characters encouraged minority characters to ignore their lowly status within America society and fight on behalf of America against the Axis powers with the weak justification that their victory would in some way be better for black Americans than if Hitler prevailed.

At the same time that cultural and societal hierarchies were playing out on the front cover of Marvel and DC comics in the 1940s and 1950s, commercial motivations were in play to prevent the establishment of a positive black superhero until the 1960s. The post-war popularity of comics was bolstered by an economic boom and an increase in the disposable income of working- and middle-class white Americans, which trickled down to children in the form of pennies. Those children were the main consumers of comic book titles, thus their continuing viability relied upon the expectations and spending power of white America. Still reeling from the era of segregation and dealing with the reality that *Brown vs. Board of Education* had not equalized the quality of education across America, black Americans had neither the spending power nor comparable literacy rates to "participate in comic reading" (Wright, 2001, p. 63). In short, the racial power structure that played out in every form of American life replicated and reinforced itself in comic books and superhero titles, ensuring that black superheroes were neither desired from a popular culture standpoint nor needed for commercial purposes.

Black superheroes came to be in a climate that was rife with racial politics (Nama, 2011, p. 36). The domestic turmoil of the 1960s, combined with the mass ownership of television sets, intersected to ensure that the protests of the civil rights movement were present in the eyes and minds of most Americans, including the media and the political elite. Preceded by a host of stereotyped black characters with various forms of power, Black Panther was introduced by Marvel comics during the Silver Age in 1966. In a stunning departure from the expected, racist rendering of Golden Age black characters, T'Challa was "a super intelligent and highly skilled hunter-fighter superhero from the fictional African nation of Wakanda" (Nama, 2011, p. 42). Testing the potential of their first intentionally radical black character, Marvel introduced Black Panther within a Fantastic Four storyline in which he uses the group as a test to prepare himself to defend Wakanda from an attack by white mercenaries. With his anti-colonial bona fides established within his origin, Black Panther evolved into a fascinating addition to the Marvel stable and a direct challenge to the notion of white superiority. Here was a prince, bestowed with the privilege of status from birth, enhanced by his hereditary superpowers, the leader of a "high tech African Shangri la," bursting forth from each page with athleticism, power, rage, mercy, intelligence, and grace (Nama, 2011, p. 43). Completely unencumbered by the choking strictures of

American racism, he "offered unprecedented and upbeat images of Africa and African people" (Nama, 2011, p. 42).

It is an important consideration that, in the creation of the Black Panther, Marvel felt unable to situate their first major black superhero as American. T'Challa is too possessed of privilege to be a convincing representation of the black American experience, and, in placing him outside of the hierarchy of American racism, he was afforded the opportunity to be less stereotypical and more revered than the average (or super powered) black American man. The juxtaposition between the drafting of Black Panther and the Falcon, Marvel's other significant black superhero introduced in 1969, is striking. A brief analysis reveals that the Falcon's possession of super heroic powers is complicated by his social position. He goes through several iterations, some of them outright stereotypical, and is forever caught in an internal resistance to the relegation of his status as Captain America's sidekick. While T'Challa is permitted unilateral movement as an outsider to the American racial nightmare, the Falcon is shackled by it and moved only in relation to the hegemonic, white, adored savior of American ideals.

The first black superhero to have his own comic run, Power Man (Luke Cage) was born in the era of blaxploitation films and was "the most inherently political and socially profound black superhero to ever emerge" (Nama, 2011, p. 55). Although he was created by a white, male production team (perfectly crystallizing the notion that blackness has always been both constructed and consumed within the constraints of the white creative power structure), Cage was viewed as a much more interesting and complex black character than ones that came before him. Cage's character was clearly steeped in a stereotypical white vision of what it meant to be black in America. The creative team situated him as a troubled black youth from Harlem, affiliated with a gang and running into constant brushes with law enforcement. His decision to go straight amounted to nothing as he was betrayed by his childhood friend and criminal lynchpin, Willis Stryker. The most significant part of Cage's origin story is his incarceration for a crime he did not commit in a prison in the deep South and his run-ins with a racist prison guard who singled him out to inflict extra brutality on him. In an attempt to kill Cage, Billy Bob Rackham turned up the dials on the experimental cellular regeneration machine that Cage was contained within and inadvertently caused a more extreme reaction, resulting in a superpowered, super strength black man, resistant to physical harm. In a nod to the insistence of Martin Luther King Jr. that there is dignity in suffering, Luke Cage emerged from the torture by his captors indestructible, cool, confident, and impervious to bullets and physical brutality. Cage's popularity was always in flux, but he remained at the forefront of his own comic for several years and appeared as a guest in numerous crossovers and Marvel comic events. Cage's origin story and experiences as a black superhero operating in the very real political and social dynamic of the time ensured that he was read as a signifier of "the troubling intersection of racism, institutional authority and broader themes associated with black political disenfranchisement" (Nama, 2011, p. 56). It is worth noting that, post 9/11 and post the founding of the "Black Lives Matter" movement, the story of Luke Cage was commissioned as a Netflix show, widely watched and critically acclaimed.

The super powering of black characters, particularly those who were American and therefore steeped in the injustice of their hereditary status, was woven into every comic in which a black character was presented or took the lead. T'Challa was viewed with reverence and appreciation, his mystical origins melding with Afrofuturism to create a character that an American audience could admire without fear but still be enchanted by. The Falcon and Luke Cage were steeped in the unique American racial brew. They were superpowered and awesome but viewed by a white audience with suspicion. It is a response that is both complicated but obvious when one investigates the cognitive dissonance and issues that arise when a fictional black American is afforded super heroic powers and possesses them within a system that deliberately and systematically sets out to disempower them.

The "problem" with black superheroes

In a society that views black bodies (particularly male) as out of control and potential threats to the social order, constructing black superheroes was historically met with fears and resistance from the white power structure. Concurrent to the difficult genesis of black superheroes but understood much later in terms of a critical race analysis lens, there were several important aspects at play in the compulsion to keep superheroes white during the years in which they were first established. These factors began to erode over time, and that erosion allowed for unique and compelling representations of black super heroic power.

The question of why it took until 2018 for a black superhero to access the Hollywood machine and be a commercial and critical success is bound up in two main areas. The first is that weaponizing black bodies with super heroic power or indeed, any power, has traditionally been viewed as an extreme threat to the white power structure in America. The second is the notion that the initial erasure of racial issues from the origin comics of the 1940s to 1960s was aggressively repeated in the wake of 9/11, a time where the white superhero genre was reinvigorated to a level of commercial success and cultural importance with a magnitude not seen since World War II.

When society "expect[s] masculinity from black men but den(ies) them the access to the institutions to achieve it" (Brown, 1999, p. 29) an insurmountable burden is placed upon men of color to both succeed within a society that systematically disenfranchises them at the same time as expecting them to mimic the behavior and attitudes of the dominant racial structure. Black men in particular are "emasculated and feared" (Brown, 1999, p. 28), which poses a significant problem when we view them within the superhero genre. Until very recently, the history of representation of minorities within comic books was one note and/or racist. It was also the belief of some cultural critics that, for a significant period of time, the very presence of black superheroes could be viewed as a "utopia," a fantasy realm in which white readers could "accept black superpowers" without ever having to contemplate what real black power and agency would look like and mean for society as a whole (Nama, 2011, p. 153). Despite the understandable reservations of many that black superheroes would always be choked by the oppressive history of racism in America and the lack of agency for people of color to tell their own story, the notion of super heroic black bodies and characters continues to tantalize with all its possibilities. It is undeniable that, given the dominance of whiteness within the superheroic genre convention and the genre's deep connections to nationalism, white supremacy, norming, and the preservation of the status quo, any attempt to imagine or rewrite blackness within the conventions of the genre offer significant "symbolism, meaning and political import" (Nama, 2011, p. 9).

The first striking aspect of *Black Panther* was that artistic control was given over to a black director, Ryan Coogler. Coogler, born and raised in Oakland, California, has been acclaimed for his work at bringing the stories of the underrepresented to life. His focus on the black community in films like *Fruitvale Station* and *Creed* situated him perfectly to take on the leviathan task of bringing *Black Panther* to the big screen. The fact that the co-writer, costume designer, producer, and significant numbers of the cast and crew were also people of color may seem like an obvious point of departure when conceiving of a uniquely black centered film, but it is still an exceedingly rare event in terms of the usual Hollywood production. The melding of a significantly diverse team to bring to life an African character in a fantasy genre that has always been white centric, conservative, and supportive of the establishment status quo was groundbreaking in itself; the fact that this team managed to produce a film of such complexity, beauty, and hope while still firmly situating it within the expectations of the super heroic cannon was a welcome surprise to many, and it began with the women.

The women of Wakanda

The representation of women in *Black Panther* is doubly impactful in the range of roles they fulfill and the fact that they are empowered, black, and African. The first woman we get a full introduction to in the film is on a secret mission to rescue women in a bordering African nation from a Boko Harem-esque terrorist group who are, presumably, in the act of kidnapping them into sexual slavery and degradation. Nakia is shown to be capable, physically and mentally tough, and is more furious with T'Challa for his intervention than she is happy to see him. Nakia only relents when she learns that T'Challa's appearance was not principally to help her but to inform her of the death of the King and his impending ritual combat. Over the course of the film it is revealed that, although Nakia loves T'Challa deeply, she is unable to reconcile that love with the sense of mission and duty that she feels toward other victimized Africans, and she leaves Wakanda to provide direct aid to women in danger in surrounding nations. Interestingly, Nakia and Killmonger are two sides of the same coin in terms of their desire to use Wakandan resources to help. However, Killmonger shows no mercy, remorse, or limit in the despicable methods he will employ to reach his goal, while Nakia's trajectory is more circumspect. Initially, she tries to convince T'Challa by reasoning with him that opening Wakanda's borders is not an automatic recipe for the destruction of the country. Steeped in the ideology of his father and ancestors, T'Challa is unable to conceive of this option until the very end of the film when he has been rescued by Nakia's courage. Nakia shows no fear as she first tries to tempt the leader of the Dora Milaje away from her post. She shows incredible presence of mind in rescuing one of the last flowers of the Black Panther herb before Killmonger can destroy them all, and she, along with the Queen and Shuri, displays vision in approaching the Jabari and offering its chief the power of the Panther. At this point, believing that she has lost T'Challa, her mission becomes the protection of Wakanda. She does this not by following the new King or the ancient patriarchal ritual that has elevated him to power but by conceiving of a different way forward in which she views M'Baku as a more acceptable alternative to lead Wakanda that the bloodthirsty Killmonger. Embedded in this part of the film is the ongoing theme that, while the men remain rigid and dogmatic in terms of how they view themselves and Wakanda's place in the world, it is the women who evolve, quickly and progressively, to create new ways of thinking, of working together, and, ultimately, to create solutions to the predicaments that the men have created. The aspects of Nakia's character that T'Challa finds most attractive, her physicality, mental tenacity, independence, and general strength, are also the ones that introduce the most significant tension into their relationship. Nakia very firmly chooses her mission over love and cannot remain in Wakanda with T'Challa. The end of the film reveals an interesting and progressive turn of events when T'Challa, knowing that Nakia cannot fulfill her mission *and* stay in Wakanda, offers to situate her mission *in* Wakanda. Having made the decision to open Wakanda to the outside world and share its technology and resources, T'Challa creates a cultural worldwide exchange that he puts Nakia at the center of. Some may read this as male agency trumping female autonomy, but, situated within the wider picture, it is actually an extremely pro-feminist ending. Nakia is the principle reason that T'Challa changes his mind; it is her mission and work, as well as the chaos that Killmonger's extremist vision of that ideology wreaks, that causes T'Challa to alter his course. It is clear that if Nakia wanted to leave, she would, but in creating a necessary role for her that also enables them to be together he removes the barrier of forcing her to choose between her love for him and her passion and offers an alternative vision of a relationship in which each couple's goals are elevated by the presence of the other.

One of the most significant representations of black African women in *Black Panther* comes in the form of the Dora Milaje. Imagined in the comic books, they were lithe, dressed in skintight suits, adorned with long flowing locks, and engaged in fighting in the unlikely choice of high heels. Although they were to be feared, the comic version of the Dora Milaje suffered from the general lack of imagination of what female characters could be (other than attractive, shapely, physically impossible women enacting the brutality of the traditionally masculine fighting trope). In the film, Coogler turns that vision on its head and presents the audience with a group of warriors who are both unencumbered by traditional societal expectations of women and, at times, actively challenging the stereotypes into which female characters are usually boxed. Introduced as warriors before anything else, they are dressed in gladiatorial robes that are designed to enhance the purpose that the women serve: violence in defense of the King. The costume choices for the women meld function with traditional African tribal adornments, and it is clear from the outset that nothing about the Dora Milaje is ornamental or designed to appease the "male gaze." The decision to shave their heads (the ultimate functional hair style for someone constantly engaged in physical violence) is a clear stylistic departure from the original comics and underscores the notion that they are a complete contrast to every female character we have seen or are expecting to see in a superhero film. Coogler, again, avoids a significant trap that female characters have been hindered by in the past when he incorporates the love interest between W'Kabi and Okoye. First, this serves as a reminder that female warriors can be sexual (as opposed to the usual virginal, pure Valkyrie type warriors we expect). Up until the fight scene we see playful, sexual, and loving interchanges between the couple. During the fight scene when their relationship is tested to breaking point by her loyalty to T'Challa and his decision to support Killmonger, every expectation of female behavior is inverted. Beaten down W'Kabi asks "Would you kill me, my love?" Pointing her spear at his throat, she replies, "For Wakanda? Without question." It is at that moment that W'Kabi specifically invokes the traditional expectation that the woman should yield her values because of her love for a man. Her response is an unexpected and firm refusal to give up her values and walk away from her duty and her sense of what is right. The expected outcome in traditional Western cinema would be for her to yield. She does not yield, and it is W'Kabi who yields to her when he realizes he is beaten. In the creation and presentation of this alternative femininity, Coogler adds to his existing stall of female characters and shows that depth, humanity, and a wide variance of behavior, capabilities, and contradictions can all be found in the women of Wakanda.

In the scenes where tribal leaders gather to consult with the King and at the ritual combat, the audience is further presented with an array of female leaders who have a significant influence on the decisions made in Wakanda. Of the four tribes making up those who participate in Wakandan politics and culture (excluding the Jabari), two of the tribes are led by women. The merchant tribe and mining tribe are represented by women in the King's council, and they both speak strongly for themselves and as representatives of the interests of their people. It is clear that in Wakanda, enormous respect has always existed for women, and within the bounds of a hereditary monarchy, there has also been an extremely progressive thread of feminism. When the hereditary system of monarchy by bloodline and ritual combat fails to deliver a leader whom a majority of Wakandans view as worthy, we see two aspects of how the women behave that distinguish them from the men. During T'Challa's defeat it is the women who display displeasure and quickly move to regroup. They reject the notion that they should accept the results of the ancient ritual and are quick to seek an alternative outcome, not accepting the patriarchal society's finality of the challenge.

Within the royal family, we see a dignified, regal, and wise black woman as the Queen (Ramonda) and Shuri, T'Challa's beloved sister, occupying the role of Director of National Science and Technology. When we are first introduced to Shuri she is dressed in casual clothing and wearing Princess Leia buns. She is also possessed of incredible intellect that is revealed in the inventions she churns out. Shuri is excited by science, thrilled by what it can do to enhance society, and shown to be utterly excellent in every aspect of innovation. Importantly, Coogler avoids the mistake of casting all the female characters as simply physically strong, and throughout the film, Shuri is seen employing her technological acumen in her defense and the defense of others.

With the introduction of these females in the first scenes of the film, we are shown a depth and breadth of talents, competencies, and strengths that are varied and empowering. The women of Wakanda exist in every role and are situated on the spectrum of female power from all out warrior to diplomat to scientific genius. They occupy all the archetypes and roles that male characters usually do in adventure sci-fi films and signify to the audience that Wakanda is a very different society than we have ever seen in terms of the value of women in relation to men and the elevation of women in many aspects – but not all – to the level of men.

Viewing the women of Wakanda through an American centric lens reveals the extremity of the contrast between the women of Wakanda and how we have been taught to view women in Western society. While the sustained effort of the feminist movement in the United States has advanced the rights and roles of women in some ways, there has always been an immense backlash from those who misunderstand the message of equality at its core. When moves toward equality are perceived as the favoring of women over men and women are still debased in media, politics, and culture, Wakanda offers a group of females occupying every role that society has to offer and doing so in a way that is expected and normalized. The fact that the women of Wakanda have no expectations of oppression for themselves is the most unique thing about them. It is something that could only exist in the alternative but convincing realities that the superhero genre allows for, and it is a truly groundbreaking vision. The fact that the women are also black and African underscores their revolutionary power. For a world that views black African women as among some of the least empowered people on the planet and has generally excluded them from the feminist movement in Western countries, the women of Wakanda are visionary in their normality.

Geography and culture

In addition to a completely original representation of African women, Coogler was also tasked with creating the landscape, culture, technology, and aesthetic of Wakanda itself. The challenge of building a convincing story and look for a nation steeped in both traditional African tribalism with the addition of extra-terrestrial advanced technology was immense, both because the story was so firmly rooted in the expectations of the superhero genre and because an African nation untouched by colonialism, violence, degradation, and stereotypes has not existed in historical recency.

In terms of the geography and architecture of Wakanda, the film shows a traditional vision of the African countryside. Wakanda's disguise is the exact expectation that a Western cinematic audience would expect to see. Intractable forests, sweeping plains, mountains, and herdspeople, living basic, nontechnological lives. When T'Challa's plane sweeps through the barrier that protects the real Wakanda from the outside world, the audience, who may be excepting some version of Westernized skyscrapers or other-worldly looking structures, are treated to a landscape of upward expansion that looks nothing like another city on earth. The aesthetic of Birnin Zana mimics the form of Western skyscrapers *if* traditional African huts and temples had been built to the heavens. For an audience used to viewing African cities as mirroring those of the capitalist West, it is an unexpected vision of what may have happened in the absence of the colonization of every single aspect of African life and culture.

The possibilities of Africa, absent colonialism, are also explored in the clothing of Wakanda. There is no single uniform, with the exception of the Dora Milaje. Every Wakandan retains some form of identifying tribal clothing, which they tailor and adjust to fit their own preferences. In the pre-production of the film, discussion about how to build Wakanda began with the agreement that architecture, clothing, weapons, and culture would all be based on the reality of the heritage of the nations that would surround Wakanda were it real. Everything in the aesthetic of Wakanda is based on real African experiences. Everything that follows is the melding of that initial decision with the Afrofuturistic feel the massive deposit of vibranium allows for. The technological aspect of Wakanda is interestingly situated in the natural. Everything technological is of the earth, underscored in the scene where Shuri sifts the sand through her fingers before she turns to show T'Challa all the technology she has managed to create from it. In contrast to the usual signifier of advanced technology in superhero films (think Batman's steel inventions and Iron Man's tech screens where he can shift information from one to another with a flick of his wrist), Wakanda's technology is organic and natural at the same time as being far superior in every way to the technology that mankind has been able to create from synthetic materials.

Culture and mysticism

The melding of the Afro-futuristic narrative with African traditionalism is a tension that plays out in several ways throughout the film. In the opening scene, a young T'Challa implores his *Baba* to tell him a story that reveals the tribal heritage of Wakanda, the mysticism of the Black Panther lore, and sets the scene for the bubbling stress that exists between the "old" way of doing things and moving away from that rigidity of thinking, while retaining respect for the founding mysticism of the nation.

The most obvious clash point for these tensions exists in the strained relationship between the modernized tribes of Wakanda and the Jabari, The White Gorilla Cult, who choose to isolate themselves from the rest of Wakanda and live in the unforgiving mountains. When the leader of the Jabari presents himself to challenge T'Challa for the throne, he directly addresses the gathered dignitaries and reveals his anger at the way Wakanda has moved away from traditionalism: "We have watched and listened from the mountains! We have watched with disgust as your technological advancements have been overseen by a child!" Somewhat ironically, it is traditionalism itself that allows M'Baku to challenge T'Challa in the first place, as leadership is not purely predicated on hereditary status. M'Baku has the right to challenge T'Challa, whose Black Panther powers are stripped from him before ritual combat, precisely because T'Challa is following the ancient, traditional lore of the country. The ritual demands that ascendance to the throne be predicated on strength and appropriateness. The fact that the tribe are explicitly referred to as a "cult" and that M'Baku sneers "where is your Panther god now" as he almost bests T'Challa indicates both a strict adherence to religion as a guiding principle of fate and a dogmatic rigidity. M'Baku survives the combat because T'Challa allows him to. Were the roles reversed, it is certain that M'Baku would have no issue with killing T'Challa. T'Challa's progressive nature elevates mercy and practicality over the need to kill, and in begging M'Baku to yield, he unwittingly ensures his own survival later on in the story as the debt M'Baku owes him is repaid.

The mysticism of Wakanda is explored mostly during the scenes in which T'Challa appears to his forbearers on the ancestral plain. The initial meeting between father and son shows T'Challa asking for and gratefully receiving the wisdom of his father. T'Chaka states: "it's hard for a good man to be king." At no point does T'Chaka tell T'Challa what he should do or how he should lead his people, and T'Challa emerges from the ritual less sure of himself than when it began. The herb that affords T'Challa and all the Black Panthers before him their mystical strength is unique in that it is a power that is given and taken away. The expectation of the superhero genre is that once powers are bestowed, they are there for good and cannot be removed by another. The distinction with Black Panther is that he must constantly be worthy of his powers, or someone who is deemed worthier will take his place. This situates T'Challa in the interesting and rare position of being a superhero who knows what it is like to not have super strength. The tenuous claim that T'Challa has to his power must constantly be reinforced by wise leadership, mercy, physical feats of strength, and above all, the preservation of Wakanda. Unlike many white superheroes, who never have to examine the source of their power or question what they must do to keep it, T'Challa must rise to the level of hero in every decision he makes and every action he undertakes. The expectations for his behavior are set much higher (as they are for black men and women all over the world), and one small mistake is much more likely to be judged harshly by the removal of his power, his throne, and his identity as Black Panther.

Finally, mysticism plays an important role in the scene when Killmonger becomes the Panther and goes to his version of the ancestral plain to exemplify the painful liminal space that African Americans exist within. Killmonger is not met by his forbearers on a sweeping plain. Although his forebearers would presumably be the same as T'Challa's (being that they are cousins), Killmonger is met in the apartment in Oakland by his father who is standing exactly in the spot he was when T'Chaka took his life. While T'Challa's ancestors all appear for him and imbue him with the legitimacy of his heritage, Killmonger's one ancestor is someone who is shown to be illegitimate and torn between two worlds, one of which he pines for but does not feel a part of and one in which he has anchored his progeny but also cannot exist within. In the scene where T'Chaka visits N'Jobu, the Prince has no accent before the king arrives. A soon as he speaks to his brother his accent changes and he sounds African. When he speaks with an American accent he is attempting to assimilate, and when confronted by his brother he is code switching. N'Jobu comes from royalty, and his African accent would reflect the diplomatic face of his country, so his switching back and forth between African and Oakland is a perfect example of the erasure of heritage, the creation of African American identity, and the switching between the two as a way to try to reclaim some aspect of a lineage that many African Americans can never really be one hundred per cent sure of. Oakland itself is symbolically significant in that it was the home of the Black Panther Party and a recognized epicenter of racial tension, poverty, and intersecting difficulties, which resulted in the desperate situation N'Jobu was trying to alleviate with his revolutionary plan.

Racist tropes

A fascinating aspect of Black Panther is the manner in which racist tropes (ones that American audiences particularly have grown up with and internalized) are presented and inverted. When Killmonger appears at the British museum to lay claim to Wakandan artifacts by force, he is confronted by a historian who is both condescending and wrong in her "knowledge" of

African culture. She ignores Killmonger's assertion that the artifact he is looking at is Wakandan and continues to show that she is both limited by her racial perceptions and further limited by the Western tendency to fetishize what it believes African culture to be. The actual villain of the piece, a white South African mercenary, Ulysses Klaue, spits out the first overtly racist line of the film: "you savages don't deserve vibranium." It is doubly ironic in that Wakandans are clearly not "savages," being far more technologically advanced than Klaue, yet, Klaue still feels superior to them. Clearly believing that natural resources are something that should be earned, even though the Western world was blessed with them far more than the African continent they carved up between them, he is the ultimate white colonizer, fearful of power in the hands of black Africans at the same time as he is convinced they have done nothing to deserve it.

While the one American character, CIA agent Everett Ross, is presented more sympathetically than Klaue and is not shown to be overtly racist, he reveals the same sense of superiority that Klaue is imbued with. After the immense display of technology and power shown by the Wakandans in South Korea, he continues to assume that Wakanda is primitive. Despite the visual reality of their superiority to him and the Americans in every way he calls Wakanda "third world" and as having "nice outfits for shepherds" etc. Shuri later calls him a colonizer to his face, and he is further enlightened as to what black Americans are subjected to every day in American society when he accompanies the women to the White Gorilla Cult. When Ross arrogantly presumes to speak (in an area in which he has no authority and even less knowledge), M'Baku grunts at him repeatedly and screams: "You cannot talk!" The black experience of everyday existence, the notion that black silence prevents violence from being visited unto black Americans is crystallized in the clever inversion of roles in this scene. Ross doesn't say another word – presumably to survive his terrifying encounter with M'Baku – and is excluded from witnessing the Black Panther ritual. Ross' presence in the lineup is sympathetic because as an individual he displays courage, the ability to work with others, and forms of racism that are inherent, subtle, and not meant with malice. It is also troublesome because he is presumptive, arrogant, dismissive of Wakandan power, and only realizes his lack of agency when the full technological array of Wakanda is revealed to him. Klaue and Ross occupy two extremes of the spectrum of racism, one overt and confident in the attitude handed down by his forbearers that black Africans and African resources are to be exploited and the other a more "polite" form of racism, one that is learned, internalized, and, while not or overtly hostile, is difficult to shake off because it is layered with a sense of white American superiority.

Isolation and emancipation and Killmonger

Established early in the film is the perception that Wakanda's greatest strength, in fact the reason for its survival, has been the assumption of a defensive, isolationist domestic and foreign policy. Allowing the rest of the world to believe that the technology rich nation is an archetypal "third world" state, lacking in resources, seems to have arrested the desires of colonizers to waste their efforts there. Several indicators of both isolationism and defense are signaled in the developing plot and are placed in direct opposition to Killmonger's ideology of emancipation through the inversion of the world power structure by violent, revolutionary means. The first thing to note is that the Wakandan power salute ("Wakanda Forever") is defensive in nature, bringing the arms up, crossed to guard the heart and vital organs from attack in a closed physical gesture. This is unlike the black power salute, which is defiant and exposes the entire body to the potential for attack. When T'Chaka appears to N'Jobu, the Dora Milaje are dispatched first to ensure that it is safe for the king to appear. Wakandans do not trust anyone with their secret and guard their resources and identities zealously. An interesting conflict arises when the audience is forced to consider how just the Wakandan policy of isolationism is when the African Diaspora, in this case Wakandans included, are suffering at the hands of colonizers and imperialists. When the United States takes an isolationist and protectionist tack, as it has recently, the rest of the world is imperiled. The United States is expected to lead the free world and adhere to certain norms. We do not expect this from Wakanda, even when its immense resources and technology are revealed. Killmonger himself views the lack of aid from Wakanda as a stunning and painful hypocrisy, but, viewed in terms of the historical tendencies of both Wakanda and the US, it is at least understandable. The United States colonized from a position of strength and power along with the European nations. While Wakanda may be engaged in an extreme form of isolationism and protectionism, the decision comes from the very real need to protect *itself*. Europe, America, and more recently China have viewed Africa, its people, and its resources as something to be plundered and exploited. Wakanda never sought to colonize, only to ensure its continued existence as the only nation state in Africa that has not been conquered and carved up by imperialists. The extremity of such an attitude is revealed in a scene when Nakia implores T'Challa to help refugees from surrounding countries by opening Wakanda up to them. W'Kabi is quick to stifle her request by reminding the King that: "you bring in refugees, they bring their problems with them." This sentiment, echoed in recent political discourse in the United States and all over Western Europe, is one of the ways in which the behavior of Wakanda's elite engenders some empathy for Killmonger's mission. Although he is merciless, trained to kill, and does so with zero remorse, he is also the bearer of an ideology that embodies several tensions including the need to help those in desperate situations, the need to save yourself, and the fine balance between altruism and utter selfishness. The fact that T'Challa rejects both isolationism and his forbearers calling him home in his second visit to the ancestral land sews the seeds for the evolution of the Wakandan tradition of isolating and ignoring. T'Chaka explains his decision, and T'Challa realizes he was wrong. The only way forward when the painful story of Killmonger is revealed is stalling the immediate threat to Wakanda, making sure Killmonger does not succeed in his plan, and slowly beginning to open Wakanda up to the rest of the world.

Killmonger

The less than heroic conduct of T'Chaka and the decision not to respond to the cries of the African diaspora situate the "villain" of the film in a fascinating, groundbreaking position. We understand on sight that Killmonger is the villain, and we expect a certain kind of genre convention to play out. The recent move toward villains who engender sympathy in Marvel films particularly reaches its zenith in *Black Panther* and foregrounds Killmonger as one of the most complex, challenging, and confounding post 9/11 villains we have seen. Killmonger is both the product of his African heritage and is, literally and figuratively, carrying the scars of his blackness as an American. The first thing he so obviously represents is a living, breathing incarnation of the liminal space in which all African Americans in America occupy. In his first scene, he attacks the British museum wearing an African mask and armed with an American machine gun. He also bears the Wakandan "mark." It is not clear how Wakandans receive the mark, but the film hints toward a ritual in which it is imbued. N'Jobu wants his son to have access to Africa and the sense of pride that comes from his homeland and has Wakandan artifacts all over his apartment in Oakland. While Killmonger feels some sense of connection to Wakanda through his father, his existence in America and the conditions he is forced to endure ensure that his connection to his roots is complicated by both his disgust at Wakanda for allowing other Africans to exist in conditions of slavery and his desire to use Wakandan resources to invert the racial hierarchy of the world. N'Jobu believes that his neocolonialist plan to help diasporic Africans and show them that the Wakandan value system is a better alternative to how they are currently living *is* being true to Wakanda. He instills in Killmonger both the Wakandan mark and his neocolonist value system and sets the wheels in motion for the clash between his son and his nephew. The relationship between N'Jobu and Killmonger mediates heavily on the notion of birth being the key to nativeness. Killmonger was not born in Wakanda, and his father fears he will never be accepted as a true Wakandan. As an African American man, his birth in Oakland is meaningless as a marker of citizenship and belonging because he was marked from birth by the American racial hierarchy as inferior to white Americans. Belonging and a preoccupation with where someone was from was an obsessive pastime in post 9/11 America, and immigrants of all ethnicities suddenly found themselves categorized by birthplace, racial appearance, level of patriotism, and heritage, always coming up short in comparison to the native born, white, flag waving American patriot. The obsession with belonging may have bubbled over for new immigrants and groups of immigrants who had previously been tolerated in American society, but it has always existed for African Americans. Post 9/11, their voices, culture, and attempts to create an alternative narrative away from the white, militaristic, patriarchal one that was prevalent was strangled by lack of attention and a lack of interest in black voices in general. Killmonger is a particularly interesting example of post 9/11 American blackness. He bears a scar on his body for each kill, which acts as a clear signifier of the scars of slavery. This visual cueing of the torment of slavery and its ongoing connection to living African Americans is further imbued with meaning as Killmonger was scarred in the service of the US Government. His service to his nation would be considered exemplary from the standpoint of the white, militaristic patriarchy. He graduated from MIT and Annapolis and became a Navy Seal before his service as a black ops soldier for the CIA. Killmonger is the "painful hyphen" in African-American; he has been imbued with a sense of his Africanness (minus actual belonging) by his father, he bears the mark of Wakanda and a war dog tattoo in honor of his father but has been used in the service of the US government, waging war against poorer countries. Killmonger is a physical manifestation of the psychic trauma that African Americans carry with them at all times as well as a living embodiment of the notion that even exemplary service to the United States and a complete assimilation of one's body and skills with the preferences of the United States still does not generate respect or acceptance. Killmonger is fully integrated into American war culture and steeped in the history and culture of Wakanda, but he belongs to neither and is accepted by neither. As for Killmonger's goals and strategy, they reveal a deep-seated mistrust of hereditary power (the kind that has oppressed black people all over the world and particularly so in America) as well as a disregard for the mysticism that gives the Black Panthers their power. When he burns the herb, he is ensuring that nobody can or will be king after he is dead, viewing his mission as one in which kings will no longer be worshipped because those enslaved by them will be free. The hard reset on the world he wants to achieve by arming the War Dogs with vibranium and having them distribute weapons to the African Diaspora echoes the neo-colonist tendencies instilled in him by his father but taken to the most extreme form. It is revolutionary that a character like Killmonger can exist in the post 9/11 popular culture landscape, let alone be so provocative and so well received. His complexity is a direct challenge to the one note narrative of white militaristic, patriotic supremacy, and, as such, his character is able to explore extremely complex themes of slavery, oppression, colonialism, emancipation, violence, and trauma. The entire story arc of Black Panther is one that sets the scene of a completely self-sufficient and superior African nation in juxtaposition with the living embodiment of the colonialist horror that was visited on every other African nation and its people. Bringing the motivations of Killmonger to the forefront of the action and presenting them unapologetically is deliberately confrontational to a mostly white audience. This point was not lost on Coogler, who presents Killmonger in both hyper-realistic and villainously operatic proportions at moments in the film. It allows for a narrative of American blackness to be brought to a mass audience and forces contemplation of past American sins. It is hard to imagine that in any other genre convention the trauma of black Americans could be so clearly and convincingly laid out for a predominantly white audience to sit through and respond as positively as they did.

The ultimate clash of the ongoing tensions built within the storyline of *Black Panther* are, of course, enmeshed in the final fight sequence. There are now two Black Panthers, one African, one African-American, both with a vision of reaching out to the rest of the world, one by peaceful means and one by violent revolution. Their dual existence culminates in Wakandans being forced to choose their allegiance and engage in a civil war against their fellow citizens, friends, and lovers. Killmonger's liminal status is again underscored in his interaction with Shuri. She taunts his illegitimacy: "You'll never be king, you're not one of us," repeating the painful mantra that he neither belongs in Wakanda nor the United States. In concert with the constant visual and verbal cueing of that illegitimacy, Killmonger's genuine pain and sorrow at his lack of belonging are revealed in the scene where he dies. He asks to be thrown into the ocean rather than saved: "as my ancestors knew death is better than bondage." This quote was identified by many as one of the most stirring parts of the film because Killmonger makes the link between himself and his ancestors – slaves (not Wakandans) – and points toward their courage and defiance in throwing themselves to death to avoid bondage. Others viewed this as a capitulation to the unrealistic notion insinuated that black Africans had a choice not to be slaves if they had just been strong enough to choose death over slavery. As *Black Panther* was released, the rapper Kanye West had caused a media storm by suggesting that the longevity of the slave trade (400 years) suggested that it had become an accepted choice for Africans. Uproar ensued, and the views of each side of this debate are played out in Killmonger's dying words. While his words are courageous and point to a choice of freedom in death, the consequences of every slave making the same choice would have been the annihilation of all African-Americans. They quite simply would not have existed; their heirs would not be an ever-present reminder of the slavery and cruelty of America, and the capitalist system would have moved on without tension or consequence. In death, T'Challa drags Killmonger to the top of a mountain to view the beauty that N'Jobu had always described to him and poses him in the Wakanda forever salute. Giving him back his Wakandan identity in death restores that which was taken away from him by T'Chaka, by his existence as the child of two worlds, and by no choice of his own.

T'Challa's ideology wins out, and as he moves forward with his plan to open Wakanda up to the rest of the world, he deliberately rejects the idea of an inversion of the existing racial order. The presence of CIA agent Everett Ross in the final battle and the aid that he is able to give the Wakandans plays on both the idea that he is the consummate representation of the American government and its complicity in keeping African Americans enslaved at the same time as being able to help T'Challa in his mission. Killmonger's vision is that the masters become the slaves, and every tactic he chooses serves this point. T'Challa's vision is to reboot the past with an understanding that there will be international cooperation with the ongoing fight to address racial inequality. He seeks to uplift the African Diaspora but in education, diplomacy, and peace as opposed to taking over the white power structure and reversing the misery. T'Challa foregrounds the capable women around him to run the Wakandan outreach centers and builds the first one at the literal scene of his father's crime to symbolize the laying to rest of the erroneous choices that T'Chaka made.

While the ending scenes of *Black Panther* formed a satisfying arc for some viewers, it also left the question of moral authority open. Audiences leaving the theater may have been happy that T'Challa's philosophy won the day, but it is clear from the critical reception of Killmonger as the villain that the 'good' superhero in this case did not arrive at his victory by vanquishing a typically evil force. This is just one of the ways in which *Black Panther* used the superhero genre in a subversive manner to create a truly unique vision of black African and American narratives. The stifling effect of the post 9/11 popular culture narrative is torn apart in the presentation of racial issues in the film, and whilst seated within and mostly conforming to the expectations of the genre, Coogler and his team managed to pull off the impossible task of bringing *Black Panther* to the screen to both critical acclaim and record box office success. In the complex melding of narrative, historical trauma, character development, feminism, and Afro futurism with a genre that was naturally prone to uphold the post 9/11 return to conservative, male-dominated superiority, *Black Panther* clearly whet the appetites of an audience that was ready to receive such complexity. With commercial success assured and further Black Panther films in the pipeline, one can only hope that the minoritized themes of the first film will continue to resonate with audiences and pave the way for other daring explorations of what it means to be African, American, Black, or Other in a world that takes its cue from a superpower that has never fully developed a post racist popular culture.

Notes

1 Two polls conducted by the Pew Research center in 2008 revealed that 10%–12% of Americans believed Obama to be a practicing Muslim.
2 The man who would take over the presidency from Obama, Donald Trump, alluded to this conspiracy theory after the Pulse nightclub massacre in 2016 – www.vanityfair.com/news/2016/06/donald-trump-obama-muslim

Bibliography

Ahmad, Muneer I. "A Rage Shared by Law: Post September 11th Racial Violence as Crimes of Passion." *California Law Review*, Vol. 92, No. 5, 2004. pp. 1259–1330.

Biakolo, Kovie. "Black Panther" Forces Africans and Black Americans to Reconcile the Past." *Buzzfeed*. February 19, 2018. www.buzzfeed.com/koviebiakolo/black-panther-is-for-everybody-black?utm_term=.dupbLbMlj#.bspQ5Q18Y.

Black Panther. Dir. Ryan Coogler. Marvel Studios, 2018.

Bobo, Lawrence D. "Racism in Trump's America: Reflections on Culture, Sociology, and the 2016 US Presidential Election." *The British Journal of Sociology*, Vol. 68, No. 1, 2017. pp. 85–104.

Brown, Jeffrey A. "Comic Book Masculinity and the New Black Superhero." *African American Review*, Vol. 33, No. 1, 1999. pp. 25–42.

Chedade, Carol. "The Racial Lesson of 9/11." 2002. https://academic.udayton.edu/race/06hrights/waronterrorism/racial05.htm.

Delgado, Richard and Jean Stefacic. *Critical Race Theory: An Introduction*. New York: New York University Press, 2012.

Garneau, Eric and Maura Foley. "Grant Morrison's Mutants and the Post 9/11 Culture of Fear." In *Ages of the X-Men*. Ed. Joseph Darowski. Jefferson, NC: McFarland, 2014. pp. 178–188.

Jones, Jeffrey M. "Blacks Showing Decided Opposition to War." *Gallup*, March 28, 2003. https://news.gallup.com/poll/8080/blacks-showing-decided-opposition-war.aspx.

Mosely, Walter. "Time for a New Black Power Movement." *The Guardian Newspaper, London*, August 17, 2002.

Nama, Adilifu. *Superblack: American Pop Culture and Black Superheroes*. Austin: University of Texas Press, 2011.

"Presidential Approval Ratings – Barack Obama." *Gallup*. https://news.gallup.com/poll/116479/barack-obama-presidential-job-approval.aspx.

Ross, Thomas. "Whiteness After 9/11." *Washington University Journal of Law and Policy*, Vol. 18, No. 1, 2005. pp. 223–243.

Smith, Jamil. "The Revolutionary Power of the Black Panther Movie." *Time Magazine*, February, 2018. http://time.com/black-panther/?xid=homepage&pcd=hp-magmod.

Tyree, Tia C.M. and Liezille J. Jacobs. "Can You Save Me?: Black Male Superheroes in Hollywood Film." *A Journal on Black Men*, Vol. 3, No. 1, 2014. pp. 1–24.

Wanzo, Rebecca. "And All Our Past Decades Have Seen Revolutions: The Long Decolonization of Black Panther." *The Black Scholar*, February 19, 2018. www.theblackscholar.org/past-decades-seen-revolutions-long-decolonization-black-panther-rebecca-wanzo/.

Wright, Bradford. *Comic Book Nation: The Transformation of Youth Culture in America*. Baltimore, MD: Johns Hopkins University Press, 2001.

6 The marginalized "other"

Mutant identities in the X-Men films

In the early 1960s, in reaction to the resurgence of superhero comics in the American market, Marvel Comics spearheaded a new kind of superhero comic, one that not only told the larger-than-life adventures of superpowered beings but also examined what it felt like to *be* one of these superheroes. With these comics, the untouchable, indestructible "gods" of the Golden Age of comics had given way to more human heroes. It was during this era that powerhouse Marvel creator Stan Lee created Spider-Man, The Incredible Hulk, Iron Man, and the Fantastic Four, all with distinct back stories that took ordinary humans and through fantastical means (radioactivity, technology, space radiation) gave them extraordinary abilities.

Amidst these human heroes with superhuman abilities soon came a superhero team that deviated slightly from the other Marvel heroes of the early 1960s. While the X-Men comics spent a significant amount of time focusing on the heroes' humanity, a hallmark of the Marvel heroes of the 1960s, that humanity was often questioned in the pages of their comic book adventures because of the genetic elements that distinguished them from the rest of the population of the Earth. "The mutants dealt with harsher realities and faced deeper existential struggles than most of their predecessors; they were not really celebrated as heroes, and often risked their lives for the sake of a world that did not accept them" (Bucciferro, 2016, p. ix).

Since the X-Men are not products of magic, chemicals, radiation, etc., in many ways, they are the first "identity politics" in superhero form. The exploits that readers explored on the pages of the X-Men comic book do not focus its narrative energy exclusively on the classic "good vs. evil" superhero trope. Instead, the X-Men comics introduce a new element to the mix, that of reflection on the interaction between the members of the team and the world in which they were considered abnormal. With the arrival of the X-Men comic, the identities of the heroes play as much of a role in their development as the morals they stand for. Breaking free from the established trope of powerful beings fighting other powerful beings, here, a group (mutants) fight to be accepted in counterpoint with humankind while struggling internally to define what being a mutant means. This focus on identity, then, takes on further weight as those identities come into conflict with societal perspectives and prejudices against them. After all, noted X-Men author Chris Clare-mont has said, "The X-Men are hated, feared and despised collectively by humanity for no other reason than that they are mutants. So, what we have here, intended or not, is a book that is about racism, bigotry and prejudice" (Wright, 2001, p. 117).

Early in their existence as a genre, superhero comics took on a particularly powerful role in representing minority identities in the symbolic sphere. As Marc Singer has noted,

> Because superhero comics have evolved their own conventions for repre-senting the dilemmas of a divided self, they have the potential to become perfect vehicles for exploring minority group identity. . . . Superhero comics can literally personify the otherwise abstract ontological divides of minority identity.
>
> (Singer, 2002, p. 116)

X-Men stories in particular open up a space for the metaphoric exploration of difference and marginality and provide a better understanding of the societal, political, and social forces that act upon a wide variety of those that lie outside the normative sphere. At the heart of this distinction that sets the X-Men apart from other contemporary superhero teams is what Joseph Darowski (2014) calls "the mutant metaphor," specifically linked to representations of minority identity. "The minority metaphor," Darowski says, "allows for exploration of issues not commonly associated with what is often considered a juvenile genre" (p. 10).

Explaining the symbolic power of the X-Men as a metaphor for a variety of minority communities (Bucciferro, 2016; DiPaolo, 2011; Lyubansky, 2008; Roberts, 2005) and social movements (DeBrandt, 2005; Skir, 2005; Trushell, 2004; Zingsheim, 2016) is a common critical position for scholars who study the mutant team. From this metaphor, which has been used to discuss race, gender, sexual orientation, disability, and a number of other minority posi-tions and movements tied to them, the X-Men draw much of their popularity and potency. The metaphor can even be understood as even more universal in scope and has been stretched to apply to anyone who has ever felt isolated or like an outsider in their own environment.

So, if the original comic's source material has tackled a variety of identities and issues, what is it that the filmic representations of the X-Men can tell us about contemporary society and the preoccupations of American cul-ture in the post 9/11 period? With the metaphor of difference and the social movements connected to it serving as their central conceit, the X-Men films reflect the concepts and issues of importance to these communities amidst an environment that, due to the fears stoked by the terrorist attacks on New York, was not always supportive of difference. If, as Ramzi Fawaz has stated, these characters, created in the 1960s "were framed as cultural outsiders and biological freaks capable of upsetting the social order in much the same way that racial, gendered, and sexual minorities were seen to destabilize the image of the ideal U.S. citizen" then the X-Men films redeploy this idea of the "cultural outsider" in an effort to resurface narratives of "other" minorities in a post 9/11 landscape (Fawaz, 2016, p. 4). This chapter will explore the US sociopolitical climate in the post 9/11 period in large part as a function of the polyvalence of the X-Men as a metaphor for race, gender, sexuality, religion, and other marginalized communities as a means of better understanding the roles these communities played in the cultural landscape of the post 9/11 era. In order to better understand what can be understood from the films, however, it is important to first start with a brief look at how these concepts have been dealt with in the comics texts that served as source material for the films. Our analysis will then explore more specifically how the individual manifestations in filmic form of this metaphor serve to communicate distinct ideas about marginalized groups in the 21st century.

When the X-Men comics premiered in 1963, Marvel Comics had already helped to stoke the resurrection of the superhero genre by introducing or re-introducing popular heroes such as Thor, Iron Man, Spider-Man, the Incredible Hulk, and the Fantastic Four to the world. When the X-Men comic premiered, it was not an incredibly successful book, but "(a)lthough the comic book initially struggled to find and audience, Marvel has nurtured the adventures of mutants into one of the largest and highest-selling areas of their publishing line" (Joseph Darowski, 2014, p. 10). Early X-Men stories focused on the typical superhero vs. supervillain type tropes, although later in the first series, the comic did begin to explore issues of prejudice and racism.[1] In 1975, after a five-year hiatus in which older adventures were reprinted to keep the title going, "Marvel decided to relaunch the title, and it did so to great critical acclaim and financial success" (Joseph Darowski, 2014, p. 11).

Once the 1975 relaunch took off, headed by writer Chris Claremont who stayed with the series for 16 years, the X-Men comics began to further explore the power of the mutant metaphor to stand in for various minority communities and social movements. In the height of second wave feminism, this new iteration of the team included "strong female characters who played more than the token supporting role traditionally allotted to women in comic books" (Wright, 2001, p. 263). Despite not dealing with issues of race until later in the original 1960s run, the Claremont series of the X-Men continued to interact with themes that could be linked to issues of race-based bigotry and prejudice. As the series entered the 1980s, these themes continued, with additional marginal groups being added to the metaphorical representations of the mutant team. The 1980s saw the "coming out" of the LGBT rights movement in reaction to the type of prejudice and bigotry the X-Men fought against in the issues of the comic, and the comic series added the LGBT movement to the list of marginalized communities it could represent. X-Men comics even took up a number of issues that arose directly from the real world conflicts that plagued the LGBT community with a storyline dealing with the Legacy Virus (an analog for AIDS) and another dealing with the mutant "cure," with various visual citations that consistently connected mutant identities with queer ones (a sign reading "God Hates Mutants" in reference to the Westboro Baptist Church's "God Hates Fags" and legislation called Proposition X like California's Proposition 8).[2] Although the specific movements and identities that can be understood through the mutant metaphor have evolved over the years of the run of the comics, what has remained consistent has been the ability for the X-Men to stand in and represent the personal, political, and societal struggles of a variety of marginalized groups. The team does "more than merely model an ideology of tolerance and diversity. Rather, they examine the causes of prejudice and intolerance and pit competing perspectives against each other" (Lyubansky, 2008, p. 77).

When, in the late 90s, due to financial struggles at Marvel comics, the rights to make X-Men films were sold to 20th Century Fox, a powerhouse film franchise was born, jump starting the superhero film phenomenon of the 21st century. When *X-Men* premiered in the summer of 2000, it was an instant success, immediately spawning sequels, which to date numbers 12 films (with a 13th forthcoming) and has grossed over $2.41 billion worldwide (BoxOfficeMojo.com).

Although the filmmakers could not have predicted at the time the franchise was launched that the cultural landscape would change so dramatically after the terrorist attacks of 9/11, the X-Men franchise has, nonetheless, provided a vehicle to examine and unpack a number of prevalent cultural issues that arose in the US following the attacks. With the change to the cultural landscape, the success of the X-Men franchise has provided a vehicle to explore themes directly tied to the attacks and the aftermath (terrorism, fear of the "Other," religious discrimination) as well as other themes that reflected the struggle of marginalized communities along lines of race, gender, and sexuality that persisted, despite often being drowned out by the cultural response to 9/11. Other superhero films of this period, which we study elsewhere in this volume, primarily create a world in which heroes become emblematic of the help/qualities the world needs, but in these films, the X-Men are not headlining heroes who are looked up to by regular citizens. In their cinematic universe, people with powers must fight for a place, and those they fight want to destroy that world in order to re-make it. A theme of "Us" vs. "Them" becomes simultaneously internal (Mutant vs. Mutant) and external (Mutant vs. Human), which draws attention to the idea that something sets this group apart from others. As noted previously, that something can be understood in a variety of ways and centers around issues of inclusion, marginality, diversity, and identity and the sociopolitical impact of these ideas in contemporary society.

X-Women

Although the superhero team made up of mutants is called the X-Men, one of the distinguishing factors of the comics series has been the way it features and centralizes issues of importance to the female members of the team. In a team initially made up of mostly men, led by a patriarchal figure in Professor Xavier, it is the X-Women that became a central part of the relaunch of the series in 1975, and since then the series' focus on the women on the team as leaders and strong heroes has remained one of the elements that distinguishes it from other superhero series.

However, beginning with the first *X-Men* film and continuing with subsequent sequels and reboots, the creative teams behind these adaptations of the comics source material have chosen to sideline the female members of the team, de-emphasizing the elements of their characters that often have made their membership on the team a dramatic change from the often male-centered or over-sexualized representation of women heroes in comic books. In a sort of regressive move, these films take these strong heroines and leaders and reduce their representation to objectified or ignored characters. In the traditionally male dominated field of action blockbuster films, superhero films, and comic book films, perhaps the sidelining of female characters in the X-Men films comes as no surprise. Film productions such as these are, after all, a money-making enterprise, and studios are hesitant to take risks to deviate from their lucrative – yet often sexist – formula. Even despite this de-emphasizing of the importance of the female characters in the X-Men films, an examination of the representations of the X-Women in the X-Men cinematic universe, specifically the characters of Jean Grey, Storm, Mystique, and Rogue, can, nonetheless, shed some light on 21st-century understandings of empowered femininity and its treatment on screen.

Jean Grey, a powerful omega level mutant telepath/telekinetic is, as we learn at the beginning of the first film, *X-Men*, one of the leaders of the team. In the opening scenes of the film, she is shown speaking in front of a congressional hearing in an impassioned way, trying to convince senators to vote down the Mutant Registration Act. In this scene, she is poised and in control but is also immediately questioned in a condescending tone by Senator Kelly, marking the first of many instances where men will attempt to silence or control Jean Grey. Later, when Jean is asked by Logan about her using Cerebro, the giant computer that enables the Professor to find mutants in the world, she says "For someone like me it's dangerous." This focus on the "danger" of Jean Grey will come to be a central theme for the first three X-Men films (and based on the preview for the newest installment as well). Throughout these films, despite her prominent position on the team (she is one of the mutants who has been with the Professor the longest) the mediation of her powers and her control by the Professor is a central conceit. In the second film, as Jean's powers grow, she loses more and more control, often putting her team in danger, and this ultimately results in her sacrificing herself to save her team. By the third film, Jean's powers have become completely unleashed, and she manifests the threat that the Professor had been trying to contain, emblematized by his exclamation to Logan, "She has to be controlled." When, ultimately, he fails to control her as intended, and her destructive power is released, Wolverine, another powerful, central male character, has to be the one to exert the ultimate control, death. Men seek to control Jean Grey, first Charles, then Logan, and even Magneto eventually comes to do the same when Jean's Phoenix power manifests and he sees an opportunity to wield her as a weapon.

While in her interactions with the Professor discourses of control are often at work, Jean is also further sidelined as a central hero of the film through her positioning as a love interest to two of the male characters, Cyclops and Wolverine. This super heroic love triangle establishes Jean as the object of the men's affection and a cause for rivalry, resulting in conflict between the men and tension between Wolverine and Jean. Highlighting how her importance to the general plot of the second film is deemphasized by the will and perspective of male characters, after sacrificing herself to save her teammates,[3] and in their grieving over the loss of such an important teammate, Wolverine tells Cyclops, "She did make a choice: It was you," effectively reducing her sacrifice and heroism to the resolution of the tense love triangle.[4] Upon resurrection in *X-Men 3*, Jean destroys Scott, effectively eliminating the romantic rivalry and setting up the dramatic tension that will culminate in Wolverine's having to kill her to save the world.

Although Jean is positioned in the films as the most powerful of female mutants and therefore seemingly in need of controlling, another example of one of the strongest women from the X-Men comics universe to be deemphasized in the X-Men films is Storm. In the comics, Storm is a Kenyan weather goddess who, in addition to being immensely powerful, is one of the key leaders of the X-Men, taking over leadership of the team at various times in the run of the comics (Cocca, 2016, p. 80). However, in both *X-Men* and *X-Men 2*, her character is reduced to a glorified babysitter and caregiver to the younger mutants at Xavier's school. Her role was so diminished from that of the source material that Halle Berry negotiated more screen time for the third film as a requisite for her returning to the franchise. However, Carolyn Cocca (2016) has pointed out that, even with additional screen time, Storm is still relegated to a supporting role and not team leader in the third film (p. 83).

Arguably the female mutant with the most central role in the six principal X-Men films is Mystique, the enemy of the X-Men in the first trilogy, and her portrayal on screen is highly problematic in these films. First, she appears effectively and inexplicably naked during the entirety of the film.[5] The choice to portray one of the principal antagonists of the X-Men in those first three films and the only female one, as naked, clearly serves to objectify her and constantly highlights her female body, coded as "hypersexual, strategic, and dangerous" (Zingsheim, 2016, p. 101). In the first trilogy, she is used as a tool of Magneto's master plan and wielded like a weapon, simultaneously objectified for her body and sexuality but also for her power to transform into anyone she desires. Her relationship to Magneto as nothing more than a tool he can use is highlighted when she loses her powers in *X-Men 3*. Upon de-powering and being left in a "normal" (and naked) human form, Magneto abandons her, effectively discarding her since she is of no more use to him. In the prequel trilogy, Mystique takes on a more central role as Charles Xavier's friend and "adopted" sister but still suffers from many of the issues with her portrayal in the original trilogy. In *First Class*, she is shown wearing clothes for the majority of the film, but she is still shown as an object to be controlled by a powerful man. In these films, Charles takes on that role. Early on, chastising Mystique, in reference to her remaining hidden from public view he says, "A small slip up is one thing. A big one doesn't bear thinking about," and later when in a bar she considers having a drink, Charles is there to mediate her interaction with the world, telling her, "You need another cola." By the end of *Days of Future Past*, Charles becomes aware of this behavior and admits to it, saying "I've been trying to control you ever since the day we met." Although Charles is the primary male controlling force for Mystique in the prequel trilogy, Magneto does continue this behavior. Once he learns that Mystique's actions are responsible for the horrific dystopian future, he is willing to sacrifice her to stop it from happening. Once again, to him, she is disposable; she is only a tool to help him achieve his goal.

These three examples are not the only ways that female mutants are portrayed in a way that runs counter to a 21st-century feminist project of gender equality and greater agency and subjectivity for female characters in popular culture, though they are definitely the most egregious. Other mutant women are treated similarly in the films. Rogue, the first mutant to appear in *X-Men*, is shown discovering her powers by threating the life of a boy, signaling that female sexuality is dangerous and must be controlled. She is also wielded as a tool by Magneto in his attempt to turn New York City into mutants at the end of that film. In *X-Men 2*, her role in the film is secondary, along with the other teen mutants, and in *X-Men 3*, her value is portrayed as part of a romantic triangle between Iceman, Kitty Pryde, and herself, ultimately leading to her decision to take the mutant cure so that she could be more intimate with her boyfriend, Iceman, further reducing her value as only a romantic foil and communicating that power and ability linked to femininity are not nearly as valuable or important as having a relationship with a boy. Her scenes were so inconsequential and secondary to the plot of *Days of Future Past* that she was removed completely from the theatrical release of the film (Holmes, 2015). Kitty Pryde, who in the comic version of *Days of Future Past* is the central hero of the plan to save the future, is reduced to utility player in supporting the men of the film who must come together to save the day.

X-Men: First Class, sees the introduction of two additional women to the X-Men universe: one mutant, the other human. However, they also fall victim to the same forces that have acted on the other women in the films. The often scantily clad mutant telepath Emma Frost, in addition to being positioned as overly sexualized eye candy (she is wearing revealing lingerie when first introduced to audiences, and in a later scene uses her sexuality to attempt to convince a Russian officer to do as she wishes), is portrayed as of secondary importance to the men in the film. In a scene on board the submarine and wearing the helmet that blocks her powers form working, Sebastian Shaw tells Emma, "I was thinking that you are the most exquisite thing I've ever seen and that this needs ice. Fetch me some. There's a good girl." In this exchange, her value to Shaw is as a subservient sexual object. With her powers "tamed" or tied to masculine will by Shaw, she is put into her place. The scene is clearly a set up for a visual gag with Emma cutting a piece off of a glacier for the drink, but it is also representative of the gender issues plaguing the other mutant women in the films. The human CIA agent, Moira MacTaggert, despite being portrayed as a strong female in a position of power and value to the team, is also put in her place by a group of high ranking men who threaten her with a "one way ticket back to the typing pool," which, given the historical moment of the film, could serve to highlight the progress made by women by contrast, but she falls victim to the controlling force of Xavier at the end when he decides to erase her memory of all interactions with the nascent mutant team. He chooses for her in order to remain hidden from authorities, manipulating her own autonomy and literal ability to think for herself.

Although the mediation, control, and sidelining of powerful women in the X-Men films (and especially in the earliest of the series) is problematic when viewed in counterpoint to the more forward thinking, feminist original source material, there is a glimmer of hope for the redemption of the X-Women.[6] In the 2016 film *X-Men: Apocalypse*, an effort is seemingly made to rectify some of these wrongs through the repositioning and redemption of the three female mutants most mishandled in the preceding films. To this end, in the film, Mystique, repositioned as a central character in the second trilogy of the primary X-Men franchise, takes on the role of heroic idol to a generation of younger mutants, including the two other primary X-Women in the film: Jean and Storm. Early on, looking at a picture of Mystique on her wall, Storm says "Great fighter. She's my hero" indicating that it is Mystique's strength that inspires the young mutant. Later, on the plane headed to fight the final battle with Apocalypse, Jean tells Mystique, "You're a hero to us. . . . Seeing you that day on TV changed my life." Mystique is constructed as a hero that is capable of inspiring a generation of mutants, in this case, two of the most important female mutants in the X-Men universe. The message of one generation of women fighting for a just cause and inspiring the next to take up the cause as well is significant, especially in light of the past treatment of female mutants in the series discussed earlier.

The most powerful moment in the redemption of the power of the female hero to inspire and lead is one that communicates the reach and scope of a community of women supporting each other and inspiring others (of all genders). After the X-Mansion is destroyed and Mystique's true form is revealed, the series of shots of the recently saved mutant children reacting to her presence are overwhelmingly female. In fact, other than the principal characters of the film, the only children that are prominently featured in close-up reaction or in group shots are all girls. Hank tells her: "They look up to you. Right now, they need you." This sequence spotlights the admiration that these young mutant women have for Mystique and constructs an intergenerational web of support and inspiration to action. In the context of the mutant superhero film, that action is, of course, the final battle against the enemy, but it is not difficult to extrapolate the message that this sequence and the redemption of Mystique as a true leader has, especially for women in the film's audience. Although she rejects Hank's words, saying "That's not what they need," it is her bravery in the final moments of the fight against Apocalypse that inspires Storm to snap out of her obedience and contribute to the villain's destruction.

For Jean Grey, whose previous appearances in the franchise have been as a force that needs to be controlled, it is exactly that power that contributes the finishing blow to Apocalypse and allows the other X-Men to destroy him. Almost defeated, Charles tells Jean "Let go. Unleash your power. No fear" in direct contrast to the portrayal of Charles' attitude toward Jean's powers in the other films. When Jean's true power is unleashed in previous films, the result is pure destruction and threat to all those around her, while here, her extreme power is what tips the battle back in the favor of the X-Men and allows them to win. Although, as discussed previously, the next film appears to see Charles back to his practice of controlling and containing Jean's feminine power, at least in this moment, Jean's true power is portrayed as a positive force.[7]

Perhaps the resuscitation of positive portrayals of feminine power and the recuperation of the strength and importance of female mutants is a sign of the times. The three years since the premiere of *X-Men: Apocalypse* has seen a shift in Hollywood portrayal of female superheroes. In 2017 *Wonder Woman* smashed all expectations of a female led (and directed) superhero film, 2018 saw another female hero headline a film in *Ant-Man and the Wasp*, and in 2019, *Captain Marvel* did for Marvel superheroines what *Wonder Woman* did for DC: showcase one of the most powerful Marvel heroes in a central leadership role.

Wolverine and masculinity

While the representation of women in the X-Men universe reflects a departure from the source material's more enlightened and progressive treatment of its female heroes, the men of the X-Men cinematic universe remain much truer to their comic book counterparts. The success of the film franchise can be closely linked to the character of Wolverine, as played by Hugh Jackman, and it is that particular male mutant who becomes the focal point of the vast majority of the X-Men films.[8] In Wolverine, the films present a complicated and complex figure who navigates a continuum between anti-hero and hero, often simultaneously exhibiting characteristics of both. He is a loner who is often relied on for the heavy (violent) lifting of the X-Men's exploits yet comes and goes at will in his search for answers about his identity. In his solo films, he acts similarly, preferring to be alone or tied to only a small number of allies, and although the character often plays a more supportive role in the comic books, it can be said that he is clearly the central character of the X-Men cinematic universe.

When Wolverine appears in *X-Men*, he is a man without a purpose, with an unsure path and an unknown identity. In this way, he is like returning servicemen from the conflicts in Iraq/Afghanistan. In their time deployed on active duty, their identity and function as a member of a team was set, but upon returning to civilian life, they often face great difficulty in assimilating into a culture and life that has become foreign and distant to them due to the trauma of service in a warzone. But, in the cases of the returning members of the military, their struggles are often due to a contrast to their identities as constructed in the service, and the expectations of civilian life. For Wolverine, his memories of his past life first as a soldier and later as a weapon have been wiped, and he must go in search of them. Without an understanding of his role in the past and how he, as an individual, crafted an identity within the context of war and conflict, he is nothing but pure rage and violence. As Logan's search for his memories progress, with the help of Charles, many of the gaps in his past are filled in as the Professor helps him reconstruct his memories. The audience soon learns that his past is entwined with that of war and military service, making him the most potent metaphor for the trauma of war but also for the values that American culture ascribes to the military, especially in the hyper-patriotic post 9/11 period. As a culture, the collective response to 9/11 was institutional (government, citizenry, military), but the real, lasting effect was on individuals who lost their lives or were physically/mentally scarred. By highlighting Logan's military service as both an individual soldier scarred by war but simultaneously a weapon of war, Logan is both the mechanism fomenting aggression and the human victim of that institutional, hegemonic force.[9]

Wolverine's most direct ties to the military are in his own service. In *X-Men Origins: Wolverine*, he is shown participating in numerous military campaigns starting with the Civil War, including World War I, World War II, Korea, and Vietnam, and his service in World War II is further highlighted in *The Wolverine*. Through this connection, his moral character and his struggles can also be tied to the individual soldier, becoming a reflection of both the mechanisms/logistics of war and the toll on the individual. Also important to understanding the military metaphor described here is how Logan functions within the military industrial complex as a tool and weapon himself. In *X-Men Origins*, Col. William Stryker takes the powerful mutant with a healing factor and naturally occurring claws and covers his bones and claws with adamantium, one of the strongest metals in the Marvel universe. In this way, Wolverine symbolizes the simultaneous function that all servicemembers have as an individual with agency whose identities as a warrior are constructed in a context of service, patriotism, duty, and many other rationales and their function as a tool or weapon of the branch of service for whom they work. Although a fictional, superpowered example, in Wolverine these two often competing forces can be seen at work. His efficacy and power is sought out and crafted in the hopes of wielding it in future conflicts, but that conversion into living weapon is done at the cost of the humanity (and ultimately memories and identity) of the hero. It is not insignificant that when, after Wolverine escapes from the laboratory at Alkali Lake, Stryker continues his Weapon X program that had created Wolverine but this time also develops a method to brainwash the mutants he experiments on so that they become even more of a weapon, free of identity and free will.[10]

Beyond his ties to military service and as an analog for American servicemembers, Wolverine's masculinity in and of itself is significant. In the films, Wolverine is constructed and represented as a masculine ideal. Physically he has a powerful and muscular bodily presence that is, outside of that of Mystique, the most revealed body in the X-Men cinematic universe. He exhibits a number of traditionally (but often stereotypically) masculine features/behaviors including facial and body hair, his iconic cigar, leather jacket, and motorcycle. He is duty bound but is also loner. He is portrayed as a fighting machine who, when needed, can go into a berserker rage but is also called upon to roles of leadership and stewardship on the team. In his interactions with a number of female mutants, he demonstrates love, both paternal (Rogue, X-23) and romantic (Jean, Mariko, random lovers from his past).

Through the contrast of the representation of empowered femininity in the figure of Jean Grey and of empowered masculinity in Wolverine, especially by means of the relationship that the two have, the differences in how American culture understands the two becomes clearer. When confronted with the fact that the Professor had been controlling part of Jean's mind to "protect her from herself," Logan reacts negatively to the news, saying "Jean had no choice." He is an advocate for her autonomy, because he was also experimented on and lost his memory of it. In this interaction, two of the male heroes, both who seemingly "have Jean's best interests in mind" argue over how she should be treated. Jean herself does not have a voice, but Wolverine becomes her "champion," tapping in to old modes of a "damsel in distress" who needs saving by the strong hero. As the masculine ideal whose significance and role in the films is a function of his rage and his instinctive, animal nature, advocating for Jean to be able to express her powers freely and without control is not unsurprising, but given the gendered power exchange it does paint a much more complex image. Wolverine is valued more *because* of his power, which derives from this animal rage, but he is a man, and this makes him desirably "dangerous" as Jean points out in *X-Men 2* when she says "Girls flirt with the dangerous guy, Logan. They don't take him home. They marry the good guy," which is particularly ironic, given the fact that Jean's danger literally destroys man after man (first Cyclops, then almost Wolverine, then Charles, then a ton of soldiers, then almost Wolverine again). However, Wolverine's destructive rage is also most often wielded to help the team to defeat the "bad guys".[11] His male privilege allows him a conduit for that primal nature. With Jean, any exploration of it results in death of "good guys."

The mutant team provides numerous opportunities to explore issues of gender but can also have a similar effect on how contemporary audiences approach issues of race. Before the climactic battle of *X-Men*, Magneto looks at the Statue of Liberty and explains to Rogue part of his philosophy. He says,

> I first saw her in 1949. America was going to be the land of tolerance, peace. . . . There is no land of tolerance, there is no peace. Not here, nor anywhere else. Women and children, whole families destroyed simply because they were born different from those in power.

Although he is attempting to justify attempting to convert thousands of people into mutants in a plot to equalize the masses, he presents a stinging criticism of contemporary American values in regard to the rights of the individual to succeed no matter their background, free from government intervention, as relates to gender (debates over women's bodily autonomy and role in positions of power) but also to race. The threat that Magneto recalls to women and children, destroyed because they were different, has echoes in the current administration that cages immigrant children because they are racially/ethnically different than the white men in power. In this example, mutancy serves as a metaphor for contemporary racial issues and can reveal a number of the cultural preoccupations with race and ethnicity that hang over the early part of the 21st century.

Post 9/11 – post-racial

As has been discussed earlier, the power of the mutant metaphor is in its polyvalence or its ability to simultaneously stand in for a variety of marginalized groups in society. And, although in the comics, that metaphor has "mutated" itself and come to represent a much wider variety of discrimination and bigotry than perhaps was originally conceived of in the early days of the comics, racial issues and the plight of people of color in the American context was the first function of the metaphor in the comics.

> The issues of race relations and prejudice were worn on the proverbial sleeve of the (comic) series. . . . The X-Men were created at a time when race and prejudice were among the most pressing issues in America. The mutants who made up the X-Men were literally a separate race in this narrative, and the issue of prejudice has long been the prevalent theme in the series.
>
> (Joseph Darowski, 2014, p. 30)

Although the early team of X-Men was not racially or ethnically diverse, the discrimination and bigotry they faced in society because of their mutations established a window through which those of a variety of backgrounds could read and understand their own struggles. Author Junot Diaz has stated, for example, that he identified with the predominantly white X-Men because of his marginalized state as Dominican immigrant (Nama, 2013, p. 254). Over time, however, the comics did become more diverse in the cultural/racial makeup of the team. In the 1975 relaunch, non-white mutants such as Storm joined the team. But, the comic would still suffer from a lack of racially diverse American mutants, keeping associations with the struggle for Civil Rights in the US mostly in the purely metaphorical sphere.

When the X-Men cinematic universe was born with *X-Men* in 2000, the filmmakers had a chance to make choices in how to feature and showcase more ethnically diverse mutants, but, as many scholars who have studied the films have pointed out (Cocca, 2016, p. 81), the film series remains predominantly white, in both the makeup of the team and in the ways in which the films reify hegemonic white power (Smith, 2016, p. 184). In many of the films, ethnic mutants are relegated to secondary or background roles and are often sacrificed. Members of Magneto's Brotherhood are predominantly MoC (Mutants of Color) and are presented as villains to further Magneto's plan (Smith, 2016, p. 187). In *First Class*, of the two MoC on the team, Darwin is killed in front of the team, and Angel turns evil. In *Days of Future Past*, it is MoC that die protecting others.

These examples reveal that, although mutation and the plight of mutants in a society that hates and fears them can be clearly understood as a metaphor for race relations in the modern era, the actual, diegetic presentation of race, through the mutants of the film, is far from progressive. This may be understood as a function of the post 9/11 period in which these films appear, in which a mythic, monolithic concept of "America" as predominantly white, protestant, etc. emerges as tied to a drive toward "unity" and support in reaction to the terrorist attacks. In the need to show a united front in the face of a domestic attack from abroad, the diversifying force of the X-Men and the mutant metaphor in general seems to give way to a more homogenous conceptualization of "Us" to be placed counter to "Them."

Although the erasure of mutants of color from significance in the ranks of the superhero team seems to acquiesce to this homogenizing drive, the films do also present a contradictory narrative as well in the function of the antagonist's plots. The goals of Magneto in the films seem to be aligned with maintaining the conceptual status quo, albeit with mutants as the hegemonic power. If, according to Cornel West (1993), in understanding the cultural politics of difference we are to "trash the monolithic and homogeneous in the name of diversity, multiplicity, and heterogeneity," Magneto's goals are firmly aligned with traditional hegemonic power (pp. 203–204). While the X-Men are supposed to be diversity personified advocating for co-existence toward progress, this symbolic role is in direct contrast with the way they are portrayed as less ethnically and racially diverse and then further problematized in the team's antagonism with Magneto and his goals of hegemonic mutant power.[12] This complex web of symbolic and overt portrayals of race establishes that diversity and civil rights in the racial/ethnic sphere are complex and resist distillation into a simple metaphor.

The contrast between Magneto's perspective on supplanting human hegemonic structures with a goal of mutant supremacy with Charles' view of harmonious integration with human society has been linked by a number of scholars to the contrast between the views of Malcolm X and Martin Luther King, Jr. (Howe, 2012, p. 48; Wright, 2001, p. 219). Both men had a view of how to overcome the oppression and discrimination that African Americans faced in the turbulent society of the 1960s but differed in both their proposed methods to achieve their goals (violent action versus nonviolent protest). Although it is in their philosophies that Charles and Erik are most often linked to the two Civil rights leaders, one moment seems to underscore this connection. In *X-Men: First Class*, Charles and Erik sit talking on the steps of the Lincoln memorial. The establishing shot of this scene begins with Lincoln's statue as the only figure in the image, and the voice of Charles speaking to his friend. The two mutants are on a quest to find other mutants out in the world. In the exchange between the two, Charles is hopeful, but Erik invokes the violence and death that he knows from experience is often the result of the conflict between two groups divided by difference.

CHARLES: Their isolation, their hopes, their ambitions. I tell you, we are at the start of something incredible, Erik. We can help them.
ERIK: Can we? Identification. That's how it starts. Then ends with being rounded up, experimented on, eliminated.
CHARLES: Not this time. We have common enemies . . .
ERIK: For now.

The establishing shot of Lincoln recalls the role that he played in the advancement of diversity in the American context and the freeing of those of African descent from slavery. Lincoln seems to represent the hope and possibility that divisions based on difference can be bridged and progress, however incremental, can be made.[13] Soon, the camera pans down, revealing Charles and Erik speaking, with a visual link between President Lincoln and the two mutants with differing perspectives. When the camera reverses to show the men from behind, however, the reflecting pool and the Washington monument are immediately seen making another visual citation, this time to Martin Luther King's iconic "I Have a Dream" speech at the march on Washington in 1963. Through this visual citation and the presentation of the two perspectives, the film links these men to the Civil Rights movement and to the complexity and diversity of opinions as to how to achieve equality and justice.

Another specific way that the X-Men films interact with contemporary issues of race and ethnicity is through representations of hegemonic power wielded to seek out and eliminate difference. In *Days of Future Past*, Bolivar Trask invents mutant hunting technology and installs it in a squadron of Sentinels that are tasked with seeking out and destroying mutants. The

Sentinel project is born out of a fear of mutants and, although initially wary, is sanctioned by the US government after Magneto's attack at the Paris Peace Accords in 1973. In the current climate, the Sentinels can be read as a metaphor for ICE, especially in the charged political climate of Donald Trump. If, before, the popular cultural imaginary as understood through representation in film and television specifically linked ICE primarily to the investigation and deportation of dangerous immigrants and criminals, Trump's conflation of all Latin American immigrants with dangerous criminals and his mandate to round up even those in society who have been making positive contributions (DREAMers, servicemembers) and innocents (imprisoned children) provides a link to the mutant hunting robots of the dystopian future. In both, fear stoked by those in power through hyperbole attempts to protect the country from a potential threat by deploying teams to seek out and "eliminate the threat." For Trump's ICE, that elimination is deportation regardless of criminal status or actual threat, and for the Sentinels, that mandate is taken to its apocalyptic end, resulting in the utter destruction of society and the near elimination of all mutants.

LGBT rights and visibility

As described earlier, because of its ability to stand in for various marginalized communities, the mutant metaphor came to include representations of queer communities in the pages of the comic, especially in the 1980s and 1990s just as LGBT issues began to appear more in the broader cultural narrative surrounding the civil rights and identities of LGBT Americans.

A number of analyses have been written linking specific elements of relevance to LGBT communities with the X-Men comics beginning in the 1960s and continuing on into present iterations of the comics. For example, in his groundbreaking book applying queer theory to the superheroic oeuvre, *The New Mutants*, Ramzi Fawaz (2016) explores, among other topics, how the X-Men comics of the 1970s provided readers with a "nuanced conception of superhuman difference . . . by imbuing its narrative with the visual and cultural politics of women's and gay liberation" (p. 34). Others have delved into specific representations of the mutant metaphor as representative of particular aspects of the LGBT community or specific story arcs that are particularly salient explorations of issues affecting the diverse LGBT community. Christian Norman (2014) looks at the appearance of the Legacy Virus as an existential threat to mutantdom as a direct metaphor for the HIV/AIDS crisis through the critical lens of biological determinism. These studies linking the LGBT historical, sociopolitical, and psychological experience of the late 20th and early 21st centuries will inform our analysis of the filmic incarnations of the mutant super heroic team, relating the source material and inspiration for these characters and their exploits and allowing for a deeper understanding of the ways LGBT issues are presented both metaphorically and more overtly in the X-Men films.

During the first two decades of the 21st century, as the X-Men films were flourishing in the cultural zeitgeist, issues surrounding the LGBT community were similarly the focus of debates, discussions, and treatments in popular culture. While the collective focus of the country was on the aftermath of the terrorist attacks of 9/11 and the ensuing "War on Terror," LGBT Americans struggled to have their voices heard and their issues taken up in the halls of power. Because of the power of the mutant metaphor to represent various marginalized communities and the clear connections between mutancy and the LGBT issues as made in the original comics source material, the X-Men films provide opportunities to explore various facets of the LGBT experience in the 21st century.

It is well-documented by a number of cultural critics that the mutant metaphor can be linked to the issues surrounding the LGBT movement. Mutants in the X-Men universe, are, after all, born with their mutations, with their powers manifesting at puberty at around the same time that most LGBT individuals begin to understand their same-sex attraction. Both groups are initially often maligned by those in places of hegemonic power (government, religion, science), and they both face discrimination in a society that does not understand them. In the pages of the X-Men comics of the 1970s and 1980s, this metaphor was made more explicit through the exploration of events and story arcs that firmly tied the mutant metaphor to the LGBT movement. The X-Men films continue the work begun in the comics to reflect and unpack a number of specific concepts and issues that surround discussions of the LGBT experience, including those of understanding queer identities, discourses of illness, the movement to achieve civil rights, transgender issues, and queer visibility.

In *X-Men 3*, a scene plays out in the living room of the Grey family as they learn that they can send their daughter Jean to Xavier's School. When Mr. Grey refers to Jean's "illness," Magneto exclaims: "Illness? You think your daughter is sick?" This scene not only reflects the experiences of many LGBT individuals as they embark on a journey of self-discovery and understanding in a heteronormative world that often does not understand them but also uncovers the specific form that ignorance has often taken: the conflation and understanding of homosexuality as illness. When homosexuality first entered the collective cultural consciousness during the earlier parts of the 20th century, it was primarily couched in discourses of illness. Before the end of the 19th century, terminology did not even exist yet to discuss the idea of homosexuality, because it was almost always understood as a deviance from what was then understood to be the normal sexual function of people. Physicians and scientists who studied the phenomenon, for example, used terms like "inversion," which referred to inverted manifestations of gender in an individual: "the masculine soul, heaving in the female bosom" (Taylor, 1998, p. 288). Still others, such as Freud, attempted to understand homosexuality as a perversion of the biological procreative imperative.[14] Even in the latter part of the 20th century, when discourses of Civil Rights were laying the groundwork for a movement to legitimize the identities of those theretofore deemed ill, homosexuality was still referred to in scientific circles as "social or sexual deviance" (Simon and Gagnon, 1967, p. 177).

It is from these discourses of illness that the mutant metaphor as a stand-in for homosexuality becomes a useful tool for understanding not only the historical context of homosexuality but also how, on into the 21st century, discourses of illness were still being used to target and marginalize the LGBT community. In the X-Men universe, after all, mutants are considered by many to be a deviation from the human norm and, for those who believe as such, a phenomenon that must be identified, isolated, and eliminated.

William Earnest (2007), in his detailed analysis of the first three X-Men films as reflective of LGBT issues points out the links to how mutancy in the X-Men universe is understood in terms of unnaturalness, or illness. He says:

> This rhetorical emphasis on the unnatural, unhealthy aspects of mutancy is echoed elsewhere. "We should love the mutant but hate the mutation," Kelly tells his fellow senators, not in the film itself but in a 30-minute mockumentary called the "Mutant Watch," aired by the FOX network to promote the film's release . . . [a] . . . reimagining of the familiar evangelical Christian trope "love the sinner, hate the sin."
>
> (p. 223)

Senator Kelly's opinion about mutants reflects the evangelical perspective that constructs homosexuality as something that must be controlled or eliminated by any means necessary. It is this perspective that has served as the inspiration behind movements to use various means to attempt to change the sexual orientation or gender identity of individuals who have expressed queer desire/expression. These practices, referred to as "reparative" therapy and often linked to religious groups (Donaldson, 2011), have been thoroughly discounted by medical professionals, yet even today, individuals can be subjected to harmful procedures that do more harm than good.[15]

In one scene in *X-Men 3*, a young Angel (Warren Worthington) locks himself in the bathroom while he commits an act of self-harm, cutting off his wings to try to hide his nascent mutant power. Upon discovering the scene, his father exclaims "Oh God, not you," eliciting a tearful response from the young mutant of, "Dad, I'm sorry." This is a scene of a young boy who wants nothing more than to avoid disappointing his father's expectations of what is normal, and to do this, resorts to self-harm, an extremely common phenomenon in LGBT youth, affecting between 13% and 45% of LGBT youth (Liu and Mustanski, 2012). What follows in a later scene is the culmination of Warren's desire to please his father and try to be "normal." In it, the winged mutant is strapped down to receive the mutant cure similar to an electroshock reparative therapy victim who believes the procedure is the only way he can be a normal part of the family even though it means killing a part of himself that makes him, him. When he struggles in his bonds, his father says, "This is what you want" and Angel replies: "No, Dad. It's what you want" before breaking free. Like so many LGBT youth who were forced and coerced into harmful therapies, it is most often a family member who cannot handle the difference in their child and wants to force their will upon them to change. In both groups, LGBT and mutant, the threat from a family member (both psychological and physical) is often greater than that from those outside the family. After all, Mystique refers to being "afraid to go to school as a child" in *X-Men*, while in *X-Men 3* she admits that "My family tried to kill me." Ultimately, Angel does escape from the threat of forced conversion and later even shows his father the kindness his father could not show him by saving him from Magneto's attack.

In these examples, The X-Men films take part in an exploration of difference, marginalization, and identity that can be closely mapped to queer identity and the struggles those identities have had with hegemonic, normative culture. The films also reflect the advances that have been made in the area of LGBT Civil Rights in a number of ways.

In an early scene of *X-Men*, Jean Grey speaks to Congress about mutation, attempting to educate the senators in attendance about the abstract concept of mutation as well as the lived experience of mutants who have revealed themselves to society. She says, "It is a fact that mutants who have come forward and revealed themselves publicly have been met with fear, hostility and violence." In response, Senator Kelly uses fearmongering tactics to scare those in attendance into supporting his Mutant Registration Act, ignoring the plight of those mutants Jean mentions who have been threatened and instead constructing an Other that is to be feared. Those familiar with the trajectory and specifics of the development of LGBT rights over the past 50 years will immediately notice the parallels, as LGBT Americans were subjected to similar rhetoric while seeking the benefits of full citizenship, free from discrimination under the law. Crusaders in and outside of government, like Senator Kelly, recall anti-gay crusaders from recent history who, often misunderstanding or misrepresenting LGBT issues, fought for the disenfranchisement of queer Americans. William Earnest likens Kelly to crusaders such as Anita Bryant and Jesse Helms who used their power and visibility to stave off the advancement of LGBT rights (Earnest, 2007, p. 221).

In 1993, after heated debates in congress, President Bill Clinton enacted the Don't Ask Don't Tell policy, which dictated that servicemembers serving in the US Armed Forces could not be fired for being gay but that they were also not allowed to publicly reveal their sexual orientation. Continuing until its repeal in 2011, the policy resulted in a forced "closeting" of gay and lesbian Marines, soldiers, sailors, and airmen and was the subject of numerous debates in and outside of government surrounding "military readiness" and whether sexual orientation was a negative factor during warfare. Although not an obvious focus of the metaphoric treatment of LGBT issues in the X-Men films, there are moments worth noting where the underlying historical reality of the policy and the debates surrounding it appear.

The X-Men films explore this policy and its impact on LGBT servicemembers once again through the mutant metaphor. In one deleted scene from *Days of Future Past*, Mystique refers to those mutants serving in the armed forces by saying "I can hide like you, but what about those who can't? It's hard to hide your powers when you're getting shot at" a familiar fear for those who chose to serve during the Don't Ask, Don't Tell policy. In *First Class*, the first iteration of the X-Men team is formed as a covert arm of the CIA. In their training and their service in this capacity, they are subjected to discriminatory treatment by other agents yet take their duty seriously, to great sacrifice in the final battle to avert nuclear war. These examples serve to highlight how the real-world LGBT experience intersected (and to some degree still intersects) with service to country. Finally, to comic effect, in relation to the struggle to hides one's difference while participating in government service, in *First Class*, after being accidentally "outed" by Charles, Hank says "You didn't ask, so I didn't tell."[16]

While political policies and issues such as those discussed earlier have been at the forefront of discussions of LGBT equality in the 21st century, in the movement for LGBT equality, one of the more recent conversations that has taken place in the public sphere has been over the rights and identities of the transgender community. Just as the visibility of transgender people in popular media has risen (in the form of openly trans actors and trans characters in film and television), in the halls of state and federal government, the ability of transgender Americans to live their truths has been debated. One of the primary forms that conversation has taken is the debate over the right for transpeople to use the bathroom that corresponds to their gender identity. The discourses of those opposed align with similar discourses on mutancy in the X-Men universe, with references to them being deviant or as having ulterior motives. Just like debates over gays and lesbians entering the public sphere 20–30 years earlier, the current political and cultural arguments center on the fear of interlopers into a gendered space and a general misunderstanding of what it is at the heart of the difference they fear.

From the perspective of transpeople in the current cultural moment, the general concept of mutancy and difference and the misunderstandings and discrimination that come with it can provide a parallel with which to relate. In the newest films, mutants like Mystique can take any form, and early on in the more recent films she chooses to appear "normal" due to societal pressure from Charles to fit in. But, through her own character arc, she discovers that her blue form, even though it may not be readily accepted by the public at large, is her truest self. Because for many transpeople, their struggle is to reconcile an internal understanding of who they are with an outward appearance read by the outside world in a specific way, the figure of Mystique is a particularly powerful one. Despite societal pressure to be something she is not, she takes the more difficult road in order to be her true self.

Mystique's positioning as a particularly salient metaphor for the transgender community takes on additional meaning in a scene from *X-Men 3*. Captured, in an interrogation room, the agent calls her by the name Raven.

"I don't answer to my slave name," she responds, giving a glimpse of the power of names and naming in questions of identity in general, especially in transgender identity. The agent responds "Raven Darkholme. That's your real name. Isn't it?" in a condescending tone revealing that he is asking a question he thinks he knows the answer to and is using naming as a tool of power. This reflects the reality of transpeople who are often misnamed and misgendered by those in a privileged position of power in order to put them in their place, remind them that they are less than, or marginalized.

In these examples, we have examined how the X-Men films have explored issues related to LGBT realities of the 21st century in a metaphorical or symbolic manner, but beginning with the source material comics, the X-Men have also provided a vehicle not only for symbolic exploration of queer identity but also for more overt representations of queerness in the pages of X-Men comics and in the X-Men filmic universe. Given the polyvalent mutant metaphor, it is not surprising that, as societal acceptance of homosexuality and other queer identities became more widespread, the diverse team of mutants would also see openly queer identified mutants join the team or come out. The first superhero of any type to reveal their sexuality was Northstar, a member of the Canadian branch of the X-Men in Alpha Flight #106 (1992). Northstar's revelation that he was gay was groundbreaking for his visibility, and the character's significance persisted, and 20 years later he became the first queer superhero to get married in Marvel's first same-sex wedding (Peeples, 2016). The marginal nature of the first gay X-Man was not insignificant, and although there have been countless X-Men in teams and titles from all of the world, the number of openly gay mutants has remained small and relatively marginal in scope. In addition to a few less central characters (Anole, Shatterstar, Rictor, Bloke, Morph) who have expressed some form of queer identity in the X-Men comics, until recently the only central characters who had come out as LGBT were from alternate universes and Earths such as Colossus from the "Ultimate" Universe, Beast in a parallel Earth, and an alternate universe version of Wolverine (Peeples, 2016). However, this changed when, in 2015, Iceman came out as gay, becoming the first central X-Man to identify as gay (Gustines, 2018).

Although there have been queer mutants in the comics for more than 25 years now, it has taken a little longer for there to be an openly queer X-Man on film. Although the character of Deadpool in the comics is pansexual (with expressed crushes on male superheroes like Spider-Man), it is a different character introduced in his eponymous film that is the more significant (Fleenor, 2018). *Deadpool* (2016) introduced the character of Negasonic Teenage Warhead to the X-Men universe, and in the sequel *Deadpool 2*, she became one half of the first LGBT superhero couple on film.

Fear of the mutant "other"

American culture in the post 9/11 period holds two contradictory concepts in its hand at the same time: that of the "melting pot" that indicates that we are all Americans no matter where we came from – especially when constructed around a patriotic imperative – and an "us vs. them" mentality that projects a fear of the (non-white, straight, Christian) Other. These contradictory perspectives problematize the patriotism and "coming together" that was a result of the terrorist attacks, raising questions such as: who does "us" refer to in "us vs. them"? The signifier of "American" should be, based on our founding concepts, polyvalent and multi-representational, but when faced with a (real and existential) threat from the outside, which had not been the case in many generations, the fear of the "other" manifested and took on a more concrete form (Muslim, Middle Eastern, brown, Other). The X-Men films, through the mutant metaphor, explore the "us vs. them" construction that surfaces or strengthens post 9/11 and in the US context most often takes the form of islamophobia or other anti-Muslim sentiment.

In the wake of the terrorist attacks of 9/11, the US saw a swift uptick in incidents of anti-Muslim bias and violence, along with violence and hate directed at any marginalized group that could be construed to be Muslim or Middle Eastern by their dress, skin tone, or other visual identifier.[17] This is not to say that there was no anti-Muslim bias in the country before 9/11 but rather that the reaction to the attacks resulted in a focused hate and animosity as Americans sought out an outlet for their fear and anger at the attack on American soil. Distrust and fear were common unifying forces in discourses surrounding terrorism, and the symbolic themes established by the films in the X-Men franchise connect to this fear of the "Other" but do not strengthen the black and white dichotomy of good versus an outside force of evil that had been the symbolic discourse of previous foreign wars. A hallmark of the "War on Terror" instead is a much more nebulous and uncertain struggle with an enemy not exclusively linked to a hostile foreign power. To this end, the struggle that the X-Men have with the Brotherhood seems to rest on an ideological difference but is much more nuanced and complex. This is especially true given the historical background of the Brotherhood's leader, Magneto.

Defined by their heroic status, which is tied to the refusal to kill or harm others when at all possible, it is not difficult to argue that the X-Men are super heroic. But for every superhero and superhero team, there must be a supervillain and/or supervillain team, and that team is, ostensibly, the Brotherhood of Evil Mutants. This rivalry is established very early on in the original run of the comics, and the Brotherhood is the primary antagonist of the X-Men in the first three films of the trilogy.[18] However, it is established fairly early on in the films that beyond being a monolithic evil force, the Brotherhood is guided by a moral and ethical philosophy that is not of violence and destruction for violence and destruction's sake but rather as a reaction to oppression and violence against mutant kind. Their methods and tactics are clearly established as outside the acceptable super heroic order, yes, but by highlighting the hate and oppression that exists in the X-Men universe from almost the very first scene of the first film, it makes it difficult for audiences to view the "enemies" of the X-Men as a purely evil force.[19] The ambiguity of the "evil" nature of the Brotherhood creates a space to question old modes of "good" and "evil." The redefinition of the superhero's antagonist(s) for the 21st century is a hallmark of the superhero film during the height of their popularity and allows for new approaches to understanding the "enemy" in the 21st century War on Terror,[20] because in this structural framework, the enemy or "Them" as "Other" becomes overly reductive, as it conflates all of the one group with a few bad individuals/smaller group. When the binary of "us" vs. "them" no longer works to explain the more complex geopolitical landscape that emerges post 9/11, then there also arises a concomitant need to *understand* the "Other" so often maligned and misrepresented in the general cultural sphere.

In the comics, other Marvel heroes fought Communists[21] overtly, but the X-Men of the comics fought "the proxy of evil mutants" who could have stood in for the enemy of the time of those comics, the communists, as well. But, when these same villains are uncoupled from the specificity of the Cold War context, they are now are able to represent a wider variety of ideological, political, and social ills. In the early comics, Magneto and his Brotherhood of Evil Mutants were presented in ways that clearly connected them to the Cold War preoccupation with Communism. If Magneto is established as a Cold War metaphor, as the clear enemy against the benevolent X-Men, his role is complicated when removed from his originating context. Now, in filmic portrayal, Magneto is no longer a monolithically evil representative of a foreign superpower. Instead, he is a former friend, a victim of discrimination, and an individual with a complex driving philosophy that is simultaneously morally bankrupt (in his desire to murder *Homo sapiens*) but also reactive to his position as a multiply marginalized individual (Jewish, mutant).

Additionally, the X-Men themselves are a group of people "outside of reality" whose conditions automatically pull them into a liminal space – not human but in a human culture. Post 9/11 – this status creates questions about how we define and understand who "we" are and what makes us so. Are we a product of our culture? The X-Men are all parts of their home cultures, but they are pulled from it, so they are simultaneously *of* somewhere else both culturally and biologically and don't quite fit in any place. Coupled with the muddying of the concept of the "supervillain" this leaves open an interpretive space to better interrogate and unpack the more complex issues that are viewed as a threat by US culture in this period.

Although the threat that is faced in the early trilogy is portrayed in a way that seems to universalize the positions presented in the films of right and wrong and good vs. evil, there are other mechanisms at play that seem to counter a universalizing force and instead anchor the struggle in a more political sphere. In *X-Men*, Senator Kelly says, "We're Americans. Let the rest of the world deal with mutants in their own way." This quote makes the mutant "problem" expressly political, not "universal". If the argument for mutancy as a threat to the world was free from politics, then it would be important for the government to seek international consensus (like Human Rights abuses now where all civilized nations agree on what crosses the line). Here, there is no universal understanding of the mutant "threat," so that re-frames the conflict as a purely political one rooted in identity politics. The explicit political connection to the reaction to the mutant threat is furthered by the appearance at various times in the films of protesters. Initially, the protesters are exercising their free speech by reacting to the fear of the mutant threat, but later the representations of protests change to include both sides. Humans protest for "Human Rights" and mutants and those friendly to them protest against things like the mutant "cure." These protests echo tea party rallies against Obama, White Nationalist rallies now, and other 21st-century rallies and protests where dominant groups protest losing rights they are not really at threat of losing.

One final way that the filmic X-Men provide a new perspective for understanding the concepts of "evil" and "enemy" in the post 9/11 context is in the interactions between some of the mutant heroes themselves. The X-Men try tirelessly to assimilate, looking for a place in the world and seeking the path of least resistance, becoming super heroic in their deeds to save the world both human and mutant alike. These deeds render them legible to the culture (they do good), a culture that understands superheroes as a concept but does not quite know what to do with "mutants," and mitigates their "othered" status. This work to make themselves legible to their culture as heroes is clearest in *Deadpool* and *Deadpool 2* as the titular character repeatedly rejects invitations to join the X-Men because of his unwillingness to follow their (heroic) code of ethics, more specifically their dictate to not kill.[22] In this rejection, Deadpool serves as a sort of symbolic bridge between the two divides, even further complicating the understanding of what it means to be "good" or "evil." In the other X-men films there are mutants who are coded as "good" mutants (the X-Men) and "evil" mutants (the Brotherhood, though as discussed earlier, even this is problematic), and the X-Men code is clearly established. But Deadpool is not "evil." He is, after all, the headliner of two blockbuster superhero films. Deadpool kills people, though, positioning him outside the moral/ethical structure that defines what it is to be an X-Man and is what keeps him from permanently joining the team, as he is invited to do on various occasions. This ambiguity aligns with the more nuanced geopolitical environment post 9/11. The films establish what mutant "goodness" looks like, so when Deadpool as a mutant who does good things cannot ascribe to the moral/ethical super heroic heart of the mutant team, the idea of what is "good" is complicated now, leaving this question hanging for audiences to interpret and understand.

Mutants and the legacy of 9/11

Up until this point in our analysis of the X-Men films as representative of a variety of issues that occupy the thoughts and preoccupations of Americans in the beginning part of the 21st century, we have relied heavily on the mutant metaphor as a symbolic representation of issues surrounding a number of marginalized communities and as a means of understanding the more complex construction of the concept of "enemy" in the new modes of the "War on Terror." There are, however, a number of moments in the X-Men films that seem to invoke the attacks of 9/11 in a much more direct way.

An important space for a majority of the heroes of the Marvel universe, New York City is also the primary physical localization of the terrorist attacks and figures prominently in a number of the X-Men films, initially as symbolic of American values and later in a sort of visual citation that seems to invoke the attacks themselves. At the end of *X-Men*, New York City is threatened by Magneto and his team. Although this is the one film of the franchise that premiered before 9/11, the centrality of NYC as a symbol of America and American ideals is key to Magneto's threat and is also that which made it a target of the terrorists on 9/11. It is not accidental, then, that many of the locations for the final showdown of the films have a symbolic purpose tied to the representation of American ideals. The Statue of Liberty of *X-Men* is the ultimate symbol of freedom and liberty, while the Golden Gate Bridge of *X-Men 3* is a symbol of access, progress, and hope. The beach in Cuba at the end of *First Class* represents the success of American diplomacy in a time when the enemy was much more clearly defined yet could be dealt with on the diplomatic plane, and the White House of *Days of Future Past* is symbolic of the leadership position of the US (though choosing the Nixon White House does problematize that understanding of leadership and respect on a more global scale).[23]

The final battle at the White House is an especially poignant scene in the post 9/11 context, especially given the established symbolic meanings of the other elements involved in the attack. In this series of scenes, Magneto uses a baseball stadium (the ultimate symbol of American culture) to create a barrier around the White House, which he then damages badly in his attempt to assassinate Bolivar Trask. Beyond the symbolic nature of an attack of this nature, by showing a badly damaged White House, it is impossible not to draw connections to the failed attempt on 9/11 to attack the White House. The "terrorist" Magneto literally envelops the "People's House" with Americanness while directly threatening the American executive branch.

Magneto is established as the primary antagonist and closest analog for the threat of terrorism but, as discussed earlier, his enemy status is constructed in a more nuanced way that problematizes a direct symbolic connection with the threat of terrorists in the 21st century. There are, however, a number of ways the films attempt to underscore Magneto's role as "terrorist" in our contemporary understanding of the word. One way is through Magneto's use of mass media. In *X-Men 3*, Magneto goes on TV and threatens the world directly, and at the end of *Days of Future Past*, he acts similarly, saying "You built these weapons to destroy us. Why? Because you are afraid of our gifts. Because we are different. Humanity has always feared that which is different. Well, I'm here to tell you, you're right to fear us. We are the future." These moments rhetorically tie Magneto to real world terrorists like Osama Bin Laden who record threats to the world to be broadcast to the world.[24]

In the use of media, the X-Men films also provide a commentary on memory and how we think about national/international incidents such as terrorist attacks. "Footage" visuals anchor the events of both *First Class* and *Days of Future Past* in a historical moment by evoking nostalgia/memory. This serves to comment on how our interaction with international "incidents" of all types are constructed from pieces of news footage in the modern era. Watching when something happens, in the modern age, we are "glued to the TV" to hear the reporters and officials calm us and explain to us. This footage in the films evokes this mode of interacting with the contemporary threats of the world and renders the reaction of the world to these events legible to a post 9/11 audience. Furthering the establishment of the mode, immediately following the revelation of mutants in *Days of Future Past*, there is a scene where a nurse shares her opinion, talking about it in a way of establishing a communal connection with others as a way to understand and unpack the gravity of a major global event.

Conclusion

The X-Men films can provide a window into a more complex conceptualization of the idea of the "Other," allowing audiences to better unpack and understand the nuances of a non-hegemonic "Other" group. By transporting this discussion and analytical process to the world of superhero fantasy, the abstract arguments about fear of that which is different can occur free from the triggering specific references to gender issues, global Islamic terrorism, domestic racial tension, or homophobia.

The global political climate saw the US's professed moral guideposts tested as the superpower fought back against an enemy that presented itself in novel ways. Like the superpowered mutants of the X-Men universe, *how* one uses real power is at the core of the X-Men mythos and parallels the constant self-reflection many Americans dealt with in the aftermath of 9/11. As a global superpower, responding to the attacks was a clear, expected response, but *how* would the US use that power? Would Peter Parker's Uncle Ben's admonition of "With great power, comes great responsibility" ring true, or would the nation be guided more by vengeance and retribution (a la Batman, the Punisher, and many more)? The moral issues and conundrums that appear in the X-Men films make a case for power, mitigated by a clear moral compass, at times instructing the American people how to move forward and at other times criticizing its government for allowing rage and revenge to obscure its morality and professed ideals. To this end, the X-Men films utilize the mutant metaphor to rhetorically represent the struggles of the marginalized in general and the specific plights of those marginalized for their gender, race, sexual orientation, gender identity, or religion. Of all of the superhero films studied in this volume, the X-Men films are the most prolific, and although each film differs in the specific elements that dictate the narrative of each iteration, the symbolic through line of the films reveals that in the face of hate, violence, and discrimination, those that take a stand to combat it can "save the world," a message that in today's turbulent times is more necessary than ever.

Notes

1 John Darowski (2014) points out that the comic did not embrace the mutant as metaphor for the Civil Rights movement until later in its initial run in part because of the makeup of the team. "Part of the problem undoubtedly would have been the challenge of having five middle-to-upper class WASP-ish teenagers serve as a commentary on the great minority struggle of the day" (p. 26).
2 For additional reading on these themes, see Norman (2014).
3 "Self-sacrifice is presented as a redeeming quality in powerful women" (Cook Overton et al., 2016, p. 125).
4 In an earlier scene, Logan had kissed Jean, and she rejected his advance out of devotion to Scott.
5 In the comics, Mystique is, like all other heroes, always drawn with clothes. Her costumes are various levels of revealing, depending on the era and the artist drawing her, but the choice by the creative team of the first film to portray her with no clothing had no basis on the original source material.
6 For an extensive study of the feminist project of the X-Men comics, see Fawaz (2016).
7 Charles does not get a complete pass in his command to Jean to "Let go." He is, after all, commanding her as her leader and mentor, in some ways wielding her as a weapon like Magneto does at the end of *X-Men 3*. The distinction is in the function of those powers in the film to a positive end. Additionally, immediately following this moment, Charles returns the memories he took from Moira MacTaggert at the end of *First Class*, a reminder that the Professor often uses his powers for what he thinks is best, even though he often later regrets doing so. He says "I'm sorry. I should never have taken these from you," an echo of his apology to Mystique at the end of *Days of Future Past*: "I've been trying to control you since the day we met and look where that's got us. Everything that happens now is in your hands. I have faith in you, Raven."
8 Of the 12 films that are part of the X-Men cinematic universe, seven of them feature Wolverine as a central protagonist, while in two others, he makes a cameo (in *First Class*, a very brief one, and in *Apocalypse* a longer, more significant one).
9 Logan's dog tags are literal markers of his identity – it is how the audience first learns his name, and they serve as symbolic representations of his identity: he gives them to Rogue to hold onto in *X-Men* so he will always be with her, and he symbolically leaves them behind with the body of Col. Stryker at the end of *X-Men 2* as he leaves that portion of his life behind, armed with a new purpose and restored memories.
10 Laboratories and experimentation play an important part in a number of the X-Men films and are a central example of the manifestation of the fear of *Homo sapiens* that *Homo superior* is either a threat to their existence or a means to gaining an advantage in preparation for global warfare. In *X-Men 2, X-Men Origins: Wolverine*, and *X-Men: Apocalypse*, these experiments are squarely centered around the US Military's desire to take advantage of mutation to win wars, despite the toll that that experimentation may take on mutants. They are, after all, not human in the eyes of the extremists like Stryker in charge of the experiments. Once Stryker specifically learns that converting mutants to weapons is too risky an operation because of the threat of their retaining their free will, he attempts to destroy them all in a mutant genocide. In *Logan*, with the mutant population dwindling, the same hegemonic forces come back around, and the ubiquitous laboratories in these films are now re-tasked with creating mutants by genetic manipulation and cloning.

X-Men 3 sees a different lab representative of the private sector that uses the scientific mode to "help" mutants who want to cure themselves of mutation but eventually become appropriated by the military industrial complex to weaponize the cure to aid in the fight between mutants and humans.

11 Wolverine's berserker rage is a trope utilized in superhero comics when a hero, usually a loner, slips into a violent, trance like state and is capable of fending off a much higher number of enemies than in a normal state.

12 This is further problematized by the fact that in their representations in the films, the brotherhood is the much more ethnically diverse group (who are ultimately killed and defeated).

13 A quote from Lincoln's first inaugural address are the first words of X2 after the opening credits sequence, recited in front of Lincoln's portrait in the White House: "We are not enemies, but friends. We must not be enemies. Though passion may have strained, it must not break the bonds of our affection." This seems to establish Lincoln and his efforts to bring divergent, disparate groups together as a significant symbolic figure early on in the X-Men film franchise.

14 See Freud (1955).

15 After being consistently criticized by numerous scientific and psychological organizations, the practice of reparative "conversion" therapy has decreased dramatically in the recent past, with one of the largest proponents of the practice, Exodus International, which was founded in 1976, ceasing operation in 2013, and the practice has been outlawed in a number of states. The harmful psychological effects of the discredited practice have been explored in the book *Boy Erased* and its 2018 film adaptation. See Conley (2016).

16 In what is, perhaps, representative of the ability that LGBT servicepeople have to serve more openly, in *Dark Phoenix* (2019), the X-Men team is known to the government and the public, and in the early portion of the film, is revered by both as heroes who step in and save the day when no one else can. The marginalized, mutant team, hunted, demonized, and discriminated against in past films, is allowed to "serve" openly. This open "service" is further underscored by the fact that the film takes place in the early 1990s, the precise time in US history when the debate over open LGBT service was taking place.

17 For an in-depth study of post 9/11 anti-Muslim bias, see: Cainkar (2009).

18 Although chronologically speaking the Brotherhood of Evil Mutants appears much earlier, as the antagonists in this more complex iteration of the mutant metaphor, it is difficult not to be reminded of the Muslim Brotherhood, which furthers the rhetorical connection to the supervillain team.

19 A young Magneto is the first mutant seen on film, and his trauma in the Nazi Concentration Camps immediately creates a sympathy in the audience, coloring the adult villain throughout. If audiences feel Magneto's anguish and pain, his plans and methods, while objectively evil and wrong, are nonetheless understandable on some level by audiences.

20 See our discussion on the exploration of "good" vs. "evil" in the Batman franchise in Chapter 1.

21 See Captain America, Chapter 2.

22 This makes him a queer character beyond the pansexuality outlined earlier in large part because he actively refuses the mutant "status quo" by choosing to occupy a more liminal space that is neither hero nor villain. The character seems to be motivated by love and a need to help people, but he does so through wonton violence and murder. This queers his character by actively challenging the dichotomy of "good" superhero or "evil" villain.

23 Although *Dark Phoenix* (2019) has its final battle take place on a train in a nondescript forest, the original ending before studio takeover issues interfered was supposed to take place in New York, outside the United Nations building, likely a deliberate choice for its diplomatic symbolism. (O'Connell, 2019).

24 In *X-Men 3*, a scene where the joint chiefs and the president watch the attack on the Brotherhood's encampment evokes a number of images of political and military leaders guiding a targeted attack on terrorism, including the iconic picture taken of the Situation room during the raid that eliminated Osama Bin Laden.

Bibliography

Bucciferro, Claudia. "Introduction." In *The X-Men Films: A Cultural Analysis*. Ed. Claudia Bucciferro. Lanham, MD: Rowman and Littlefield, 2016. pp. ix–xxii.

Cainkar, Louis A. *Homeland Insecurity: The Arab American and Muslim American Experience After 9/11*. New York City, NY: Russell Sage Foundation, 2009.

Cocca, Carolyn. "Containing the X-Women." In *The X-Men Films: A Cultural Analysis*. Ed. Claudia Bucciferro. Lanham, MD: Rowman and Littlefield, 2016. pp. 79–91.

Conley, Garrard. *Boy Erased: A Memoir of Identity, Faith, and Family*. New York: Riverhead Books, 2016.

Cook Overton, Barbara, Athena de Pré, Loretta L. Pecchioni, and John H. Overton. "The Curious Case of 'Dr.' Jean Grey, Mystique, and Mariko." In *The X-Men Films: A Cultural Analysis*. Ed. Claudia Bucciferro. Lanham, MD: Rowman and Littlefield, 2016. pp. 121–134.

Dark Phoenix. Dir. Simon Kinberg. 20th Century Fox, 2019.

Darowski, John. "'Evil Mutants Will Stop at Nothing to Gain Control of Mankind!': X-Men, Communists and Cold War Containment Culture." In *The Ages of the X-Men: Essays on the Children of the Atom in Changing Times*. Ed. Joseph J. Darowski. Jefferson, NC: McFarland, 2014. pp. 17–29.

Darowski, Joseph J. *X-Men and the Mutant Metaphor: Race and Gender in the Comic Books*. Lanham, MD: Rowman & Littlefield, 2014.

Deadpool. Dir. Tim Miller. 20th Century Fox, 2016.

Deadpool 2. Dir. David Leitch. 20th Century Fox, 2018.

DeBrandt, Don. "Parallel Evolution." In *The Unauthorized X-Men: SF and Comic Writers on Mutants, Prejudice and Adamantium*. Ed. Len Wein. Dallas: BenBella, 2005. pp. 113–122.

DiPaolo, Marc. *War, Politics and Superheroes: Ethics and Propaganda in Comics and Film*. Jefferson, NC: McFarland, 2011.

Donaldson James, Susan. "Mormon 'Gay Cure' Study Used Electric Shocks Against Homosexual Feelings." *ABC News*, March 30, 2011. https://abcnews.go.com/Health/mormon-gay-cures-reparative-therapies-shock-today/story?id=13240700.

Earnest, William. "Making Gay Sense of the X-Men." In *Uncovering Hidden Rhetorics: Social Issues in Disguise*. Thousand Oaks, CA: Sage Publications, 2007. pp. 215–232.

Fawaz, Ramzi. *The New Mutants: Superheroes and the Radical Imagination of American Comics*. New York: New York University Press, 2016.

Fleenor, S.E. "The History of Deadpool's Pansexuality." *SyFyWire*, June 1, 2018. www.syfy.com/syfywire/the-history-of-deadpools-pansexuality.

Freud, Sigmund. "The Psycho-genesis of a Case of Homosexuality in a Woman." In *The Standard Edition of the Complete Psychological Works of Sigmund Freud*. Ed. and Trans. J. Strachey. Vol. 18. London: Hogarth Press, 1955. pp. 145–172 (Original work published in 1920).

Gustines, George Gene. "Iceman Came Out. Now He's Coming Back in His Own Series." *The New York Times*, June 28, 2018. www.nytimes.com/2018/06/28/books/iceman-new-comic-book-series.html.

Holmes, Adam. "Why Rogue Was Pulled Out of X-Men: Days of Future Past." *CinemaBlend*, 2015. www.cinemablend.com/new/Why-Rogue-Was-Pulled-Out-X-Men-Days-of-Future-Past-72508.html.

Howe, Sean. *Marvel Comics: The Untold Story.* New York: Harper Collins, 2012.

Liu, R.T. and B. Mustanski. "Suicidal Ideation and Self-harm in Lesbian, Gay, Bisexual, and Transgender Youth." *American Journal of Preventive Medicine*, Vol. 42, No. 3, March 2012. pp. 221–228.

Logan. Dir. James Mangold. 20th Century Fox, 2017.

Lyubansky, Mikhail. "Prejudice Lessons from the Xavier Institute." In *The Psychology of Superheroes: An Unauthorized Exploration*, Eds. Robin S. Rosenberg with Jennifer Canzoneri. Dallas: BenBella Books, 2008. pp. 75–90.

Nama, Adilifu. "Color Them Black." In *The Superhero Reader*. Eds. Charles Hatfield, Jeet Heer, and Kent Worcester. Jackson, MS: University Press of Mississippi, 2013. pp. 252–268.

Norman, Christian. "Mutating Metaphors: Addressing the Limits of Biological Narratives of Sexuality." In *The Ages of the X-Men: Essays on the Children of the Atom in Changing Times*. Ed. Joseph J. Darowski. Jefferson, NC: McFarland, 2014. pp. 165–177.

O'Connell, Sean. "Original Dark Phoenix Ending Included Skrulls and a 'Huge' New York Battle, According to Tye Sheridan." *CinemaBlend*, June 10, 2019. www.cinemablend.com/news/2474641/original-dark-phoenix-ending-included-skrulls-and-a-huge-new-york-battle-according-to-tye-sheridan.

Peeples, Jase. "11 Uncanny Gay and Bisexual X-Men." *Queerty*, May 27, 2016. www.queerty.com/11-uncanny-gay-bisexual-x-men-20160527.

Roberts, Adam. "Lee, Kirby and Ovid's Metamorphoses." In *The Unauthorized X-Men: SF and Comic Writers on Mutants, Prejudice and Adamantium*. Ed. Len Wein. Dallas: BenBella, 2005. pp. 139–151.

Simon, William and John H. Gagnon. "Homosexuality: The Formulation of a Sociological Perspective." *Journal of Health and Social Behavior*, Vol. 8, No. 3, September 1967. pp. 177–185.

Singer, Marc. "'Black Skins' and White Masks: Comic Books and the Secret of Race." *African American Review*, Vol. 36, No. 1, 2002. pp. 107–119.

Skir, Robert N. "X-ing the Rubicon." In *The Unauthorized X-Men: SF and Comic Writers on Mutants, Prejudice and Adamantium*. Ed. Len Wein. Dallas: BenBella, 2005. pp. 19–28.

Smith, Jason. "Mutating Minorities: White Racial Framing and Group Positioning." In *The X-Men Films: A Cultural Analysis*. Ed. Claudia Bucciferro. Lanham, MD: Rowman and Littlefield, 2016. pp. 179–192.

Taylor, Melanie A. "'The Masculine Soul Heaving in the Female Bosom': Theories of Inversion and The Well of Loneliness." *Journal of Gender Studies*, Vol. 7, No. 3, 1998. pp. 287–296.

Trushell, John M. "American Dreams of Mutants: The X-Men – 'Pulp' Fiction, Science Fiction, and Superheroes." *Journal of Popular Culture*, Vol. 38, No. 1, 2004. pp. 149–168.

West, Cornel. "The New Cultural Politics of Difference." In *The Cultural Studies Reader*. Ed. Simon During. London: Routledge, 1993. pp. 203–204.

Weston, Kath. *Families We Choose: Lesbians, Gays, Kinship.* New York: Columbia University Press, 1991.

The Wolverine. Dir. James Mangold. 20th Century Fox, 2013.

Wright, Bradford W. *Comic Book Nation: The Transformation of Youth Culture in America.* Baltimore: Johns Hopkins University Press, 2001.

X2: X-Men United. Dir. Bryan Singer. 20th Century Fox, 2003.

X-Men. Dir. Bryan Singer. 20th Century Fox, 2000.

X-Men: Apocalypse. Dir. Bryan Singer. 20th Century Fox, 2016.

"X-Men." *BoxOfficeMojo.* www.boxofficemojo.com/franchises/chart/?id=xmen.htm.

X-Men: Days of Future Past. Dir. Bryan Singer. 20th Century Fox, 2014.

X-Men: First Class. Dir. Matthew Vaughn. 20th Century Fox, 2011.

X-Men: The Last Stand. Dir. Brett Ratner. 20th Century Fox, 2006.

X-Men Origins: Wolverine. Dir. Gavin Hood. 20th Century Fox, 2009.

Zingsheim, Jason. 2016. "Shape-Shifting Identity: Mystique's Embodied Agency." In *The X-Men Films: A Cultural Analysis*. Ed. Claudia Bucciferro. Lanham, MD: Rowman and Littlefield. p. 101.

Conclusion

In the various and varied iterations of the Spider-Man origin story, young Peter Parker is confronted with the words of his Uncle Ben: "With great power, comes great responsibility." Through these words, Peter finds his heroic path, seeking to use his powers to help ordinary people in his neighborhood and his city. In the years that followed the terrorist attacks of 9/11, the American public was faced with the task of reflecting on its place in the world and the ways in which the country had used the privileged position in its interactions on the global stage. The reactions and developments that arose from this catastrophic and horrific event were simultaneously both overt and political (War in Iraq and Afghanistan, Patriot Act, new regulations and legislation) and more subtle and cultural (patriotic displays, terrorism as film and television theme, "freedom fries"), but whether in the grander geopolitical realm or the realm of popular culture, the impact of the attacks reverberated through all aspects of American life.

When asked about the rise in escapist films after 9/11, Don Hahn, a Disney producer, points to the need for escapist entertainment saying, "We'd rather be entertained and movies can take us away from that and have us escape from that . . . Maybe that's why we are seeing so many super-hero movies, so many 'Captain America', 'Iron Man,' because those characters can defeat bad guys" ("Hollywood shies away . . ."). We have explored here, however, that these superhero films serve a function to audiences beyond just a two hour respite from the real world. They allow audiences to approach issues and ideas in a more abstract way, challenging them to process the myriad and complicated concepts that are now an ever-present part of American life in the 21st century.

In this study, we have chosen some of the more significant films of this era to analyze in an attempt at better understanding how superhero films over the last almost 20 years have tackled the issues of contemporary American culture. However, the films that we chose to focus our study on represent only a portion of the numerous superhero texts produced over the past two decades. Given this proliferation, it would be impossible to tackle every superhero film, television program, and comic exploring contemporary, relevant cultural issues. There are, however, a few additional films and television programs worth noting here, as we conclude, which continue the threads that we have explored here.

In his chapter exploring the superhero comic book response to the 9/11 attacks, "Spider-Man at Ground Zero," Bradford Wright describes a comics scene of Spider-Man looking at the ruins of Ground Zero and calls it "one of the most shocking images ever to appear in a comic book; shocking, because it is real" (Wright, 2003, p. 287). Marvel Comics' choice to use the character in this way was likely due in large part to the hero's close connection to New York City. Many Marvel heroes are either based in New York or spend significant amounts of time there, but the "Friendly Neighborhood Spider-Man" is the most closely associated with the city, as his powers have him clinging to skyscrapers and swinging through the various iconic parts of the Big Apple. So, when New York was attacked in the real world, Spider-Man's reaction was representative of the everyman's reaction. The filmic iterations of the character that have appeared in the years since the attack have not been as overt with ties to the real world attack, but, as we have seen in various other films we have studied here, the Spider-Man films serve a similar, though more abstract, purpose.

Spider-Man (2002) was the first major superhero film to be released after the terrorist attacks, and although filmmakers took the opposite approach from Marvel Comics by removing an advance trailer for the film that depicted Spider-Man capturing a helicopter full of bank robbers in a web between the Two Towers, the film and those that followed featured the city of New York prominently (Wright, 2003, p. 287). In these films, the superhero, representative of the regular "everyman," saves the citizens of New York City from the smallest petty crime to the largest supervillain, while also a student. The seven films featuring the character have featured the character exploring the joy of helping people, more so than any other superhero film, highlighting the importance of altruism and helping others in a dangerous world. Also significant is filmmakers' increasing focus over the years of the production of these films on the youth of the character, both in the storylines (the newer films are firmly anchored in high school melodrama) and in their casting increasingly younger actors to play the webslinger. Tom Holland's performances in standalone films and in the Avengers films as well seem to embody the spirit of millennial America. This Spider-Man is mentored by Tony Stark, and in that father/son type relationship the films explore generational shifts through dialogue that clearly portrays the character as much younger than the other heroes, while pointing the way forward for future generations as they mourn the losses of the past through Peter Parker's dealing with the loss of his mentor, Stark. As the first major arc in the Marvel Cinematic Universe comes to a close, looking forward to the future, Holland's Spider-Man is perhaps the most emblematic of how the youth of today must learn from their predecessors, while making their own way.

The grief that Peter Parker must deal with described earlier is one of many reactions tied to the processing of grief, loss, and trauma explored in the most recent *Avengers: Endgame* (2019). If *The Avengers* (2012) provided audiences with a symbolic attack on New York in which the heroes save the day, *Endgame* brings the heroic reaction down to a much more human level, in its portrayal of grief and loss. In the aftermath of *Avengers: Infinity War* (2018) in which half of the population of the universe is snapped out of existence by the villain Thanos, the remaining heroes are shown processing and dealing with grief in distinct ways. Black Widow takes up the mantle of leader and throws herself into her work, focusing exclusively on the job that she must do as the de facto leader of the team. Captain America, continuing the therapeutic role explored in *Civil War*, attends a grief counseling group where ordinary people process their losses by supporting each other in their grief. Thor becomes a hermit and seemingly allows his grief to make him withdraw from the world, resulting in a life of videogames, junk food, and beer. Tony Stark gives up the superhero life as well and retreats into family, moving to a remote area and raising his child with Pepper Potts. Hawkeye becomes a more ruthless version of his previous self, abandoning any moral code he had developed up until that point as he seeks out criminals and murders them for the being allowed to live when his family was snapped away. Although taken to the hyperbolic extreme, each of these reactions represents the varied real-world ways that people deal with extreme trauma and grief. By showing the superpowered examples of moral goodness and right each seeking out ways to process their own grief and trauma, audiences can be inspired to embrace their own healing processes from a variety of traumas both cultural and personal. Superheroes have always served as models of strength and morality, and in these particularly poignant scenes, they are shown to be, in essence, human as well.

When *Wonder Woman* premiered in 2017, the arrival of the first feature length superhero film centering around a female hero marked a significant shift in the superhero landscape due in large part to the female led creative team and the story of the film, which highlighted empowered femininity in ways theretofore unseen. While we have discussed extensively the ways that *Wonder Woman* explored issues of gender, feminism, and female power in the 21st century, these explorations did not stop with the Amazon Princess. With the release of *Captain Marvel* (2019), Marvel Studios continued this work by featuring the superpowered Captain, who is, arguably, one of the most powerful heroes in the Marvel universe, male or female. The significance of such a powerful figure standing out in a field dominated by men is further underscored in the film through Carol Danvers' back story, which anchors her development in the military context. Before being taken to space and trained as part of an intergalactic fighting force, Danvers is a pilot in the US Armed Forces, and the filmmakers make a point to demonstrate how she, as a female pilot, is not held back by her gender, even though aviation during the time of the film is a male dominated field. Her development as a pilot is guided by her mentor, Dr. Wendy Lawson (Annette Bening) and supported in her private life by other strong female allies. *Captain Marvel*, therefore, can be seen as continuing the work begun with *Wonder Woman*, which appears to be on track to continue with future sequels and other female centered superhero films.

Similarly to the development and explosion in popularity of superhero films in the past 20 years, the two major comics publishers, Marvel and DC, have simultaneously explored many of the same themes and ideas as their big budget films (and some new ones) in the various television programs based on the two super heroic universes. The nature of episodic television, where each week a new adventure awaits or where an aspect of a character can be developed and explored, coupled with the widespread prevalence of streaming media services, provides numerous opportunities for creative teams to create a wide variety of superhero stories for audiences. Although the blockbuster films may benefit from larger budgets and a wider audience, the nature of episodic television can allow for more flexibility in storytelling, and, since usually months separate the writing of an episode and its air date on TV instead of the years a film may take, superhero television can be more immediately relevant to changes or developments in societal issues. A few brief examples of how superhero television has taken up many of the themes and concerns dealt with on the big screen reveal that these programs, while providing ample opportunity for lighter entertainment, do attempt to deal with many of the same ideas as their big screen siblings.

In the area of gender, the *Supergirl* television series has taken deliberate steps to highlight women in all areas of the program. In a series centered around the younger cousin of the man of steel, Supergirl, the program places women in prominent positions, both good and bad, oftentimes subverting the more male centered tropes of the films and television programs focusing on Superman. Here, Supergirl grows up in a household full of women (her adopted father disappears during her youth) with a sister and adopted mother (played by big screen Supergirl Helen Slater) serving as her Earth family. When she is able to connect with her Kryptonian roots, it is her mother who visits her in a hologram to give her guidance. Kara's (Supergirl's alter ego) boss is a high-powered female media mogul, Cat Grant, and in later seasons, the director of the Department of Extra-Normal Operations is her adopted sister, working under a military general, also a woman. Even in the political realm of the show, the president of the US is a woman (played by former Wonder Woman, Lynda Carter). Even the hero's villains are predominantly female, with various evil Kryptonians, including her aunt and Lillian Luthor (mother to Lex). The foregrounding of powerful, important female characters in a show centered around a female hero allows the show to explore a variety of themes such as family, discrimination, gender inequity, healthcare, immigration, and many more. Furthering its apparent commitment to featuring stories centered around female heroes, the CW network will be premiering *Batwoman* in fall 2019.

When *Batwoman* premieres, the series will be the first superhero program or film centered around an LGBT character, as Kate Kane (Batwoman) is a Lesbian military vet who takes up the mantle of the bat to fight crime in Gotham City. How specifically the show will weave the Batman mythos into the adventures of Batwoman is yet to be seen, but featuring the character in this way brings issues around gender and sexuality to the forefront of super-hero media. Although *Batwoman* will be the first superhero program that features an LGBTQ+ character in its titular role, various superhero televi-sion programs have included LGBTQ+ heroes and allies in supporting roles. *Arrow's* Mr. Terrific is a gay hero, *Legends of Tomorrow's* White Canary is a lesbian, and *Supergirl* had the distinction in 2018 of presenting the first trans-gender superhero, Dreamer. Dreamer's storyline in particular was an example of how the fantastical world of super heroics can explore the often complex facets of LGBT identity in that the hero, an alien living on earth, gains her powers through matrilineal succession. On her planet, one woman in each generation of "Dreamers" inherits superpowers. When the powers skip the older sister of Nia, an open transwoman, the program underscores the idea that gender identity is not anchored in biology. The mystical inheritance that Nia is granted symbolically legitimizes her gender identity, sending a message that all gender identities should be respected and valued. The featuring of these LGBT characters in superhero television serves an important purpose in bringing these marginalized identities into the forefront. This is especially significant when viewed in contrast with superhero films of the same era, where the exploration of LGBTQ+ identities and experiences has been, to date, limited to the realm of the symbolic – as we have discussed here – or in very small measures.[1]

In addition to exploring issues of gender and LGBTQ+ identities, episodic superhero television has also continued the work being done in film in exam-ining other marginalized identities. DC's *Black Lightning* and Marvel's *Luke Cage* center these two superhero series on two of the more prominent black superheroes of the comics world. Each hero's primary mission in the two programs is to protect his respective city/neighborhood (the fictional Free-land and NYC's Harlem, respectively). These two programs place primacy on the challenges facing the African American community in the US today through a focus on racism, the broken criminal justice system, gentrification, poverty, family struggles, class, among others. The ideas and issues that can be explored in feature films in a more symbolic way are literally brought down to the more granular, detailed level, as both Black Lightning and Luke Cage fight oppression for the benefit of their neighbors, family, and friends.

Similarly, the more symbolic explorations of issues of disability in films such as the X-Men saga are made much more concrete and representational in superhero television programs such as *Daredevil* and *Doom Patrol*. In *Dare-devil*, the blind superhero protector of NYC's Hell's Kitchen straddles the two worlds of disability and superpowers while protecting the citizens of NYC both in his lawyer secret identity – Matt Murdock – and his super identity as Daredevil. In *Doom Patrol*, almost every hero on the superhero team struggles with some sort of "super" disability, including the wheelchair bound leader of the team, Dr. Niles Caulder, Rita Farr (Elasti-Woman) who suffers from crushing anxiety due to her difficulty in controlling her physical form, Kay Challis (Crazy Jane) who suffers from multiple personality disorder where each personality has a different superpower, Cliff Steele (Robotman) who survives a car crash only to have his brain implanted in a robot, and Larry Trainor (Negative Man) who must live life wrapped in bandages.[2] Each of these characters must come to terms with their bodily and psychological difference on an individual, personal level, while navigating a world that views them as freaks to be feared. Once again, hyperbolic superhero narrative provides audiences with a means to approach the complex lived experiences of various disabilities.

Superhero television provides an excellent platform for the exploration of various aspects of identity and the more immediate nature of these programs as far as their timeline, episodic structure, and ability to delve into more nuanced narratives, especially those of a more political nature. As mentioned earlier, objectively, *Supergirl* is the most politically grounded of the superhero television programs today, with the most recent season constructed around a commentary on immigration, xenophobia, authoritarian power, and the role of the media in the age of Trump. The series did this by centering the narrative of the show around an "Earth First" movement of humans whose lives had been impacted by the presence of aliens in the world. The parallels between the rise of the white nationalist movement in the US are obvious and intentional, with charismatic internet media personalities fomenting hate against all aliens based on the negative actions of the few and the appearance of the "Children of Liberty," masked humans who seek out to intimidate and commit acts of violence against aliens. Clearly characterized as the villains of the season, the anti-alien group and its leader, Agent Liberty, are supported by a large group of human citizens, with Agent Liberty even gaining legitimacy by being named Secretary of Alien Affairs by the president of the United States. The struggle that Supergirl and her allies face against a group that derives their animosity from real tragedy inflicted on them by aliens is clearly evocative of the current political movement where anti-immigrant sentiment is fomented by media personalities, legitimized by the president, and where those whose views are antithetical to the mission of certain agencies are named to be their head (EPA, Secretary of Education, etc.).

Superheroes have had a presence in popular media beyond their comics' source material since almost the beginning of their existence. The value in these stories for adaptation and interpretation in other media was an almost immediate result of their appearance on the American cultural landscape of the mid 20th century, with animated stories and live action serial films appearing first, soon followed by numerous animated television programs, live action episodic adventure shows, and a few notable examples of big budget feature films. In all of these examples before the turn of the 21st century, these programs and films were either completely marketed toward children and youth or promoted as nostalgic throwbacks to childhood for adults who might seek an escape with their favorite heroes. It is only recently, in the post 9/11 period, that American culture has embraced superhero media as a genre unto itself, providing audiences, many of whom have been introduced to superheroes for the first time through the numerous films and television programs, with rich source material from which to explore the complex social, political, and psychological realities of this period. With the billions earned to date, superhero media is most definitely here to stay, at least for the immediate future. If the narratives of the past 20 years are any indication, they will also likely continue to evolve and change, providing audiences with a commentary of their contemporary realities while entertaining audiences worldwide.

Notes

1 In the press buildup to *Avengers: Endgame*, co-director Joe Russo seemed to hint that the film would present Marvel's first LGBT hero (Megarry, 2019). However, once the film premiered it became quickly obvious that *Endgame* was not the platform for this. Instead, the film included a very brief appearance by an ancillary character who confessed to losing his male significant other in the snap during a therapy session led by Captain America. The resulting response to that nod to "diversity" without really attempting to break through that specific superhero barrier has been less than stellar, with many highlighting the various ways Marvel has failed to represent LGBTQ+ superhero visibility, in many cases filming scenes that did so and then removing them from final film cuts (Pollard, 2019).
2 Negative Man is also presented in flashbacks as secretly gay in his previous life as a pilot, providing the character with an intersectional identity to be explored.

Bibliography

"Hollywood Shies Away from 9/11-inspired Movies." *Agence France-Presse*, September 4, 2011. https://entertainment.inquirer.net/12201/hollywood-shies-away-from-911-inspired-movies#ixzz5pQnICTun.

Megarry, Daniel. "Could Avengers: Endgame Feature Marvel's First LGBTQ Superhero?." *Gay Times*, April 5, 2019. www.gaytimes.co.uk/culture/120712/could-avengers-endgame-feature-marvels-first-lgbtq-superhero/.

Pollard, Alexandra. "Marvel Doesn't Deserve a Pat on the Back for Avengers: Endgame – It Has Ignored Queer People's Existence for Too Long." *Independent*, May 2, 2019. www.independent.co.uk/arts-entertainment/films/features/avengers-endgame-lgbt-gay-character-joe-russo-marvel-mcu-a8896341.html.

Wright, Bradford W. *Comic Book Nation: The Transformation of Youth Culture in America*. Baltimore: Johns Hopkins Press, 2003. p 287.

Index

Made in the USA
Las Vegas, NV
29 July 2023

75407511R00096